FORGING WAR

The Media in Serbia, Croatia and Bosnia-Hercegovina

D1494666

May 1994

ARTICLE 19
International Centre Against Censorship

© ARTICLE 19

ISBN 1 870798 22 8   LAW

Printed in the Great Britain by The Bath Press, Avon

The real culprits in this long list of executions, assassinations, drownings, burnings, massacres and atrocities furnished by our report, are not, we repeat, the Balkan peoples. ... The true culprits are those who mislead public opinion and take advantage of the people's ignorance to raise disquieting rumours and sound the alarm bell, inciting their country and consequently other countries into enmity. The real culprits are those who by interest or inclination, declaring constantly that war is inevitable, end by making it so, asserting that they are powerless to prevent it. The real culprits are these who sacrifice the general interest to their own personal interest, ... and who hold up to their country a sterile policy of conflict and reprisals.

From the report of the International Commission to Inquire into the Causes and Conduct of the Balkan Wars of 1912 and 1913 sent by the Carnegie Endowment for International Peace.

AUTHOR NOTE

MARK THOMPSON, journalist and writer, was born in Sheffield in 1959, and educated in London and Cambridge. From 1986 to 1989, he was a deputy editor of the European Nuclear Disarmament Journal. He is the co-editor, with Louis Mackay, of *Something in the Wind: Politics after Chernobyl* (London: Pluto Press, 1988). His book, *A Paper House: The Ending of Yugoslavia*, was published by Hutchinson Radius and by Vintage Books in 1992.

AUTHOR'S ACKNOWLEDGEMENTS

Thanks for many kinds of help and advice are due to Agencija ARGUMENT, Neven Andjelić, Ljiljana Bačević, Hrvoje Batinić, Edina Bečirević, Jonathan Bousfield, Srbobran Branković, Lee Bryant, the Centre for Anti-War Action (Belgrade), Ivan Zvonimir Čičak, the Civic Initiative for Freedom of Expression (Zagreb), Ben Cohen, the Croatian Helsinki Committee for Human Rights, Velimir Čurguz, Filip David, Pascale Delpech, Dubravka Dostal, Milan Gavrović, James Gow, Gordana Grbić, Zdravko Grebo, Ervin Hladnik-Milharčić, Bojana Humar, the Institute for War & Peace Reporting (London), Gordana Janković, Vesna Kesić, Mihajlo Kovač, Jasmina Kuzmanović, Lazar Lalić, Gordana Logar, Ivan Lovrenović, Tihomir Loza, Petar Luković, Branka Magaš, Vlada Mareš, the Media Centre (Belgrade), Branka Mihajlović, Goran Milić, Branko Milinković, Paul Miller, Aleksandar Milošević, Branislav Milošević, Žarko Modrić, Peter Morris, Branka Pražić, Senad Pečanin, Mirko Pejić, Nenad Pejić, Elena Popović, Samantha Power, Press Now (Amsterdam), Žarko Puhovski, Ivica Puljić, Dušan Puvačić, Maja Razović, Dušan Reljić, Ines Sabalić, Mladen Sančanin, Isidora Sekulić, Dušan Simić, Jagoda Splivalo-Rusan, George Stamkoski, Jonathan Sunley, Gordana Suša, Tatjana Tagirov, Biljana Tatomir, Christine Thompson, Vanessa Vasić Janeković, Jela Jevremović, Aleksandar Vasović, Dragan Velikić, Mark Wheeler, Martin Woollacott; and to those others who prefer not to be named. Particular thanks are due to Vlado Azinović and his family; Ivana Djordjević, Srdjan Dvornik, Noel Malcolm, Milica Pešić, and Miloš Vasić; to Frances D'Souza (Executive Director), Carmel Bedford, Helen Darbishire, and all at ARTICLE 19; and to Sanja, who made this book possible. Responsibility for opinions and errors rests with the author alone. (Corrections and comments will be welcome at the ARTICLE 19 address.)

ARTICLE 19 gratefully acknowledges the support of the Soros Foundation for this publication.

This book was edited by Ann Naughton and designed by Susan York. Maps and cover were designed by Louis Mackay.

CONTENTS

Acknowledgements ii

Preface *by William Shawcross* vii

Maps xiii

Introduction 1

Chapter 1   THE MEDIA IN FORMER YUGOSLAVIA   5
Ownership and Control 7
Media Freedom, Law and Censorship 8
The Press 13
Journalists 14
Radio and Television 15
The Rise of Television 16

Chapter 2   THE PAN-YUGOSLAV NEWS MEDIA   22
Background 22
Tanjug 22
Borba 31
Yutel 38

Chapter 3   SERBIA SETS THE PACE   51
Introduction 51
Background: Kosovo 53
Media and the Law 58
Non-Legal Actions Against the Media 62
The Press 63
    Printing and Distribution 65
    The Politika Paradigm 67
        Coverage of Serb Rebellion in Croatia 70
        Coverage of Internal Opposition 73
        Coverage of Plitvice 75
        Reporting Borovo Selo 76
        Reporting Slovenia's and
            Croatia's Independence 78
        Supporting the Drive for Volunteers 79
        The War in Bosnia 80
            Zvornik 81
            The Bread-Queue Massacre 83

Television 84
    Introduction 84
    Serbian Radio-Television (RTS) 86
    Calls for Reform at RTS 88
    Law on Radio-Television 91
    RTS Purges Since 1991 91
    The Format of the News 93
    Television and the President 96
    Coverage of the President's Volte-face
        on the Vance-Owen Plan 96
    Hazards of Reporting the War in Croatia 99
    Coverage of the War in Bosnia 101
        Language and Tone 102
        How RTS Presented Serb Territorial
            Conquest in Bosnia 104
        How Negative Information was
            Omitted and Obscured 105
        RTS Coverage of Attacks Against Serbs 111
        Selection of Studio Guests 111
    Other Television News 112
    Radio 117
        Local Radio 120
    News Magazines 122
    Conclusions 124

Chapter 4   CROATIA CATCHES UP   130
    Background 130
    Media and Government Control 132
    Media, War and the Political Leaders 134
    Journalists and War 136
    Media and Law 138
    Privatization of Media Companies 145
    HINA News Agency 146
    Broadcasting 149
        Croatian Radio-Television Law 149
        Croatian Television 152
            Profile of the Television Chiefs 155
            Profile of Journalists 156
            Regulating Language and Tone 159
            Regulating Images of War 162
            Vukovar 164

Coverage of War in Bosnia 166
Regional and Local Television 168
Radio 169
   Croatian Radio 169
   Local Radio 172
The Press 176
  The Vjesnik Group 176
  Vjesnik and *Večernji list* 179
   Coverage of War in Croatia 181
   Coverage of War in Bosnia 183
  The Regional Press 185
   Slobodna Dalmacija 185
   Novi list 188
   Glas Slavonije 190
  The Weekly Press 191
   Slobodni tijednik and *Globus* 191
   Danas 194
   Feral Tribune 197
Conclusions 198

Chapter 5   **BOSNIA-HERCEGOVINA LEFT BEHIND**   201
Introduction 201
Media Before the Onslaught 206
The Transmitter War 207
The Communications Breakdown 209
Media in the War 211
Media and Censorship 214
Terminology in the Media 217
News Agencies 218
  BH Press 218
  The Bosnian Army Press Centre 219
Television 220
  Introduction 220
  Attempts to Split Up the Service 223
  War in Croatia 224
  TV Journalists and the
   Question of Impartiality 227
  War Conditions 231
  Television News Under Government Control 234
Radio 237
  Private Radio 238

    Amateur Radio 241
The Press 243
    Oslobodjenje 243
    Slobodna Bosna and *Ljiljan* 247
    Dani 249
Serb Media 250
    The SRNA News Agency and
        Kanal S Television 252
    Radio 258
Croat Media 259
Conclusions 263

Glossary 267

PREFACE

by William Shawcross

Propaganda, used especially to incite national hatreds and fears, has been one of the most important weapons of war in the annihilation of former Yugoslavia. Consider this example.

In March 1994, Ana Mladić, 23-year-old daughter of General Ratko Mladić, the ruthless commander of Bosnian Serb forces, apparently committed suicide. The semi-official Bosnian Serb newspaper *Jedinstvo* exploited the young woman's tragic death in characteristic manner. The author declared himself ready to "protect the profession and the glitter of the general's stripes". Noting that Ana Mladić shot herself, he declared that she had left this world with "a thunderous roar, just like when her Daddy is defending his people". Asking why she had to die, the author announced:

> And then came fate. A terrible fate. Perhaps relentless? War: the Serbs are fated to die. I ask, was it possible that a youthful heart which had just started to beat with the joy of life, should bear the burden and tears for brethren fallen throughout the former Bosnia-Hercegovina, was it possible to bear all those fears for her dear father's life, for General Ratko Mladić who led his armies wherever it was necessary to prevent a new and more terrible death for the Serbs? Was it possible that Ana Mladić could tolerate all those 'peace makers' and similar trash in the Serb capital of Belgrade? She was surrounded by them day and night, as a student in Belgrade. Her young, healthy spirit and honourable patriotism, and the 'Serbian milk' which she had fed upon, found it difficult to bear all that which destroyed, undermined and slandered the battle of our and her brethren in the Serb land west of the watery arteries of the Serbian cause : the Drava, Danube, Drina and Sava rivers. That is the reason why a burgeoning bud and a parent's heart had to wither ... .

This mawkish obituary displays in all its grimness what Mark Thompson calls the "self-pitying, morbid and vengeful" nature of Serbian nationalist discourse. It has dominated Serbian propaganda for several years now, to terrible effect.

Now, another example of the nature of the Serbian media. Soon after Ana Mladić's death, her father directed the brutal Serb assault upon the Muslim enclave of Goražde, on the Drina river in eastern Bosnia, or as Serb propagandists saw it, Western Serbia.

There were no Western journalists, let alone television crews in Goražde. And so, unlike, for example, the February marketplace massacre in Sarajevo, the attack could be seen only at a tangent on the world's television screens. The perspective was that provided by Radio-Television Serbia (RTS), one of the Belgrade government's most powerful instruments of war.

RTS showed vistas of the town, with the Drina running through it, taken from Serb military positions on the surrounding hills. Goražde, in the Serbian vision, seemed to be basking in sylvan peace. There were no pictures of the mayhem being inflicted on the town as Serb shells hit it. No one could see the wounded in the hospital being wounded again as Serb missiles struck the building.

When RTS interviewed Bosnian Serb soldiers, they were portrayed as plucky little defenders of an embattled territory rather than as part of a vicious military machine assaulting a predominantly civilian enclave, which was supposed to be under UN protection.

That is the norm not the exception in Serbian television coverage. Thus in October 1992, a film of the Serb attack on Jajce actually showed Serb artillery fire on the town but the commentator talked only of shells from the Croats and Muslims in the town. The reporter, defying logic, declared that "[t]he Muslims and Croats are trying to threaten the positions of the Serb army. The Serb army has already reached the outlying houses."

RTS is a lying machine designed to inspire, provoke and underwrite nationalist fears and hatreds. So is Croatian Radio-Television. The Bosnian government also publishes propaganda and distortion. Indeed, while the Serbs pretended nothing untoward was happening in Goražde, Bosnian propaganda almost certainly exaggerated the scale of the attacks and the number of casualties.

In 1993, the Serbian Information Minister, Milivoje Pavlović, stated that RTS tied Serbian communities in Greece and Hungary to one another and to all Serbs in the diaspora:

Preface

> Thanks to the advantages of the electronic media, RTS provides for a precious level of spiritual unity of all Serbs worldwide in the times, when neither justice nor truth prevail, but are regulated, if not contaminated by Serbophobia and other products from the kitchens of the creators of the new world order.

In fact, the catastrophe of former Yugoslavia demonstrates more powerfully than anything else that those kitchens have created even less order in the new world than in the old. That amorphous entity, "the international community" has proved quite incapable of formulating still less executing any coherent policy. Instead, humanitarian aid has been used to fill the political vacuum left by Western governments.

Forging War is not a typical ARTICLE 19 report. It is a detailed and often horrifying account of how, throughout the fall and destruction of former Yugoslavia, propaganda and lies have been amongst the most potent weapons of the Serbian and Croatian governments. Mark Thompson, the author of *A Paper House: The Ending of Yugoslavia* was ideally placed to observe this process at first hand. The book demonstrates that the war could not have been begun, or sustained, by Serbia without the co-option of the Serbian media as the willing creatures of the Milošević government.

Forging War shows how propaganda has enabled the Croat government to portray itself (falsely) as the last bastion of Western "democratic" values; it has enabled the Muslim dominated government of Bosnia to present itself only as an innocent victim, which it has not always been; and, above all, it has enabled the Serb authorities (in both Belgrade and Bosnia) to encourage all Serbs to see themselves as the tragic, blameless scapegoats in an international conspiracy to destroy the Serb people and their homeland.

In Belgrade communist methods married to nationalist ideology have from the start of the conflict deliberately whipped up Serbian fears of "*ustaša* hordes" in Croatia and of "Muslim fanatics" in Bosnia. In the old days, arguments were between "liberals" and "conservatives", even "Stalinists"; now all debate has been reduced to ethnicity. Petar Luković, the deputy editor of the independent magazine *Vreme*, said: "Three years ago we used to be part of Europe. Now we are millions of light years away."

ix

In his book, *Bosnia, A Short History*, Noel Malcolm writes that, having stayed in Muslim, Croat and Serb villages throughout Bosnia over fifteen years, he did not believe that the country was forever seething with ethnic hatreds. But he could see why simple Bosnian Serbs had been forced by RTS to believe that they were under threat from *ustaša hordes* and fundamentalist jihad. The independent Belgrade journalist, Miloš Vasić said that if all American television had been taken over by the Ku Klux Klan: the USA too would have war in five years.

The main Serbian media, and in particular RTS, have been harnessed to the wheel of the government's territorial ambitions. Over the years journalists of independent views, who questioned the insidious and destructive official agenda, have been demoted, targeted for public condemnation or sacked. There do remain brave independent journalists and media throughout former Yugoslavia. These media do an astonishing job in keeping alive a spirit of dissent against the prevailing, nationalist orthodoxies which are as dreary as they are brutal.

In the formerly autonomous region of Kosovo, the Serbian government runs an apartheid system for the 90 per cent Albanian population; the Serbians have suspended civil life. Universities and schools have been closed, Albanian judges and doctors have been dismissed; Albanian language television has been suspended, and many (though not all) Albanian newspapers have been closed down.

In Serbia the Milošević regime has done its best to limit if not destroy independent media by imposing swingeing taxes, restricting access to more powerful broadcasting transmitters and cutting supplies of newsprint and fuel to the independent media. The economic crisis caused by sanctions has hit news-stand sales of all papers, and galloping inflation has destroyed revenues, the collection of which the government systematically delayed.

Recently the threats against both foreign journalists and independent media in Belgrade have become more strident. In April, as NATO threatened to strike Serb targets in Bosnia, the Belgrade government revoked the credentials of 13 foreign journalists in Serbia, and threatened to close the Soros Foundation in Belgrade (a major funder of the independent press in the former Yugoslavia), while uttering more ominous threats than ever against the independent media there.

The official media assiduously propagate the lie that the opposition and the independent media, not the government and its allies, are responsible for all the afflictions of the nation. In May 1992, Stojan

Preface

Cerović of *Vreme* wrote accurately that the director-general of RTS, Milorad Vučelić,

> can now calmly invite the opposition to say whatever it wants on television, because he knows that ... anybody who explains the truth can do so only at his own cost. Reality sounds like the blackest anti-Serbian propaganda, and anyone who describes it will frighten people and turn them against him.

In Serbia, as elsewhere in the Balkans, often the only source of uncensored news is from foreign satellite television. These are vital but inconstant sources of information. The United Nations mission to former Yugoslavia, UNPROFOR, has considered setting up its own radio station. Indeed, the UN Special Rapporteur, Tadeusz Mazowiecki, recommended in 1993 that "[t]he information blockade which prevails in the region should be broken. Support should be given to initiatives taken by independent groups, both within and outside the former Yugoslavia, which aim to provide objective information."

The UN did this to great effect in Cambodia, where its Radio Untac played an important part in convincing ordinary people that they could vote freely and ignore the threats of the opposing factions. In former Yugoslavia it could provide at least a partial antidote to the toxin of propaganda which has, by poisoning societies, created the conditions for war and 'ethnic cleansing'. The only indigenous antidotes, and they have not been powerful enough, have been the independent media.

Without strong, independent media, civil societies cannot be rebuilt in Serbia, Croatia or Bosnia, and the threats to Kosovo and Macedonia will remain. *Forging War* is intended as a statement in support of all those who have tried to tell the truth about the wars in Croatia and Bosnia, both inside and outside this pulverised land.

In January 1994, the director of the SaGA company (the makers of the widely-syndicated "A Street in Sarajevo" documentary series), Ademir Kenović explained his fear of what racial propaganda had done and would do:

> I feel we are on a skyscraper on the 19th floor and there is a fire burning on the 2nd floor, getting fiercer and fiercer, burning harder and harder. When

I said this two years ago, journalists looked at me as if I was pretending to be in some very important place. I wasn't.... But Bosnia is not an island - this is not Reykjavik. We will not be able to stop the flames burning through [the Balkans]. The world is making in Bosnia a paradigm of hell. Maybe something like this burning flame will appear in a different point. But it is impossible to stop. When you have it in one place it is bound to break out in another.

Forging War should serve as a warning of the terrible, destructive power of incitement to ethnic hatred when the mass media are controlled by nationalist governments. The countries of former Yugoslavia are not the only ones in Europe now facing a similar risk. Truth may be "the first casualty" of war, but in Serbia it was deliberately wounded when the government co-opted the media to encourage war. The warning signs could be seen abroad, but they were too long ignored. Truth's subsequent death by a thousand cuts from all sides — Serbian, Croatian and Bosnian — has made the conflict ever more ferocious and intractable.

4 May 1994

William Shawcross is Chairman of the International Board of ARTICLE 19, the International Centre Against Censorship.

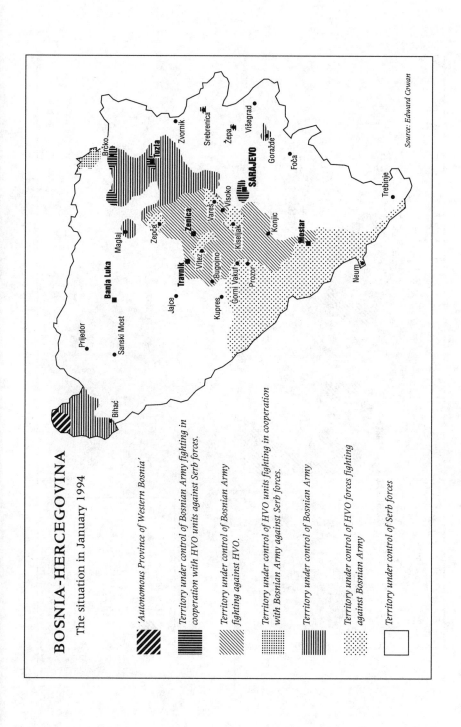

BOSNIA-HERCEGOVINA

The situation in January 1994

'Autonomous Province of Western Bosnia'

Territory under control of Bosnian Army fighting in cooperation with HVO units against Serb forces.

Territory under control of Bosnian Army fighting against HVO.

Territory under control of HVO units fighting in cooperation with Bosnian Army against Serb forces.

Territory under control of Bosnian Army

Territory under control of HVO forces fighting against Bosnian Army

Territory under control of Serb forces

Source: Edward Cowan

Prijedor

Sanski Most

Bihać

Banja Luka

Jajce

Kupres

Gorni Vakuf

Prozor

Maglaj

Zepče

Travnik

Vitez

Bugojno

Kiseljak

Zenica

Vareš

Visoko

Konjic

Mostar

Neum

Trebinje

Brčko

Tuzla

Zvornik

Srebrenica

Žepa

Višegrad

SARAJEVO

Goražde

Foča

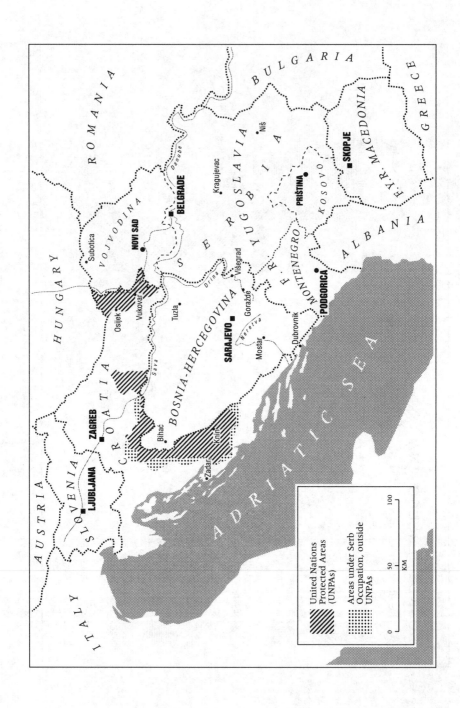

ROMANIA

BULGARIA

GREECE

HUNGARY

F.Y.R. MACEDONIA

VOJVODINA

Subotica

NOVI SAD

BELGRADE

Kragujevac

Niš

SKOPJE

Danube

S E R B I A

PRIŠTINA

KOSOVO

Osijek

Vukovar

Tuzla

Drina

Višegrad

ALBANIA

MONTENEGRO

PODGORICA

Goražde

Sava

BOSNIA-HERCEGOVINA

SARAJEVO

Moracva

Mostar

Dubrovnik

ZAGREB

C R O A T I A

Bihać

Knin

LJUBLJANA

SLOVENIA

Zadar

AUSTRIA

ITALY

A D R I A T I C   S E A

United Nations
Protected Areas
(UNPAs)

Areas under Serb
Occupation, outside
UNPAs

100

50

KM

0

INTRODUCTION

Media loom large in accounts of the war that killed Yugoslavia, and they will figure no less in histories of the conflict. There are several reasons for this. Since the war began in summer 1991, it has been waged among peoples and by people who had lived peacefully as compatriots in Yugoslavia all their lives (except those born before 1918, and except for the period 1941-45, when Yugoslavia was carved up among Germany, Italy and their fascist allies). A campaign of intense propaganda was needed to mobilize the population, to make war thinkable in Yugoslavia, let alone inevitable.

Neither side fighting in Croatia, and none of the three sides in Bosnia-Hercegovina (hereinafter Bosnia), was strong (or resolute) enough to win outright victory. Media coverage has therefore been manipulated to sustain domestic public support for the struggle. The systematic capture and destruction of transmitters proved how much store the warring sides set by the electronic media.

It is a fact of modern history that Balkan wars cannot be resolved without the close involvement of outside powers. All sides in Croatia and Bosnia understood very well how important political and public opinion in Western Europe and North America could be, in deciding the final outcome. Some key developments in the war came in reaction to media coverage. The first film of a Serb-run concentration camp in Bosnia, in August 1992, apparently elicited UN Security Resolution 770, allowing for "all necessary measures" to ensure the delivery of humanitarian aid in Bosnia. News film of victims of the marketplace massacre in Sarajevo in February 1994 brought the NATO ultimatum which ended the bombardment of the city. On a few occasions, media participated directly in the political process. When Bosnia's president, Alija Izetbegovic, was kidnapped by Serb forces on 2 May 1992, his release was negotiated live on TV Sarajevo.

Domestic and international media coverage was therefore a strategic concern, and not only for the warring sides: a British officer who commanded UN forces in Bosnia believes that media "[s]ometimes served the useful purpose of being present to record agreements [between the sides] — there were sometimes no other records. Being held accountable in the forum of world opinion can occasionally be a powerful means of persuasion and agreements made on camera are more difficult to break."[1]

The war has been saturated with media. It has been a very accessible bloodbath, in 'the heart of Europe'. Foreign journalists could reach battlefields and sites of genocide by car, a few hours' drive from Vienna, Venice and Munich. Some have become famous for their work in Croatia and Bosnia. On the other hand, the former Yugoslavia has been the most dangerous place in the world for journalists; by the end of April 1994, at least 38 journalists had been killed in the war.[2]

Lastly, and overall, the fate of the media has been an allegory of the war itself. Like the nations of Yugoslavia, the media were thoroughly mixed. The press was distributed throughout the country. Television and radio signals spread across republican borders, interweaving in the atmosphere as the nations mingled on the ground. Media 'campaigns' were the forerunner of military campaigns. Verbal violence engendered physical violation. Many media were purged of independence and dissent, in brutal ways that anticipated the purging ('cleansing') of territories.

Forging War is focused upon two aspects of this extensive subject: the relationship between media and government, both before and during the war; and the connection between this relationship and the 'messages' carried by the media.

The report's survey is limited to three of former Yugoslavia's six republics, not for brevity's sake alone. The war has been waged among three nations of former Yugoslavia: Serbs (plus some Montenegrins), Croats and Muslims. It was in the republics belonging to these nations that public opinion was a crucial factor in the war and in the crisis that preceded it.

Serbia's more or less willing partner in arms has been the tiny republic of Montenegro. (Together they proclaimed a 'new' Yugoslavia, the Federal Republic of Yugoslavia, on 27 April 1992.) While Montenegro's part in media combat has lacked nothing in fierceness, it has not mattered greatly. Montenegro's material contribution to the war could not be decisive, and anyway Serbia has decided Montenegro's fate since 1989. Montenegrin government-controlled media have danced to a tune

---

[1] Lt. Colonel Bob Stewart, *Broken Lives. A Personal View of the Bosnian Conflict* (London: Harper Collins, 1993), 180.

[2] According to Committee to Protect Journalists, New York, 3 May 1994.

composed in Belgrade. For the same reason, media in the two formerly autonomous regions are largely excluded from consideration in the Serbia chapter.

Regarding Slovenia, the '10-day war' in that republic in summer 1991 was, with hindsight, a mere overture to the conflict in Croatia (which, notwithstanding the casualty statistics, was itself something of a prelude to the war in Bosnia). Slovenia's media played an important part in democratizing that republic in the late 1980s: the so-called Slovenian Spring. The youth press broke a taboo by denouncing corruption in the Jugoslovenska Narodna Armija (JNA, Yugoslav People's Army). This example inspired independent-minded journalists in other republics, yet Slovenia's media, like Macedonia's, stood outside the Yugoslav 'media war' for the same national, cultural and demographic reasons that Slovenia and Macedonia stood apart from the Serbian-Croatian-Bosnian knot. Their media made no difference to political options and public opinion in Croatia, Serbia and Bosnia.

The book aims to be as accurate, analytical and useful as the constraints of space will allow. The density of dates, acronyms, titles, quotations and references is therefore unavoidable. (The glossary is intended only as an elementary aid.) The research for this report, including interviews with staff and former staff of media in the three republics, was conducted from August 1993 to January 1994.

Mark Thompson
4 May 1994

Chapter 1

THE MEDIA IN FORMER YUGOSLAVIA

The media in the Socialist Federative Republic of Yugoslavia (SFRY) were more abundant, varied and unconstrained than in any other Communist state. By the 1980s, these media were, with scarcely an exception, controlled at the republican level and geared for republican audiences. Political control was usually less blatant and oppressive than in other Communist states. Readers, listeners and viewers in the SFRY enjoyed "a much greater content variety than ... anywhere else in eastern Europe".[1]

The media were controlled, indirectly if not directly, by the League of Communists of Yugoslavia, through the League's branches in the six republics (Bosnia-Hercegovina, Croatia, Macedonia, Montenegro, Serbia, and Slovenia) and two autonomous provinces within Serbia (Kosovo and Vojvodina) which composed the federation.

By 1989 when a federal law was enacted to allow the foundation of private companies, including media companies, there were nine television stations, one for each unit of the federation plus one for the Italian minority in Slovenia and Croatia. There were 202 radio stations, comprising a federal station broadcasting mainly in foreign languages (Radio Yugoslavia), six republican stations, and regional and local stations (in theory, one per municipality of 10,000-250,000 inhabitants). News and political commentary made up 28 per cent of total radio broadcasting output.[2] There was also Tanjug, a state news agency with a worldwide profile.

There were 27 daily newspapers, including two devoted to sports and one to economic affairs; 17 major news magazines; hundreds of local papers and special interest periodicals (for example, 108 publications for

---

[1] G Robinson, *Tito's Maverick Media: The Politics of Mass Communication* (Chicago: University of Illinois, 1977), 213.

[2] Federal Secretariat for Information, *Handbook on Yugoslavia* (Belgrade: 1987), 215.

religious communities). Some 69 per cent of the printed media were in the Serbo-Croatian, Serbian or Croatian languages.

There was also an abundant output of books. "At the end of the 1980s, Yugoslavia was fourteenth in the world according to the number of published books and brochures."[3] Importation of the foreign press was generally permitted "without hindrance or limitation ..., contrary to practice in most socialist countries".[4]

As political power was devolved from the central organs of the federation to the republics and autonomous regions, during the 1960s and 1970s, the media were also decentralised. One observer reported, in 1981, that "local coverage of local affairs is very much the rule. I noticed several examples of quite inadequate reporting in the Belgrade press of the speeches of regional officials." The press was "increasingly informative and regionally differentiated ... . Analysts of Yugoslav affairs must read republican media — not just the Belgrade press — accordingly."[5]

The long term meaning of the devolution of Yugoslavia's media was already clear in 1977 to Gertrude Robinson, who wrote:

> In this country's multinational setting, content is selected with ethnic priorities in mind; this fosters hermetic points of view [which] could be potentially destructive of federal unity by undermining the search for and definition of mutually acceptable political alternatives.[6]

Events have confirmed Robinson's worst fears, in large part because the devolution of power was incomplete and contradictory; it was intended to accommodate liberal reformist tendencies without undermining the political monopoly of the League of Communists. The result was that the League of Communists in each of the eight units of the federation was empowered without being democratised; and what happened to the League happened to the mass media.

---

[3] Id. at 191-192.

[4] Robinson, supra note 1 at 42.

[5] A Ross Johnson, "Impressions of post-Tito Yugoslavia: a trip report", 5(2) *South Slav Journal*, Summer 1982.

[6] Robinson, supra note 1 at 191 and 199.

Yugoslavia became an alliance of regional oligarchies[7] producing the political deadlock which followed the death of Josip Broz-Tito, "President for life", in 1980. In terms of the mass media, a curiously mixed process of fake and genuine diversity got underway. As the republican Communist elites became overtly competitive and critical of each other and of the federation, the media were allowed to become critical too. The media were manipulated to enhance the republican elites' authority, usually by appealing to national sentiments. These appeals had to be devious, until nationalism became admissible at the end of the 1980s. (In Macedonia for instance, the League of Communists repeatedly played the national card by attacking the alleged nationalism of Macedonia's own Albanian population.)

Meanwhile the full weight of repressive legislation was still used to silence critics who attacked the 'wrong' targets, above all, the republican authorities themselves. However, astute journalists were able to create space for genuinely independent work by exploiting new divisions among the authorities. The whole process was further complicated because politics had specific features in each republic and autonomous region; what was sayable or printable in one unit of the federation, could incur a prison sentence in another.

Ownership and Control

Private companies did not legally exist in Yugoslavia until the end of the 1980s. However, very few companies belonged to the state; nor did the League of Communists own anything except its extensive office space. The ideologists of Yugoslav Communism had devised the concept of 'social property' as a distinctive model of public ownership which would avoid the 'state capitalism' of Soviet-style command economies. 'Social property' had no titular owner; in theory it belonged to the whole of society, which entrusted it, so to speak, to segments of society (companies, cultural and sports associations, professional institutions, hospitals, schools and so forth) for use on behalf of the whole. Regarding its application to companies, the chief ideologist, Edvard Kardelj, defined social property as

---

[7] This phrase was coined by Branko Horvat, a Croatian economist who now heads the Social Democratic Union, a small opposition party.

"simultaneously the collective, class property of all workers and a form of individual ownership by everyone who works". This abstract, almost metaphysical category of ownership was supposed by its creators in the 1950s to hasten what Marx had called "the self-government of the producers". Yugoslavia would become the world's first truly democratic socialist state.

Yet this democratization was intended to proceed without the League of Communists losing its monopoly as a political party.[8] The League kept its "leading role" as "the organised vanguard consciousness of the working class and the working class people generally". In theory, therefore, the League of Communists alone was entitled to negotiate between the whole of society and its segments employed in companies. In practice, the League enjoyed the prerogatives of ownership. Naturally, this influence was zealously exploited in areas of high strategic importance. One such area was certainly what Yugoslav ideologists termed the "public information system"; in other words, the media.

Media Freedom, Law and Censorship

The concept of media freedom in the constitution and laws, was that the media were free to support the existing political system in the prescribed ways. Article 166 of the last Yugoslav Constitution (1974) guaranteed "freedom of the press and other media of information and public expression, freedom of association, freedom of speech and public expression". Article 203, however, listed limitations on these freedoms which were so far-reaching and vaguely defined that they ensured arbitrary powers of prohibition for the authorities.

> No one may use the freedoms and rights established
> by the present Constitution in order to disrupt the
> foundations of the socialist self-management
> democratic order ..., to endanger the independence of
> the country, violate the freedoms and rights of man

---

[8] The only leading Communist who argued against this continuing monopoly was Milovan Djilas, in 1954, who was expelled from power and later jailed for a total of nine years.

and the citizen ..., endanger peace and equality in international co-operation, stir up national, racial, or religious hatred or intolerance or abet commission of criminal offences, nor may these freedoms be used in a way which offends public morals ... .

In legislation, the same pattern applied. The Law on the Prevention of the Abuse of Freedom of the Press and Other Media prohibited dissemination of publications which could be construed as threatening "the foundations of self-management social order", or as offending the honour and reputation of states and their representatives, or revealing military secrets. The Law on the Circulation of Foreign Mass Media and Foreign Information Activities prohibited foreign publications which jeopardized the "foundations" of the political system. Laws on domestic media prohibited publications which jeopardized or even "might jeopardize" public order and safety.

Articles in the Federal Criminal Code (and incorporated into the republican criminal codes) also bore directly upon media freedom. The most notorious example was Article 133, which needs to be quoted in full:

> (1)   Whoever, by means of an article, leaflet, drawing, speech or in some other way advocates or incites the overthrow of the power of the working class and the working people, the unconstitutional change of the socialist social system of self-management, the disruption of the brotherhood, unity and equality of the nations and nationalities, the overthrow of the bodies of social self-management and government or their executive agencies, resistance to the decisions of relevant government and self-management bodies which are important for the protection and development of socialist self-management relations, the security and defence of the country, or whoever maliciously and untruthfully portrays socio-political conditions in the country — shall be sentenced to a term of imprisonment ranging from one to ten years.

(2)   Whoever commits an offence mentioned in Paragraph (1) of this Article with assistance from abroad or influenced by people abroad, shall be punished by imprisonment for at least three years.

(3)   Whoever sends or infiltrates agitators or propaganda material into the territory of the SFRY in order to commit an offence mentioned in Paragraph (1) of this Article shall be punished by imprisonment for at least one year.

(4)   Whoever produces or duplicates hostile propaganda material with the intention to distribute it, or whoever has such materials in his possession knowing that it is intended for dissemination, shall be punished by imprisonment for at least six months and not more than five years.

This Article was invoked in many of the high-profile prosecutions of dissidents in the 1970s and 1980s, including, for example, Franjo Tudjman and Vladimir Šeks in Croatia, and Alija Izetbegović in Bosnia. The first human rights petition in Yugoslavia to gather more than 100 signatories called for the abolition of Article 133.[9]

There were other Articles which could be invoked against the written or spoken word. Articles 116 and 117 of the Criminal Code specified sentences of at least five years and at least one year respectively, for anyone who committed an act aimed at the secession of part of the SFRY, or at subjugating the SFRY to another state. Article 157 incriminated anyone who "defames the SFRY, its flag, coat of arms, or anthem, its highest organs or their representatives, its armed forces or their commander-in-chief". The penalty was three months to three years in prison. Article 150 penalized defamation of foreign states, their symbols and leaders.

---

[9] This was in autumn 1980. N Popov, "Freedom of public speech. First stirrings", *Republika*, Sept. 1993.

The person and work of Josip Broz-Tito were protected by law from criticism. Article 136 prohibited "association for the purpose of hostile activity", a catch-all formulation which contradicted Article 166 of the Constitution. Article 134 penalized "whoever by propaganda or in any manner incites or fosters national, racial or religious hatred or antagonism" with one to ten years imprisonment. Incitement to resistance (violent or non-violent, no distinction was made) to "legal decisions or measures of government organs or public officials" was punishable by similar sentences. Criminal Code definitions of state secrets, official secrets and military secrets were broad and vague; indeed, military secrets included "data which have not been declared a military secret but whose disclosure could cause harmful consequences for the armed forces" (Article 224).

Pre-publication censorship in the SFRY was authorized in Article 4 of the Law on Prevention of the Abuse of Freedom of the Press. This article required publishers to provide the local Public Prosecutor's office with two copies of every publication before it was released to the public. The Prosecutor could place a temporary ban on any publication. The matter was then referred to the local court which decided whether the issue could be distributed.[10] Article 19 extended the Prosecutor's banning powers to radio, television and other media. Often, publications were banned after distribution. This led to copies being collected from news kiosks and even from individual subscribers at their homes. In court, the Prosecutor could invoke any law in order to sustain the ban. The Federal Prosecutor could also order a ban, which in this case applied throughout the federation.

Using these means, many publications were banned, even at the height of the reform movement, around 1970. The principal targets of these bans were student, literary and religious periodicals.[11] During the 1980s, however, Yugoslav media often flouted the law and the will of the authorities with impunity, despite this formidable battery of provisions to prevent and deter media from transgressing the "precisely defined limits" of their freedom, "in the spheres of foreign policy, national mythology,

---

[10] P Ramet, "The Yugoslav Press in Flux", in P Ramet (ed.), *Yugoslavia in the 1980s* (Boulder, Colorado: Westview Press, 1984), 111.

[11] An interesting list of bannings between 1959 and 1976 was published in G Schopflin (ed.), *Censorship and Political Communication: Examples from Eastern Europe* (London: Pinter, 1983).

religious policy, and nationalities policy".[12] The key cause of this seeming liberalization has been mentioned already: to wit, the transformation of the League of Communists into a "coalition of inadequately co-ordinated, at times even mutually opposed, republican and provincial party leaderships which do not shrink from *public* squabbles and recriminations".[13]

Lastly, reference must be made to the phenomenon of self-censorship, which appears to have been strong in the SFRY. Reasons for this lie deep in what S P Ramet calls the "national mythology" of Tito's Yugoslavia. One element of the mythology was the claim that the country's achievements, and even its existence, rested upon constant vigilance against an array of powerful international enemies, on both sides of the Cold War divide. Another element was the boast that self-management socialism was the first and only democratic socialist system, which uniquely empowered every citizen to participate in working and political life. A third element was the myth that Tito's Partisan army, during the Second World War, had waged a pure struggle against domestic opponents and foreign aggressors who were all fascists or collaborators alike. These and other myths, whose appeal was often greatly enhanced by Yugoslavia's anomalous status in the Cold War, were fostered by the League of Communists, then milked for every drop of legitimation which they could confer upon the political system.

Such was the background of the following retrospective tribute to self-management socialism, by Croatian journalist Slavenka Drakulić: "It was the most perfect system among the one-party states, set up to internalize guilt, blame, failure, or fear, to teach how you yourself should censor your thoughts and deeds and, at the same time, to make you feel you had more freedom than anyone in Eastern Europe."[14]

---

[12] Ramet, supra note 10 at 104. Ramet adds to this list "a category of subjects which may not be discussed at all", including "military and trade secrets, the exact amount of the foreign debt, and the Belgrade office of the UNHCR, which handles some 2,000 refugees from the Soviet bloc annually." There were also blacklists of persons who could not appear in the media; in Croatia, for example, this list included prominent victims of 'normalisation' after the 'Croatian Spring' (see Ch. 4 infra).

[13] K Čavoski, 8 *Index on Censorship,* 1986.

[14] S Drakulić, *How We Survived Communism and Even Laughed* (London: Hutchinson, 1992), 6.

The Press

The main daily newspapers were founded by the Socialist Alliance of Working People (SAWP) or passed into its control after 1945. The SAWP was a "socio-political" mass organization comprising trade union, youth, student, women's and war veterans' associations in each republic, under the political 'guidance' of the republican League of Communists. For these newspapers, which included the federal title *Borba*, *Vjesnik* and *Večernji list* in Croatia, *Politika* and *Politika expres* and *Večernje novosti* in Serbia, and *Oslobodjenje* in Bosnia, the republican SAWP appointed the director, the editor-in-chief and the managing editor. Regional and local newspapers were founded by municipal authorities where the League of Communists' influence was equally decisive. News magazines either belonged to newspaper companies or to associations within SAWP, notably to the youth and student associations.

Article 167 of the 1974 Federal Constitution stated that: "Citizens, organisations, and citizens' associations may, under conditions specified by statute, publish newspapers and other publications." Article 30 of the 1985 Federal Law on the Fundamentals of the System of Public Information likewise declared that "citizens and their associations may, under the conditions determined by law, publish newspapers and impart information through either media". In practice, the legal conditions excluded would-be media of which the League of Communists disapproved.[15] Permission had to be given by the SAWP and, in some republics, also by municipal authorities, who could veto any project on very vague grounds, virtually without right of appeal.

Content of the media was monitored by editorial councils, two-thirds of whose members were drawn from outside the medium. A variety of external bodies also had a monitoring role and were required to issue annual reports on the functioning of the press. These included the Commission for Ideological Work and the Commission for Political-Propaganda Activity in Information, both attached to the Central Committee of the League of Communists; the Section for Information and

---

[15] An Associated Press bulletin dated 22 June 1985 mentioned that a father and daughter had been refused permission to publish a private newspaper on the ground that "there is no justification for the project". Helsinki Watch, *Violations of the Helsinki Accords: Yugoslavia* (New York: Nov. 1986).

Public Opinion of the SAWP; the Committee for Press, Radio and Television of the Central Committee of the SAWP; and the republican branches of these bodies.[16]

Journalists

The official Code of Journalists of Yugoslavia defined a journalist as a "socio-political worker who, conscientiously adhering to the ideas of Marxism-Leninism, ... participates in the establishment and development of socialist self-management society". Journalists thus had an integral and instrumental place in the political system, a system which was opposed in principle to media independence. Theoretically, journalists served the whole of society through their commitment to the unending struggle for more and better self-management socialism. In practice, they were expected to serve the League of Communists by helping to garner the widest possible support in society for the policies of the government. A high degree of political orthodoxy was thus demanded of journalists. As late as 1989, when membership of the League of Communists had fallen below 10 per cent of the population as a whole, more than 80 per cent of journalists were members.[17] Membership was not an index of personal conviction, but a certificate of reliability.

In this context, obedience was presented as responsibility. In an interview published just after his death in 1980, President Josip Broz-Tito answered a question about "the role and tasks of the youth press". His reply reiterated the classic guidelines for Yugoslavia's news media in general. The youth press

> should be as far as possible in harmony with the revolutionary development of our society and generally committed ... . [It] holds an important place in the ideological and political education of the young. But its responsibility is equally great. For it

---

[16] Ramet, supra note 10 at 416.

[17] S P Ramet, "The Role of the Press in Yugoslavia", in J B Allcock, J B Horton and M Milivojevic (eds.), *Yugoslavia in Transition: Choices and Constraints, Essays in Honour of Fred Singleton* (New York and Oxford: Ber Ltd), 414-441.

must act in full accord with the League of
Communists, explain to young people the activities
we are engaged in, the problems we confront and the
measures we are now taking to tackle them.[18]

Journalists should only be critical, therefore, insofar as the League
of Communists itself was critical. To criticise the League would be, in
these terms, no less than a professional betrayal.

Two current consequences of the Yugoslav concept of 'committed'
journalism may be mentioned. The first was noted by Gertrude Robinson
back in 1977, in her remark that in Yugoslavia "media professionals still
view themselves as the rightful custodians of public knowledge, rather than
as facilitators of public debate".[19] The second effect is the phenomenon
of journalists who 'converted' from one authoritarian dogma (self-
management socialism) to another (one-party nationalism) as easily as
changing a suit of clothes.

Radio and Television

Broadcasting frequencies in Yugoslavia were controlled and
distributed by the federal government. Each unit of the federation had its
own radio and television service, under the name of its capital city. These
stations were 'socially owned', and, as in newspaper companies, the staff
had, via the Workers' Councils, a nominal role in ratifying the
appointment of executives who were selected by the republican parliament.
In reality, the League of Communists' influence was decisive; if staff
voted for the 'wrong' candidate, the League could oblige the procedure to
be repeated until the desired appointment was obtained. There were
unwritten conventions that the director-general of the service, and
sometimes the editor-in chief of television, were members of the Central
Committee of the republican League of Communists. Administrative
control of the stations was exercised by the republican Ministries of
Information.

---

[18] Quoted in XX(1) *Socialist Thought and Practice*, 1980.

[19] Robinson, supra note 1 at 230.

Content was vetted as closely as executive appointments. "Television is a medium in the service of the state and is, therefore, under strict censorship", wrote Croatian writer and dramatist Ivo Bresan. "If anything is to appear on TV it has to pass hundreds of officials and readings. What is permitted in a book cannot be stated on stage. What is not allowed in the theatre can pass in a movie, but what passes in a film cannot be shown on TV."[20]

The Rise of Television

"The development of television began in the 1960s, and it rapidly became the most widespread and influential medium of public information."[21] Sales of TV sets rose during the 1960s by 60 per cent, and the number of local radio stations rose by a multiple of 11. By 1974, 90 per cent of the population was watching television.[22]

Television grew up within the decentralized pattern which was being implemented in other media. Each republic had its own station and, by the mid-1970s, so had the two autonomous regions of Vojvodina and Kosovo. Autonomy was so far-reaching that "the republican stations cannot even agree on the desirability of fostering a 'sense of national unity' among their people", as Robinson noted. "All they are willing to concede is that they need an umbrella organisation to co-ordinate practical problems of programme development and scheduling." The stations were "equal and organizationally independent, deciding autonomously what programmes their audience want to watch and listen to".[23] The frequencies were shared among the stations, leaving only one federal frequency which the Jugoslovenska Narodna Armija (JNA, Yugoslav People's Army) could activate in an emergency.

In accord with the Titoist method of national balancing (specifically, in this respect, 'compensating' the Serb nation for

---

[20] *Vjesnik*, 15 April 1989, quoted in 53-54 *CADDY Bulletin*. CADDY is the Committee to Aid Democratic Dissidents in Former Yugoslavia.

[21] Federal Secretariat for Information, supra note 2 at 215.

[22] Robinson, supra note 1 at 33, 47, and 49.

[23] Robinson, supra note 1 at 50.

federalism), a quota system by nationality was observed in executive positions in the broadcasting service in those republics where Serbs were a constitutive people, namely Croatia and Bosnia, as well as in Serbia and the two autonomous provinces. In Zagreb, the ratio was 1:1. If the director-general of broadcasting was a Croat, the director of television would be Serb, and vice-versa. Likewise in Novi Sad and Priština: respectively a Serb and Hungarian, and a Serb and an Albanian. In Belgrade, Serbs held both positions. In Sarajevo, the position of editor-in-chief of television was added to the ratio, so that a Serb, a Croat and a Muslim would hold the top three positions.

Jugoslovenska Radio-Televizija (JRT, Yugoslav Radio-Television) was the federal body that co-ordinated the television schedules, including exchange of programmes. Until the late 1980s almost all programmes were broadcast on all stations, not necessarily at the same moment. Basic scheduling was agreed at twice-yearly meetings. The editors for different categories of programming, including news, politics, sport, culture and documentaries, also convened each month.

Co-ordination of programming was tightest among the Serbo-Croatian language services, meaning TV Belgrade, TV Zagreb, TV Sarajevo, TV Titograd, and half each of TV Novi Sad and TV Priština (which also broadcast in Hungarian and Albanian respectively). TV Ljubljana produced programmes only in Slovenian, and TV Skopje only in Macedonian.

At first, television news for all the Serbo-Croatian stations was produced by TV Belgrade. TV Zagreb, for instance, was allowed only to supplement this with a programme of republican news. Then Zagreb gained the right to make its own news every Tuesday and, later, every night, while other stations' news programmes were shown by rota on Zagreb's second channel.

Goran Milić, a former news editor at TV Belgrade news and the most famous television presenter in Yugoslavia, describes the Serbo-Croatian stations' co-operation in news and current affairs:

> Monday, let's say, was for foreign policy programmes; one station made the programme, and all six stations would show it. Small stations like Titograd didn't have the licence-fee revenue to produce as many programmes as the big stations, so Belgrade and Zagreb might take 15 weeks each out

of 52, Sarajevo probably had 11, Novi Sad seven, and Titograd four. But for prestigious programmes like the Tuesday talkshow, everyone wanted equal time. It was cheap to produce, and you could present your republic's policy in five other federal units. And each station produced the evening news programme for all five stations once a week; everyone was in favour of that.

There was some jealousy among us, because we thought the little stations were too privileged. The other stations [TV Ljubljana, TV Skopje, plus the Hungarian service in Novi Sad and the Albanian service in Priština] always went along on Tito's state visits abroad, while the Serbo-Croatian stations, who were covering roughly 80 percent of the Yugoslav audiences, had a rota for covering important events, so they sent one journalist.

Costs were shared in the proportion of the licence fees, so there were different interests. Take sport. Titograd was always voting for live coverage of some football match abroad. That would cost US$20,000 or more, of which Titograd was only liable for 3 per cent. For them it was a good deal! Or expensive foreign movies, Titograd paid 2 per cent of the fee, while Belgrade paid 28 per cent and Zagreb, 22 per cent. So there was rivalry, there were problems, but it was not unbearable. And the compensation of working in a larger station was that you could be more popular and you had more advantages as a journalist.

During the 1980s, every kind of co-operation among the republics became controversial, and television schedules were no exception. Controversy and competition were most intense in news and current affairs programming. Milić again:

The system was that each station contributed one story to the Sunday evening news. After Tito's death it became obvious that the different stations were using Sunday evening to present their republics' priorities.[24] Croatia would send a story about tourism, shipbuilding or the question of foreign currency. Sarajevo would go back to history and speak about Partisan heroes, the Non-Aligned Movement, keeping the image of Tito alive. Titograd and Skopje talked about underdeveloped areas. Novi Sad would report about agriculture, and Belgrade, about the stupid disintegration of the economy. TV Belgrade's idea was centralization of economy and politics, and always insisting on Yugoslavia, Yugoslavia ... .

There was also the political magazine programme on Thursdays: an hour or 90 minutes, with several subjects chosen by one station, presented as the mirror of that republic. So, every fifth Thursday, you could see what, for example, Bosnia thinks according to the criteria of the station's and the republic's social point of view.

For internal politics, the system was that everyone took the domicile station's report about an event, and broadcast it untouched. If the Central Committee of the League of Communists of Bosnia-Hercegovina had a session, TV Sarajevo might broadcast several hours of coverage, and the other stations would probably run a five-minute report in their news, *but as a rule those five minutes were prepared by TV Sarajevo.*

At the same time the bigger stations were putting correspondents in the most important republics. Belgrade had them in Zagreb and Sarajevo, later in Ljubljana, not in Montenegro or Macedonia but yes, in Kosovo. Zagreb had its correspondent in Belgrade, as had Sarajevo later. Otherwise, if a

---

[24] It should also be added that the variety of perspectives on the Sunday news did not merely reflect political arguments among republics; the stations also sought something 'characteristic' from each other.

situation was especially troubled or interesting, you might send a reporter, but basically, within the Serbo-Croatian stations, not.

"Then came Kosovo", Milić continues:[25]

> The principle was that TV Priština should report from Kosovo, but just before Slobodan Milošević [then leading the League of Communists of Serbia] started the attack on Kosovo's autonomy [in 1988], TV Belgrade installed a correspondent in Priština with a direct link to the Serbian capital. This correspondent was a very tough nationalist and his reports were independent of the Serbo-Croatian service of the domicile station, TV Priština.

TV Belgrade was not breaking with the schedule negotiated by JRT; it merely replaced TV Priština's reports about Kosovo with its own reports, and fed these into the federal system as part of its own output. The other stations reacted by sending their own reporters to Kosovo. "For the first time," Milić emphasizes, "political events in one federal unit were covered by five, six or even eight crews."

This was in 1987. One reason the other stations reacted so quickly to TV Belgrade's stratagem was, says Milić, their anger at the station's biased representation of a key event in Yugoslavia's disintegration. In April 1987, Slobodan Milošević visited Kosovo; during a speech to a crowd of local Serb people who were skirmishing with the cordon of police, he uttered a sentence of support for the crowd: "No one shall beat you again!" The sentence became famous immediately, thanks in part to TV Belgrade.

"The other stations were mad that TV Belgrade used its monopoly of coverage to show only the police pushing the demonstrators, not the crowd stoning the police", Milić explains:

> That was the crucial moment. After that, the joint programmes on Tuesday, Thursday, even the foreign

---

[25] See also Chapter 3, section on 'Kosovo'.

politics on Monday, were used so that instead of a report about non-alignment or the US economy to whatever, there would be 'world reactions to Kosovo', with Belgrade showing a wholly positive picture and Zagreb negative.

Abused from within, the JRT rota arrangement was too fragile to last. It broke down during 1988. The first station to withdraw was Zagreb, and Sarajevo followed. Federal co-ordination still worked for sport, culture, movies, everything except politics. Zagreb continued to show other stations' news and current affairs programmes, including some from Serbia, but it gave no station *carte blanche* to broadcast whatever it liked, in a given slot.

In 1989, when Serbia's leadership succeeded in cancelling the regional autonomy of Kosovo and Vojvodina, and in changing the leadership in Montenegro, TV Novi Sad, TV Priština and TV Titograd were turned into mouthpieces of TV Belgrade, itself a mouthpiece of the Milošević's government. "What we had at the beginning of 1990," says Milic, "was eight TV stations in which four worked as one, directed from one centre, and four others each covered its own territory."

The manipulation and breakdown of consensus in Yugoslav television foreshadowed a similar breakdown in the organs of federal government, likewise drawn from the six republics and the two regions. The federal parliament and the federal presidency, a "collective head of state", were not abolished or reformed in 1989 when the League of Communists of Serbia captured the two autonomous regions and engineered a new leadership in neighbouring Montenegro. Rather Serbia used its quadrupled vote to try and impose its own agenda. Like the television schedule consensus, the organs of government became unworkable because other republics refused to collaborate in their own domination though they also declined to unite in defence of democratic principles; for Serbia's behaviour had inflamed national ambitions of their own.

Chapter 2

THE PAN-YUGOSLAV NEWS MEDIA

Background

A separate front in the 'media war' waged by the leaderships in
Serbia and Croatia was reserved for their campaigns to capture or
undermine pan-Yugoslav news media, media which were supposed to
service and address the whole federation, without privileging any of its
units or nations over others.

The key pan-Yugoslav news media were Tanjug, the state news
agency; *Borba*, a daily newspaper; and Yutel, a short-lived television
station. Despite their differences, these three media represented a unified
information space throughout Yugoslavia. In 1990 and 1991 republican
leaderships which wanted to extend their power within Yugoslavia or to
break up the federation, and which were mustering their electorates behind
these designs, had to confront the question of what to do about Tanjug,
Borba, and Yutel.

Tanjug

Tanjug was Yugoslavia's only news agency. Its name is an
acronym of Telegrafska Agencija Nove Jugoslavije (Telegraph Agency of
New Yugoslavia), founded by Tito's Partisan command during the Second
World War and later built up as the information flagship of the new
federation. By the 1970s its daily output of "40,000-odd words for local
and 45,000 for international customers" gave Tanjug eighth place "in the
international news market, after the five international super agencies,
China's Xinua, and Egypt's Middle East News Agency".[1] With its

---

[1] G Robinson, *Tito's Maverick Media: The Politics of Mass Communications in
Yugoslavia* (Illinois: 1977), 68-69. The five super agencies were Reuters, Agence
France Presse, TASS, Associated Press and United Press International.

handsome headquarters in Belgrade, its network of bureaus and correspondents throughout the federation, and offices in some 50 countries worldwide by the 1980s, Tanjug was practically as well as politically unchallengeable. It served all the influential daily papers, all the television stations, and the chief radio stations in Yugoslavia.

While the quality of staff and their reports was always variable, since the 1960s (as Yugoslavia liberalized) Tanjug gained a reputation which no other Communist country's news agency could approach. As the state agency of a party-state, however, Tanjug was always vulnerable to explicit use as a political instrument. At moments of crisis, "indirect censorship" could be "reimposed, sometimes through Tanjug channels handing down the official foreign policy line".[2]

There was a "division of labour between Tanjug and the [domestic] print media", with the agency "specializing in foreign news and verbatim accounts of plans, government reports, and speeches of national interest, and the papers using their own reporters to interpret local news in a more individualistic manner".[3] Domestic political coverage showed Tanjug in the most orthodox light ("Tanjug does not cover human interest, religion, culture and crime.").[4] Abroad, its reporters had more opportunity to use initiative, not least because the Yugoslav agency "lost its monopoly on foreign news reporting during the 1960s", when the main newspapers started posting correspondents abroad.[5]

As the Yugoslav crisis deepened through the 1980s, the republican leaderships turned to their own national constituencies, and ideological pressure on the all-Yugoslav media relaxed. Tanjug's journalists and editors took the opportunity to continue building the professionalism of the agency.

According to Yugoslav law, the federal government appointed Tanjug's director and editor-in-chief; self-management practice required that the latter appointment then be approved by the employees. In autumn 1990, Federal Premier Ante Marković tried to replace both appointees, but his choice of new editor-in-chief was vetoed by the employees (who preferred the deputy editor of the international desk, Dušan Reljić). The

---

[2] Id. at 36.
[3] Id. at 33.
[4] Id. at 160.
[5] Id. at 86.

old editor, a Bosnian appointed in the mid-1980s, kept his place. The new director, a Macedonian, was well regarded by his staff but he had little authority in day-to-day editorial matters.

The March 1991 street protests in Belgrade were well reported by Tanjug, with none of the hysteria and abuse that the Serbian press displayed.[6] The editor responsible for this coverage was Dušan Reljić. However, the deputy editor-in-chief, Dušan Župan, was leading an attempt to change Tanjug into a pro-Milošević agency.

Despite resistance among the staff, by autumn 1991, says Reljić, "the group which wanted to ally Tanjug with Milošević was openly collaborating with the secret police". This group forwarded the agency's bulletins, as these were written, to the state security services. The director was stigmatized as a Macedonian nationalist, the Bosnian editor-in-chief was accused of rehabilitating fascism, and their ousting was engineered in December 1991. Župan took editorial control; the new director was Slobodan Jovanović, editor of *Politika ekspres*, the daily paper that had led the media attacks against Tanjug. Journalists who persisted in resisting the enforced changes "were relegated, sidelined and pressured to leave", says Reljić, who was among the chief resisters. His role in producing objective coverage of the March upheaval also counted against him. He was accused of being an agent of the Vatican and of Hans-Dietrich Genscher, the German Foreign Minister, then pushing for Croatia and Slovenia to be recognized as separate states.[7]

Demoted, Reljić quit and joined Belgrade's independent news weekly *Vreme*. With hindsight, he locates the moment when Tanjug began

---

[6] On Serbian press coverage of the March 1991 demonstrations, see Ch. 3, section on 'Coverage of Internal Opposition' infra.

[7] Genscher was a favourite target of media abuse in Serbia at this time. One example: the popular weekly news-feature magazine *Intervju* depicted Genscher on its cover of 13 Dec. 1991 as Count Dracula, complete with fangs. (Noted by I Banac, "The Fearful Asymmetry of War: The Causes and Consequences of Yugoslavia's Demise", 121(2) *Daedalus*, [Spring 1992].) 'Vampirical' was a favourite epithet of Serb propaganda against Croatia and its supporters, as examples in Ch. 3 show. Radovan Karadžić, the Bosnian Serb politician, described the war in Croatia as a war against a "vampirised fascist consciousness". (N Malcolm, *Bosnia: A Short History* [London: 1994], 228.) This propaganda notion (of Croats as 'undead') took wide effect; apart from drawing upon the rich Balkan folklore about vampires, the propaganda echoed a favourite political myth of Serb nationalists: that Croats (like Slovenes) had battened parasitically upon Yugoslavia and its truest guardians, the Serbs.

to run downhill: 9 March 1991, when the first reports arrived from the streets that the Jugoslovenska Narodna Armija (JNA, Yugoslav People's Army) had arrived to confront the demonstrators. The agency's chiefs refused to issue the reports until the JNA was shown on television, by which time Tanjug was already two hours behind other media.

The republican bureaus' reports varied in quality and impartiality. The Kosovo desk took a Serbian nationalist stance in the 1980s, while the Sarajevo desk reflected, up to the brink of war in Bosnia, the traditional anti-nationalism of the League of Communists in that republic. In Croatia, the bureau gained a reputation for professionalism. By April 1990, the 15-strong Tanjug bureau in Zagreb was providing some 30 per cent of the agency's total domestic output. After the elections, the victorious Hrvatska Demokratska Zajednica (HDZ, Croatian Democratic Community) led by Franjo Tudjman, began at once to subvert Tanjug. Ministers wouldn't talk to Tanjug, on the pretext that it was a Serbian tool, despite the fact that all except one of the employees were Croat by nationality.

HINA's first director, Josip Šentija, says the idea of a Croatian news agency dates from February 1989, when the HDZ was drafting a strategy for power. "That was the will, even then ... to get rid of all Yugoslavism, meaning Tanjug, too, as the state Yugo-agency which was doing what it did, in information, propaganda, politics, the secret services, on the home front and abroad as well."[8]

In November 1990, Tanjug was served with an eviction order from its Zagreb offices, on the pretext that the government departments on other floors of the building needed more space. The real motive emerged in February 1991, when the whole building was given to HINA, the new Croatian state news agency.[9] With its 200-line telephone cable, the Zagreb office was the distribution centre for all Tanjug subscribers in Croatia and also for subscribers to Reuters' on-line business service.

A decision to move to new premises was repeatedly stalled by the bureau chief, Mirko Bolfek. Bolfek suddenly departed Tanjug in April 1991, to become editor-in-chief at HINA. Žarko Modrić, a respected local journalist who succeeded Bolfek as the bureau chief, led the four remaining journalists to a new office. Most of the staff had already left

---

[8] J Šentija, *Slobodna Dalmacija*, 8 June 1993.

[9] Hrvatska Izveštajna Novinska Agencija (HINA, the Croatian News Reporting Agency).

during the winter of 1990-1991, intimidated by anonymous phone calls, warnings from other colleagues, and threats to their families.

According to Modrić, in 1990 the main Croatian media were still publishing Tanjug reports, sometimes without naming the source, and they continued their subscriptions until August 1991. "When the war started [in August] we were actually more independent than before", Modrić says. "Belgrade couldn't exert any pressure on us, and the Zagreb government didn't try. Some individuals refused to speak to us, but officially we had no problem with access to the President, the government and parliament." The government's aim, Modrić believes, was to pressure Croatian media to stop using Tanjug, rather than to prevent Tanjug operating. The bureau continued to function normally although its telecommunications services were now contracted to the post office. Modrić was on occasion prevented from entering the post office by workers claiming to have lost relations in the fighting.

Regional correspondents in Osijek and Dubrovnik were more vulnerable to pressure, and they had stopped working by August. Other offices in Pula, Split and Rijeka also fell silent. When telephone links with Serbia were cut in September 1991, copy had to be faxed to Sarajevo and thence to Belgrade. Even so, Modrić recalls, his report of the 7 October rocket attack on the President's palace in Zagreb was put on the wire in Belgrade only 35 minutes after the explosion.

Modrić was called a *četnik* in Croatian media while the Serbian dailies *Politika ekspres* and *Večernje novosti* branded him a Croatian nationalist. The pro-Milošević faction at Tanjug's headquarters called him an *ustaša*.[10] He resigned in December, when it became clear that Tanjug's director and editor-in-chief were about to be replaced. One Tanjug correspondent remains in Zagreb, faxing his copy to Belgrade via Vienna. In 1991 and 1992, the government tried to coerce him to leave by sending soldiers to intimidate him in his office, which has also been attacked and robbed. According to Vladimir Gajić, the chief editor at Tanjug's domestic desk (which comprises, significantly, Serbia, Montenegro, Bosnia-Hercegovina, and the self-declared 'Serb Republic of Krajina'[11]), the last man in Zagreb, however, has "big problems, because he's a Serb.

---

[10] For *četnik* and *ustaša*, see Glossary.

[11] Krajina is the Serb-controlled area of Croatia.

He was mobilized to fight in the Croatian Army early in 1993. Luckily his contacts in the ex-Ministry of Information were able to save him."

There also remains a correspondent in neighbouring Slovenia. Tanjug's reporter in Ljubljana has managed to retain his spacious office and works without problems. Gajić says that Slovenia's state radio and television even subscribe to Tanjug.

Tanjug's fate in Bosnia was different again. Zlatan Husarić was a Tanjug journalist in Sarajevo for 15 years, until 1 August 1992, when telephone links with Serbia were cut and contact became "technically absolutely impossible", according to Gajić. Then the office was attacked for the second time, and the journalists accepted defeat.[12] A year later, Husarić learned that Tanjug had sacked its Sarajevo bureau on 1 August.

Tanjug's Sarajevo bureau of six reporters tried to work normally through the first four months of war in Bosnia. When they realized that the Belgrade desk was altering their reports so as to exonerate the Serb side and incriminate the government side, the journalists objected. Belgrade ignored the protests, and the reporters tried another tack: they "simplified" their reports. Asked what this meant in practice, Husarić said that "for example, we would write 'Sarajevo was bombarded today'", without identifying the Serb aggressor. Husarić's account is hard to doubt: currently the director of the BH Press Centre,[13] the government news agency in Sarajevo, he has more motive to deny any self-censorship by himself and his Tanjug colleagues than to overstate it.

An example of this self-censorship is a report by Tanjug bureau staffer Mirjana Mičevska, dated 2 May 1992. It paints a mild but still typical Tanjug view of the stricken city:

> Life in Sarajevo has come to a complete standstill
> after nearly two months of armed clashes which have
> raged in the capital of the former Yugoslav republic
> of Bosnia-Hercegovina. The fear and uncertainty are
> equal for Muslims, Serbs, and Croats, who are all

---

[12] In the first attack, on 13 April 1992, "the Sarajevo offices of [Tanjug] allegedly were demolished and robbed. The Serbian press in Bosnia-Hercegovina and Serbia accuse the 'military formations of the former Bosnia-Hercegovina' of the attack." Helsinki Watch, *War Crimes in Bosnia-Hercegovina: A Helsinki Watch Report* (New York: Helsinki Watch, 1992), 129.

[13] On the BH Press Centre, see Ch. 5 infra.

fleeing in large numbers from a war which was imposed on them and of which they are all victims. Snipers are shooting at everything that moves, not choosing their victims ... . Almost all the shops and warehouses have been looted. War profiteering has taken root and looted goods are brought out onto improvised counters and offered for enormous prices ... .

Nowhere does Mičevska's piece (as published) say who is doing this, to whom, or why.

The reporters' self-censorship testifies to a naïve calculation: better if some of the truth gets out than none at all. It also reflects the profound confusion and sense of disbelief reigning in Sarajevo during the first months of the assault; a confusion about the aims and meaning of the war, which baffled political and military brains as well as journalistic ones.[14]

Asked if it was true, as Husarić alleges, that copy from the Sarajevo desk was rewritten in Belgrade, Vladimir Gajić said, "From his point of view, maybe. I understand his position." He went on to explain that "many reports" reaching their desk during that period "were coloured with propaganda. Whenever sources were omitted or dubious, we cut in other information from other sources."[15]

This is a self-serving response; it does not account for the polemical, prejudicial terms which Tanjug adopted from the outset. Armed forces of the legal and internationally-recognized government were "Muslim forces", "*mujahedin*", "Muslim-Croat forces", "Muslim extremists", "Muslim paramilitary organizations", or at best the "Bosnia-Hercegovina Territorial Defence forces loyal to the republic's Muslim-Croat leadership". The government was "the Muslim-Croat Government". President Alija Izetbegović was "leader of Bosnian Muslims", "President of the Muslim-Croat Presidency", or "the pro-Muslim Presidency".

These terms framed an overall perspective: that a Muslim-Croat coalition had caused the "inter-ethnic" war by obtaining independence

---

[14] See Ch. 5, section on 'TV Journalists and the Question of Impartiality', infra, for discussion of the impartiality debate in Bosnia.

[15] V Gajić to author, 14 Oct. 1993.

without "Serb consent"; and that the Bosnian Serbs had only reacted to a blatant threat, and were defending themselves, at first with JNA help. This perspective, which distorted every detail, was constantly reiterated in bulletins during April and May 1992.

Secondly, Tanjug's output shows that Gajić's use of the term 'dubious sources' has meant in practice 'non-Serb' sources. 'Serb sources', 'police sources' (in Serb-controlled areas), 'Yugoslav Army sources' or plain 'army sources' could, apparently, get any story onto Tanjug's wires, as if these sources were immune to the 'propaganda' which Gajić was so alert to excise.

Serbian public opinion has been of the utmost importance to the Serb strategy in Bosnia; Tanjug has largely monopolized Serbian press coverage of the war, and it has worked tirelessly with the Srpska Demokratksa Stranka (SDS, Serb Democratic Party) in Bosnia and the Srpska Republika Novinksa Agencija (SRNA, the Serb Republic News Agency) to keep Serbia's public actively or at least passively on-side.[16] Milorad Komrakov, a news editor at TV Belgrade, told ARTICLE 19 that Tanjug bulletins form the basis of 90 per cent of TV Belgrade's news reports.[17] Branka Mihajlović, a former colleague of Komrakov, who has become an outspoken critic of Serbian television, puts the matter thus, "Tanjug is the great problem for independent news in Serbia. Studio B and TV Politika use it because there is no alternative."[18] *Borba* journalist Gordana Logar says that her paper uses Tanjug when the paper has "no other source" for a story, meaning no other Serbian or international network news source.[19] Such sources are relatively rare for *Borba*, let alone for smaller, less well known media.

---

[16] The SDS is the political party which won most Serb votes in the 1990 elections in Bosnia-Hercegovina. Under the leadership of Radovan Karadžić, the party joined a three-way coalition government. It proceeded to undermine that government by declaring Serb autonomy across large tracts of the republic, by colluding with the JNA to arm Bosnian Serb irregular forces, and finally, from early April 1992, by serving as the political front for an all-out assault against the republic.

SRNA is the news agency of the 'Serb Republic of Bosnia-Hercegovina' proclaimed by the SDS on 27 March 1992.

[17] Milorad Komrakov to author, 11 Oct. 1993.

[18] B Mihajlović to author, 30 Sept. 1993. Studio B and TV Politika are the only rivals to State television news in Serbia.

[19] G Logar to author, 8 Oct. 1993.

By the autumn of 1993, Tanjug had correspondents in Banja Luka and Zvornik; others were planned for Pale, Trebinje, and Jajce. There were stringers in Bijeljina, Brčko, Prijedor, Doboj, and Petrovac. All these reporters had open telephone lines to Belgrade. No other medium could compete with this coverage in the Serb-controlled, 'ethnically-cleansed', 70 per cent of the republic.

In its strategic omissions and distortions, Tanjug's front-line reporting was almost indistinguishable from that of the foremost Serbian media. "Clashes" and "battles" were favoured words; "fierce fighting" constantly "raged" in contested areas. Passive constructions abounded, as in "Sarajevo roads are blocked". Sarajevo's attackers were not identified: "movement through some parts of the capital is dangerous because of snipers" (22 May 1992). The agency was fond, too, of sedative information: a return to "normal life" in Zvornik ("which is under Serb control") on 7 May 1992; "another quiet night" in Sarajevo on 22 May 1992.

Asked about Tanjug's silence on the identity of Sarajevo's besiegers during these first months, Vladimir Gajić muttered that "some people in Belgrade" had wanted it this way because they mistakenly thought it was "patriotic" and in "Serbian national interests".

Until 1989, as much as 40 per cent of Tanjug's revenue came from the federal government, the remainder from subscriptions. By 1991, subscription revenue had risen to 80 per cent.[20] It has since fallen sharply, and its economic situation is gloomy. Since 1992 the 50 Tanjug bureaus outside former Yugoslavia have been reduced to only 15, "including a couple of stringers", says Goran Opačić at the Tanjug desk in Belgrade's International Press Centre. The inner purging of doubters continued in 1993. According to the Belgrade Centre for Anti-War Action, 12 Tanjug foreign correspondents were dismissed "because of their political attitudes" early in 1993.[21] When the Federal Minister of Information warned in July 1993 that "destructive hyperinflation" was threatening Tanjug, he was serving notice that more cuts should be expected.[22]

---

[20] D Reljić to author, 5 Oct. 1993.

[21] 1 *Bulletin Voice*, April 1993.

[22] Tanjug bulletin, 22 July 1993.

Tanjug's near monopoly has been artificially prolonged by the Serbian government but has eroded, even under war conditions, as it must when there is such a demand for news and Tanjug offers such a poor service. Using desktop technology, the *VIP News Report*, a daily news digest in English, is the first private-enterprise rival for Tanjug's English-language subscriptions in Belgrade. In 1994, FoNet was started by a former Tanjug correspondent. Registration is more difficult for Serbian-language agencies, but they continue to appear: the Alternativna Informativna Mreža (AIM, the Alternative Information Network) in Paris, a new agency in Montenegro, and others.[23]

Borba

As the news organ of the League of Communists of Yugoslavia, the daily *Borba*, based in Belgrade, was printed in huge numbers in the postwar years: 650,000 in 1949.[24] These copies went largely unsold and unread, according to Branislav Milošević, the paper's current deputy editor. Despite some liberalization in the 1950s, *Borba* did not become the official all-Yugoslav newspaper until 1964, when ownership passed to the Socialist Alliance of Working People (SAWP).[25] *Borba*'s reputation for unalloyed tedium continued; it was the paper that JNA officers and professional communists should be seen to read. The paper on Tito's desk, in the Tito Memorial Museum, is *Borba*. It was more than coincidence that *Borba* should have furnished, as late as 1987, classic proof of what the Croatian journalist Danko Plevnik calls "the deep complicity between the secret services and journalists" in Yugoslavia.[26]

---

[23] AIM, with its headquarters in Paris, is an agency using local journalists in four of Yugoslavia's former six republics, particularly journalists whose views have led to their dismissal from government-controlled media.

[24] Robinson, supra note 1 at 33.

[25] On the SAWP, see glossary.

[26] Plevnik is describing how a notorious economic scandal in Bosnia was leaked via a *Borba* correspondent in Serbia. The scandal was trumped up by politicians, in Belgrade and Sarajevo, in order to disgrace a popular Bosnian politician-entrepreneur. The journalist committed suicide soon afterwards. (D Plevnik, *Hrvatski obrat* [Zagreb: Durieux, 1993], 33.)

Things were changing, however, with the arrival of a new editor, determined to wake the paper up. During the Central Committee session in 1987, which saw Milošević take power in the League of Communists of Serbia, *Borba* printed every statement, including those critical of the Milošević tendency. According to veteran *Borba* journalist Gordana Logar, the paper lost many bulk subscriptions in Serbia because of its refusal to salute Milošević's victory.

In 1988, the important step was taken of ending the separate edition in Zagreb (in Latin script), and instead combining the Cyrillic and Latin scripts in every issue, as if proving through typography how the paper transcended national-cultural differences. It was an indication of new vigour when, in 1988, the paper ran a series of articles exposing "the decadent lifestyle of top Communists ... including the [federal] Prime Minister, Branko Mikulić".[27]

This sort of material brought reprimands from the apparatchiks and Serbian nationalists at the SAWP; on 13 April, for instance, *Borba* was told that its "editorial errors will not be tolerated".[28] When Mikulić's successor, Ante Marković, launched his economic reforms in 1989, *Borba* was an obvious candidate for privatization. The federal government bought some 17 per cent of shares, banks 15 per cent, and employees 12 per cent. The rest was bought by businesses, themselves unprivatized.

At that time, Logar remarks, "everything and everyone in Serbia were against Marković. Businesses close to the regime were making hostile takeover bids. We appealed to readers to buy shares, which weren't expensive. We printed purchasers' names every day ... it became a society column". She says some 3,000 readers bought 7 per cent of the shares.

By 1990, open elections in Croatia had brought Franjo Tudjman and his HDZ party to power, and the Serbian media were campaigning on behalf of the Serb minority in Croatia. *Borba* tried to remain impartial when the rest of the Belgrade press had abandoned any constraint. Its reporting, for example, of the proclamation by radical Croatian Serb leaders of "Serb autonomy in Croatia" was balanced; the Zagreb correspondent's reports from Knin, the rebel Serb stronghold, struck an ironic note about wild accusations of Croatian aggression (1 October and 4 October 1990).

[27] *The Guardian*, 23 April 1988.
[28] 52 *Caddy Bulletin*, March-April 1989.

The Belgrade riots in March 1991 showed *Borba* at its most independent. Relying heavily on Tanjug's objective reports (see above), the paper coolly described events without denigrating the protesters, let alone condemning them. Its headline of 13 March identified the role of police violence: "How the police settled accounts with the demonstrators of 9 March." Logar says sales leapt to 150,000, and that for the first time the paper "gained a new readership of young people."

Borba's finest hour came in April, when Croatian police and several civilians were killed in Borovo Selo, near Vukovar, at the eastern edge of Croatia.[29] Unlike the Serbian and Croatian media, *Borba* investigated the story. Its reporter examined President Tudjman's allegation that "*četniki* imported from Serbia" had been involved. He followed the trail of clues to Nova Pazova in Serbia and there interviewed Vojin Vuletić, "general secretary" of the paramilitary Serbian *Četnik* Movement, who revealed that the Movement had a "staff" in Borovo Selo which had indeed participated; specifically, one Vojislav Milić had taken part.[30] The reporter also learned from a Croatian Serb source that Serbian paramilitary volunteers were already in Borovo Selo, and from the vice-president of a nationalist opposition party, Srpski Pokret Obnove (SPO, Serbian Renewal Movement), that 700 of its volunteers were active in eastern Croatia.[31] The reporter's initiative in pursuing this story, and the paper's independence in publishing it, are all the more commendable when contrasted with the main Belgrade media's coverage, as Chapter Three shows.

This impartiality served to annoy both sides. According to Logar, 40 or 50 of the paper's news kiosks in Croatia were ransacked in spring 1991, before the war started, presumably by the same gangs which destroyed Serb property, both public and private, across the republic (some of these gangs were organized by the branches of the HDZ ruling party that had been undermining Tanjug for a year before Borovo Selo).[32]

---

[29] On Borovo Selo, see Ch. 3, section on 'Reporting Borovo Selo', infra.

[30] The Serbian daily *Politika ekspres* had mentioned Milić on 3 May as "a Serb from Nova Pazova". See Ch. 3, id.

[31] *Borba*, 4-5 May 1991.

[32] See, for example, the report of the violence in Zvornik in Ch. 4, section on '*Vjesnik* and *Večernji list*' infra.

Borba's vulnerability in Serbia was illustrated by an incident around the end of 1991. After the paper ran a report on the paramilitary leader Željko Ražnatović, known as "Arkan", and his volunteers (who were to play a ghastly role in the first onslaught on northern Bosnia in March and April 1992), Arkan arrived at the editor's office with two armed and uniformed bodyguards. They demanded that either *Borba* print an interview with Arkan, or they would "liquidate" Gradiša Katić, author of the offending report. There was no question of calling the police, since Arkan's secret service connections were common knowledge. *Borba* duly ran an interview, trying to lessen its effect by publishing alongside a second interview, with Dobroslav Paraga, leader of the neo-fascist Croatian Party of Right.

A team of researchers from Ljubljana University, Slovenia, who monitored Croatian and Serbian media during the war in Croatia, found that *Borba* tried "to maintain a 'rational' attitude to the war, publishing comprehensive information, including objective reports on the reactions of the Croatian government to individual events", a dimension missing from government-controlled media in Croatia.[33] This attitude carried over into its coverage of the war in Bosnia, where, however, it was harder to sustain. This was in part because the only Yugoslavia which *Borba* could represent (after Slovenia and Croatia were recognized as states in January 1992) was Greater Serbia in all but name; and partly because the conflict in Bosnia was aggression masked as civil war. *Borba*'s coverage confirmed that, even more than in Croatia, the policy of presenting both sides as equal obscured the character and aims of Serbia's aggression.

Lagging far behind the pace of events on the ground, *Borba*'s typical editorial tone in April 1992, the first month of war, was furnished by two front-page headlines: "Tragic events in Bosnia-Hercegovina - Bloody struggle between war and peace" (6 April), and "Bosnia-Hercegovina in the vortex of civil war: Bloodshed in Sarajevo" (7 April). Typically, the Bosnian whose views were most sought-after by *Borba* at this stage was the movie director Emir Kusturica, who was twice given space in *Borba* to express his opinions from Paris: "There is no solution to the situation in Bosnia-Hercegovina as long as national parties are in power" (6 April); "trust in the JNA must be restored", and young

---

[33] M Malešić (ed.), *The Role of Mass Media in the Serbian Croatian Conflict*, Psykologist Försvar Report 164 (Stockholm: 1993), 44.

Bosnian males should join the JNA "to defend Bosnia-Hercegovina" (13 April). Kusturica and *Borba* shared an arrogant and desperate reluctance to trust non-Serb reports from Bosnia.

Borba's coverage was almost as distorted and propagandist as the Politika group's press. On 9 April it carried SRNA bulletins about the "new genocide against the Serb people". It ran reams of Tanjug reports, for example about "pogroms of Serbs in Srebrenica" (15 May). *Borba*'s report of 2 April from Bijeljina, where Serbian paramilitaries massacred Muslims in the first days of April, merely noted that "Muslim extremists were on the loose." Reporting the situation in Višegrad on 2 April, shortly before the JNA and Serb irregulars massacred Muslims, *Borba* described an even fight between Serbian paramilitaries and Croat extremists, then allowed a spokesman from the SDS to have the last word. The information that paramilitaries from Serbia were involved was not given in the *Politika* press.

Borba's correspondent in Zvornik, M Lazarević, was especially pernicious, reporting "violent skirmishes" instead of the actual massacres taking place, and quoting only Serb sources, such as an unsupported claim of 28 April that the "armed Muslim groups" included HOS [Croatian neo-fascist militia], Kurds, *Šiptars*, Bangladeshi and Pakistani mercenaries.[34] Lazarević's coverage was in full harmony with the *Politika* press coverage of Zvornik.[35] *Borba* blamed the victims for their plight; its reports of 11-12 April stressed how many mistakes President Izetbegović had made, and how anti-Serbian he was.[36]

Unlike other Belgrade papers, however, *Borba* gave column space to Bosnian Muslim politicians (though not those from the ruling Stranka Demokratske Akcije (SDA, Democratic Action Party); and it covered anti-war protests in Belgrade. On 7 April it even ran an inside-page headline "Serb terrorists attack Sarajevo", quoting an SDA source. It is also true that Željko Vuković, one of *Borba*'s two correspondents in Sarajevo, attributed the 27 May 1992 bread-queue massacre to the Serb

---

[34] On *Šiptars*, see Glossary.

[35] See Ch. 3, section on 'Zvornik' infra.

[36] The argument implied by such writing, as by Kusturica's views, was that the Muslim nationalist ideas of Izetbegović and his SDA party meant that Bosnia itself, both as reality and as idea, was less worthy of being defended. It was an implication often encountered among Serbian oppositionists.

side: not explicitly, but to those forces "which have been bombarding Sarajevo for 51 days already".

Vuković and his colleague Natka Buturović escaped from Sarajevo towards the end of 1992, after *Oslobodjenje* published an anonymous bulletin from the "Armed Forces of the Republic of Bosnia-Hercegovina". The bulletin asked how "the *Borba* correspondents" and unnamed "journalists and editors at RTVBH"[37] were still working in Sarajevo?[38]

This intimidation may explain why Vuković later adapted his Sarajevo reports into a book, *Ubijanje Sarajeva* (Killing Sarajevo), which manifests a bitterness against all sides. Interestingly, he changed his mind about the bread queue massacre. "There is no proof, nor can there be, to show who fired upon the people queuing for bread", the book states, then explains why the question of responsibility is wide open: "The truth about the massacre remains, of necessity, a secret."[39]

It was a measure of the Serbian government's control over the media, and its determination to block every significant dissenting comment on the war, that *Borba* was repeatedly criticized "by citizens' groups and extremist political interests" during the pre-election campaign at the end of 1992. The ground for these accusations (which featured on TV Belgrade news) was that *Borba* had started the war, no less, by "inflaming opinion [in Bosnia] hostile to Serbia".[40] Yet this dangerously unpatriotic paper carried a weekly interview with Radovan Karadžić, 'President' of the 'Serb Republic'.[41]

Minor harassment continued in 1993. In one small provincial town purchasers of *Borba* saw their names being listed at the central kiosk, a classical police-state deterrent, and the paper's Subotica correspondent was called in to the police station for an informal talk about her work.[42]

---

[37] RTVBH is Radio-Television of Bosnia, the state broadcasting medium.

[38] *Oslobodjenje*, 18 Sept. 1992.

[39] Ž Vuković, *Ubijanje Sarajeva* (Belgrade: 1993), 75-76.

[40] European Institute for the Media (EIM), *The 1992 Federal and Republican Elections in Serbia and Montenegro: Coverage by Press, Radio and Television*, A Report by the Media Monitoring Unit (Manchester & Dusseldorf: EIM, Jan. 1993), 28.

[41] Branislav Milošević told the author that ending this weekly feature was one of the changes made at *Borba* by the new management in August 1993.

[42] *Borba*, 21 July and 17-18 July 1993, respectively.

The economic crisis and the exodus of educated Serbs, escaping war and sanctions, has damaged *Borba*'s readership, but the paper appears to have lost fewer sales through economic hardship than the other Serbian national dailies.[43] Before and after its heyday of March 1991, *Borba* was selling some 50,000 copies daily but the figure has since slumped to 30,000 or less. In summer 1993, paper shortages reduced the print run to around 7,500.[44]

A less obvious cause of the sales slump is the price freeze on newspapers, set by the government. In October 1993 the price was 250 dinars, "about eight [German] pfennigs", explained Branislav Milošević, "while the unit production cost is 12 or 15 pfennigs. The more we print, the more we lose. Our sales in Belgrade could easily be doubled, but we have no motive to try." *Borba* has to pay three times as much for newsprint as a government-controlled paper like *Večernje novosti*.

As well as living hand-to-mouth, the paper's staff are overshadowed by the permanent risk of capture by the Serbian government. The federal government (controlled by the Serbian government) still owns 17 per cent of stock. In 1993 rumours abounded that other shareholders were helping the federal government to dominate the paper. "On 8 July, Slavko Čuruvija became acting editor-in-chief, replacing Manojlo Vukotić, despite a vote of no-confidence from the editorial staff the previous day. Dušan Mijić (whose Finagra company owns 37 per cent of *Borba*'s stock) was appointed to head the new management of the newspaper with the support of the government, raising concerns about the future editorial direction of the publication."[45]

Despite a change of editor-in-chief, under Mijić's pressure, as yet the paper has not quite capitulated. The federal government's decision at the end of 1993 to sell its stock revived fears of a takeover by government-controlled businesses. (Its motive was probably simpler: to avoid liability when the paper's heavy losses for the past financial year were announced at the end of February 1994.) At present, *Borba* is probably more useful to the Serbian government as the only semi-independent daily in the new Yugoslavia (posing no threat to anything)

---

[43] Information from Srbobran Branković of the Public Opinion & Marketing Centre at the Institute for Political Studies, Belgrade.

[44] S Markotich, Radio Free Europe/Radio Liberty Research Report, 4 Feb. 1994.

[45] IFJ/FIEJ Centre, Ljubljana, 14 July 1993.

than as a martyr for free media. There is also an ideological reason for the government to leave it alone. Although *Borba*'s Yugoslavism is now spectral and passive, it has not formally been disowned. Why should the government curb the only Yugoslav newspaper before the veil of Yugoslavism is dropped from the reality of a Greater Serbia?

Yutel

Yutel was a federal television station which started its short troubled life in October 1990, amid high hopes. By contrast with Tanjug and *Borba*, which were conceived to serve the information system in a one-party state, Yutel's political goal was to speed Yugoslavia's passage toward full democracy. By aspiring to the highest standards of journalism, Yutel would show all facets of the truth to all of Yugoslavia's fractured and bewildered public. It would remind people, by force of objective programming, why Yugoslavia should stay together.

The main figure behind Yutel was Ante Marković, the Federal Prime Minister. The director was Nebojša Bato Tomašević, a former diplomat turned emigré publisher (based in London) who was well-connected among Belgrade political circles. The editor-in-chief was Goran Milić.

After Marković took office, in March 1989, it soon became clear that he faced a communications problem. Yugoslavia's mass media were dominated by republican governments which had no obligation to promote the federal government and no motive to do so unless its priorities coincided with their own. His programme of radical economic liberalization threatened their power both practically (undermining party-state monopolies) and ideologically (revitalizing the idea of Yugoslavia). His vision of a democratic and civic future directly challenged Serb and Croat nationalist projects, respectively to dominate Yugoslavia and to break with it.

National media in Serbia and Slovenia, which otherwise attacked each other, would attack Marković simultaneously.[46] "His speeches weren't shown on television," Milić remembers, "the Prime Minister

---

[46] P Tašić, *Kako sam branio Antu Markovića* (*How I Defended Ante Marković*) (Skopje: 1993), 42-44 and 146.

couldn't be seen."[47] Since there were no federal frequencies available to the government, Marković negotiated with all the stations to give him a weekly programme in their schedules, entitled *Ask the Federal Government*. "It was boring, it deliberately avoided polemics, so it was ignored", says Milić; and it was manipulated by the stations. When, on 15 November 1990, Marković made an important speech about a trumped-up scandal involving the Bank of Kosovo, the three Serbian TV stations refused to relay it; TV Belgrade showed a football match instead. Even Croatian TV delayed transmitting the speech. TV Belgrade was due to host *Ask the Federal Government* the following day, but refused to allow the Premier to appear on the programme, allegedly for technical reasons.[48] It is worth recalling that Western media at this time were portraying Marković as the undisputed political leader of Yugoslavia.

The government was thus tempted to divert start-up funds for a new TV station from the federal budget, via the relevant committee in the Federal Assembly. Marković began discussing the project with the republican TV stations in March 1990. Yutel director Tomašević remembers a constant round of almost fruitless talks with media and political leaders, trying to persuade them to let Yutel use the dormant third channel of their frequencies. "The idea was that each republic would have its Yutel production studio", he says. "I even thought these studios could be inside the republican stations. Eventually TV Ljubljana agreed to that"; but only TV Ljubljana.[49]

Then Tomašević tried to persuade the JNA to allow Yutel to use its frequencies and parallel network of transmitters. The JNA was interested, hoping to exploit Yutel's brand of pro-Yugoslav idealism to advance its own agenda of Communist or Serb-nationalist centralism. "When the JNA realized Yutel wasn't what it wanted, it backed off, saying its frequencies were needed for aircraft navigation", Tomašević says.

These failed negotiations, however, produced an agreement for Yutel to buy or lease editing equipment, cameras, and mobile transmitters from the JNA. "Every single solid thing we had, in terms of technical equipment, was from the army", says Jela Jevremović, Milić's deputy. "We were supposed to get much more but there was already a split between

---

[47] G Milić to author, 27 Aug. 1993.

[48] Tašić, supra note 47 at 44.

[49] N B Tomašević to author, 20 Dec. 1993.

JNA radicals who wanted a Greater Serbia, and moderates who were for Yugoslavia and socialism. So we never got the rest of the stuff."[50] It was "really bad" equipment, according to a Yutel journalist in Croatia. Much money was later spent hiring better cameras and editing systems from private firms. Milić says the JNA wanted $22 million for a set of 12 mobile transmitters. Marković accepted but never paid, and the JNA only delivered one, which couldn't be used because Yutel could not obtain a licence. He said that the other eleven "were later given to the Bosnian Serbs."

Yutel had no option but to seek piecemeal arrangements with the republican stations, only one of which, TV Sarajevo, in Bosnia-Hercegovina, was ready to lease facilities on a commercial basis.[51] The other stations reluctantly agreed to transmit Yutel for one hour per day; only TV Skopje in Macedonia freely co-operated.

The federal government signed a contract with TV Sarajevo, worth 160,000 Swiss francs per month, entitling Yutel to rent an editing suite and, for one hour daily, a studio. This extortionate fee was paid, like everything else at this stage, from the federal budget that Marković had arranged. According to board member Milan Gavrović, even for the five-month period when Yutel was transmitted throughout Yugoslavia, advertising revenue never covered more than 18 per cent of costs.[52]

At the end of 1991, when Marković resigned and the federal income abruptly ceased, Yutel faced debts of US$200,000, says Milić. "I settled at once with TV Sarajevo to pay 2,000 Swiss francs a month instead of 160,000 and they were very pleased," says Milić, "because they had been blackmailing the federal government, not us; we were very popular in Bosnia."

Meanwhile Tomašević and Milić had recruited a team of editors, reporters and technicians from around Yugoslavia, some 50 in all. Yutel

---

[50] J Jevremović to author, 30 Aug. 1993.

[51] TV Sarajevo could make this offer because it had managed to escape direct government control; it also needed to boost its income. (See Ch. 5 for more on TV Sarajevo.) The choice also suited Premier Marković, who was hoping for mass electoral support in Bosnia-Hercegovina. In July 1990 at Kozara in Bosnia, the site of a famous partisan uprising, Marković had announced that federal multi-party elections would be held, and he would contest them with his own party, the Reform Forces. Those elections were never held.

[52] M Gavrović to author, 4 Nov. 1993.

had other attractions, however, not necessarily compatible: scope for political idealists and for believers in Marković; a chance to work as "professionals" (within a framework of Yugoslav ideology); a ticket on the federal gravy train; a potential audience of five million, "which would be absolutely the record in Yugoslavia", says Milić. "All the people we recruited believed in Yugoslavia and wanted to save Yugoslavia", says Tomašević.

Obstacles remained. The JNA had agreed to adapt the former Museum of the Revolution as Yutel's transmission centre in Belgrade. The building was duly stripped out, drawing criticism from the Serbian press, which claimed Yutel was destroying Yugoslavia's heritage; but the refitting was inexplicably delayed. The business of registration, licences, and permits gave further scope for wrapping Yutel in red tape.

Eventually Yutel gave up on Belgrade, switched the transmission centre to Sarajevo, and began broadcasting on the evening of 23 October 1990, a month before the elections in Bosnia-Hercegovina.[53] "Good evening, Yugoslavia!", said the editor, though only a quarter of Yugoslavs could receive the broadcast. Dušan Mitević, general director of Radio-Televizija Beograd (RTB, Radio-Television Belgrade), had told a press conference that day that TV Belgrade would not be transmitting Yutel for the considered reason that "the other TV stations won't, except Sarajevo and perhaps Skopje".[54]

That first transmission displayed Yutel's editorial approach to good effect. A Croatian television journalist reported the situation in Knin, the centre of Serb extremism in Croatia; then a journalist from the Serbian government-controlled daily *Večernje novosti* was invited, as a studio guest, to comment; he said the report from Knin had been fair.

The daily hour of news was to herald a full schedule of "films, series, sports, education, documentaries, children's and other programmes".[55] Milić says that Marković was, from the outset, thinking in terms of a "wider Yutel movement, in the sense of Yutel culture, Yutel publishing, a Yutel reformist party". The longer-term technical goal was

---

[53] By ominous coincidence, 23 October was also the day when Serbia's parliament imposed duties on imports from Slovenia and Croatia, the gravest escalation in an economic offensive which had begun in 1989.

[54] *Slobodna Dalmacija*, 24 Oct. 1990.

[55] *Borba*, 23 Oct. 1990.

a satellite television station: Marković and the Yutel board knew from their fruitless discussions around the republics that only a satellite could ensure continued access to the people. None of these goals were realized.

Ruling party opinion in Serbia and Croatia was thoroughly hostile. Tanjug alleged that the newborn station was "flagrantly violating all valid norms of federal and [Serbian] republican laws on communications".[56] In fact it had been unable to obtain the necessary licences in Serbia, so TV Belgrade, TV Novi Sad and TV Priština had an excuse to renege on their agreement. TV Zagreb had a similar pretext: the Croatian Ministry of Information never allowed Yutel to register as a public medium.

The federal government was already having to deny that Yutel was "government television" which was untrue insofar as there was no bias in favour of Marković: Tomašević remembers Marković complaining more than once that Yutel neglected his government. Financially, though, the station was highly vulnerable to this charge, and Serb politicians and media knew it. Their counterparts in Croatia laid different charges: that Yutel was a front for the JNA and the Great Serbian centralist conspiracy.

Goran Milić was considered the natural choice to lead Yutel's team of journalists. A Croat, long resident in Belgrade, president of the Serbian Association of Journalists, very pro-Yugoslav, much travelled, well connected, (and handsomely telegenic), Milić was not only a star; probably no one else would have been acceptable to all the republics as Yutel's editor-in-chief. And he wanted the job.

Milić maintains that Yutel proved its editorial independence immediately, by excluding Marković's party from coverage of the election campaign in Bosnia-Hercegovina:

> After that, and because of that, TV Ljubljana took the programme. We were showing Slovene stories in Slovenian, subtitled in Serbo-Croatian. They could see we were fair to Slovenia. Our audience there reached 45 per cent of the TV audience, even though they were recording us and showing us at 11.30 at night. Only Sarajevo and Skopje ever broadcast us live.

---

[56] *Borba*, 25 Oct. 1990.

With Yutel showing in three republics, public interest grew in the others. Under this pressure, Croatia granted a provisional licence early in 1991, then Serbia and Montenegro followed suit. For some four months Yutel was seen all around the federation except in Kosovo. Then Croatia dropped it in mid-May, ostensibly because of Yutel's anti-Croatian coverage of aggression in Slavonia. Serbia and Montenegro took the opportunity to follow suit.

In Serbia the programme was transmitted on TV Belgrade's second channel, at around 2 or 3 a.m., after a long musical intermission, Milić says, "so everybody would fall asleep before we came on". Moreover, the second channel does not reach Kosovo, so that region only saw Yutel by tuning into TV Skopje's broadcast, visible in southern Kosovo. Later, an independent channel, Studio B, whose transmitter covers only Belgrade and its environs, showed Yutel at the friendlier hour of 10.30 p.m. for a few months.

Although Tomašević says that "Belgrade was the most difficult place" for Yutel, the situation in Zagreb was only marginally better; staff were harassed by the authorities but the office was never attacked by nationalist gangs, as happened twice in Belgrade in November 1991. In Zagreb, however, the undermining continued without respite. Eventually Hrvatska Televizija (HTV, Croatian Television) agreed to broadcast Yutel's programme but only at 1 or 2 a.m. (the newspapers omitted Yutel from the TV schedule), also after a long soporific interlude of classical music. HTV forbade its employees to work for anyone else, meaning Yutel; and Yutel journalists were harassed by the police. Milan Gavrović, Yutel's first manager in Croatia, says the situation was so bad, they could not recruit a professional cameraman (the Belgrade studio had three cameras, Sarajevo two, and Zagreb only one). Tatjana Tagirov, who succeeded Gavrović, remembers that Croatian journalists preferred unemployment to working for Yutel, whose staff were banned from the TV centre in Zagreb; Tagirov would have to wait outside the building to hand over the day's cassette of reports for transmission to Sarajevo.[57]

There was wide distrust among Croats of Yutel, as there was of all things Yugoslav. (By the time Yutel appeared, Serbia had been pursuing national ends under cover of defending and strengthening Yugoslavia for three years.) Marković had insensitively aggravated matters by appointing

---

[57] T Tagirov to author, 23 Aug. 1993.

Milan Gavrović, a Serb born in Serbia, to manage the operation in Croatia. Moreover, none of his team was a 'pure' Croat. These facts were ready-made propaganda for government-controlled media in Croatia.

Yutel's viewing figures were lower in Croatia than anywhere else; no more than 27 per cent, Milić estimates. "We got no advertising at all in Croatia except from Slovenian companies", says Gavrović. The Yutel team, no admirers of Milošević, were unable to convince a large Croatian audience that Yutel was not fundamentally anti-Croatian, if only because its editorial method tended to equate Croatian 'separatism' with Serbian 'extremism'. Of Yutel's coverage of the Borovo Selo incident, for example, Milic says: "Our reports were balanced, but that balance was not acceptable to Croatia." HTV, by refusing to transmit Yutel (except for a period of three or four months), ensured that Yutel never had a real chance to present its case.

The pursuit of media 'objectivity', in the very Yugoslav sense of a neutral path bisecting national extremes, was not only an elite activity with a diminishing appeal; it positively aided the party which presented the conflict to the watching world as family business, an internal affair, at worst a civil war between extremists.[58]

An example of Yutel editors' hankering for "objectivity", calling a plague on both houses, occurred in the run-up to open conflict. On the morning of 6 May 1991, a large demonstration against the army brought some 50,000 people onto the streets of Split, Croatia's second city. The JNA responded with a show of force, and a young JNA conscript was killed.

---

[58] A young British journalist who worked for *The Daily Telegraph* in Croatia in summer 1991 has described with almost disarming frankness how Western journalists were ensnared by this conception of objectivity.

"From a hotel room it was easy to dismiss both sides as being equally at fault. Time and again reports appeared in Western newspapers quoting Belgrade Radio, which said that the Croats had attacked, and then quoting Zagreb Radio which said that the Serbs had attacked. By quoting both sources you [as a journalist] have covered your reputation ... *Because both Tudjman and Milošević were former communists-turned-nationalists, with a similar disregard for the ways of democracy, no journalist wanted to come down on either side.* After a few days in Osijek I visited Dalj, where 60 Croats were killed for the loss of three or four Serbs.... . So fearful was I of losing balance that I wrote a report which would have fitted neatly in a Serbian newspaper." (A Russell, *Prejudice and Plum Brandy: Tales of a Balkan Stringer* [London: 1993], 214-215. (Italics added.)

While Yutel's faith in objectivity had more to do with a certain idealism than with inexperience or ignorance, the italicized sentence applies to Yutel too.

The Croatian TV news bulletin at 2 p.m. included footage of an enraged demonstrator standing atop a JNA vehicle with his hands round the driver's neck. According to Vanessa Vasić Janeković, an assistant producer in Yutel's Sarajevo studio, everybody else assumed (incorrectly, it emerged) that this sequence identified the killer and his victim. Yutel news, that evening, repeated the sequence, several times, with a spoken commentary, "This is the killer!". The item provoked such anger in Croatia that a senior Yutel journalist hurried to Split to try and repair the damage.[59]

The editors had abandoned professional standards without even noticing. As the conflict escalated, differences amongst them widened. Those such as Jela Jevremović (a Croat) who came to regard the pursuit of a neutral perspective as itself a snare, were regarded by others, such as Gordana Suša in Belgrade and Dževad Sabljaković in Sarajevo, as unprofessional and frankly biased. And problems were growing all the time, not only financial and technical (the obsolete JNA equipment) but political, as access to war areas became more tightly restricted, especially for the domestic media and, most of all, for an uncommitted medium like Yutel. Nevertheless, Tanja Tagirov says the Zagreb team achieved some fine reports from Slavonia, "with no propaganda, showing ordinary people and victims on both sides".

Jevremović's moment of awareness occurred in eastern Croatia after the killings at Borovo Selo:

> I was working in Belgrade, and when Borovo Selo happened, I wanted to go. Our camera was stolen at a Croatian village barricade, and we went to Vinkovci to report the theft. Vinkovci was funeral city. Parents were bringing their 19-year-old sons in to register as reserve policemen. All of a sudden I saw war a hundred kilometres from Belgrade, which people there weren't aware of and nor was I. It had already started, and we had missed it.

---

[59] V V Janeković to author, 10 Sept. 1993.

Yutel's general approach to the Croatian war, Jevremović says, took the typical soft Belgrade line, "ethnic animosities causing conflict, with the JNA separating the warring sides".

Milić says, with hindsight:

> We understood little by little that Yutel was like trying to have a single television station for Hitler, Stalin, and Churchill, broadcasting for all three in one language, or in one language with subtitles, putting Himmler on screen, then cutting to Churchill, and then saying 'And now the football results.' It was impossible.

At the time, however, Milić adhered steadily to his notion of "symmetry" (Suša's term), polite to the JNA, taking "personal care that Milošević was never once shown in a bad light on Yutel" (Jevremović), and "treating Tudjman the same way" (Mirko Pejić, Yutel's news director in Sarajevo).[60]

As an editorial example of this "impossibility", Milić mentions the case of Dalj, a village near Osijek where 60-80 Croatian militia and civilians were killed by the JNA and Serb irregulars on 1 August 1991. One of Milić's Sarajevo staff, Ivica Puljić, complained about Yutel's report from Dalj: "A reporter arrived from Belgrade, showed the burnt-out houses and so on, without ever identifying who [was responsible]".[61] Milić elaborated:

> We sent a reporter from Belgrade because Dalj wasn't accessible from Zagreb. He filmed around, and interviewed a gravedigger: 'How many people have you buried recently?' 'That's hard to say,' says the gravedigger, 'four or five in the past few days.' He was a Croat, surrounded by Serbs. If he says 'I've buried 50 people', he's dead the next morning. We hoped viewers would understand the whole situation,

---

[60] G Suša and M Pejić to author, 1 Oct. 1993.

[61] I Puljić to author, 25 Aug. 1993.

look at the gravedigger's face, and judge for themselves if he was telling the truth. We couldn't do more. It was wrong, but nothing more was possible.

Another example is from Vukovar, the Danubian town obliterated by bombardment in the autumn of 1991. Three days after the ruins were 'liberated' by the JNA, a Yutel reporter, Ljerka Draženović, got in from Belgrade by accompanying an Italian TV crew. She filmed a long report blaming the JNA and Serb irregulars. A few days later, another of the Yutel team in Belgrade got permission from the JNA to visit Vukovar on condition he film an interview with the local official responsible for reconstructing the town. (Yutel's relations with the JNA had deteriorated so far by this stage that access to the front line was generally impossible.) Milic gave the go-ahead, hoping that viewers would understand the constraints on Yutel and make allowances. Others at Yutel interpreted his decision as a typical attempt to balance the earlier report with a pro-Serb piece. Nor does Milić now defend his decision; the mandatory interview was, he says, "disgusting".

Differences within Yutel, and outside pressure, multiplied when Bosnia-Hercegovina was attacked in April 1992. Bosnia was the republic where Yutel was truly popular; its editorial balance appealed especially to Muslims, caught between Serb and Croat territorial ambitions, and to anyone who supported the sovereign integrity of the republic. Milić reckons Yutel's regular audience reached 70-80 per cent.[62] He claims that advertising revenue was considerable up to the moment of attack (further evidence of Bosnian disbelief that the worst could happen). In Sarajevo on 28 July 1991, Yutel organized the "Yutel for peace" rally, the biggest such rally in Yugoslav history; 70,000 people turned out, despite a cloudburst.

Yutel combined Croatian and Serbian footage of controversial events, so the audience could observe the discrepancies. The station's own coverage of the crisis in Sarajevo in the first days of March 1992 won

---

[62] Nenad Pejić, editor-in-chief of TV Sarajevo until the end of April 1992, reckons that Yutel's regular audience was 700,000. Pejić says there were approximately 1.2 million television sets in the republic. If so, and if the second figure is corroborated, Yutel's proportion was nearer 60 per cent: still extraordinarily high. (N Pejić, "The Role of Television in a Period of Ethnic Television" 51-52 *South Slav Journal* (1992), 25.)

high praise from the most independent-minded Bosnian newspaper, *Slobodna Bosna.*

Milić describes Yutel's basic dilemma, when the attack came:

> Every side wanted foreign journalists to come and testify to their good intentions. The JNA called reporters to film what it wanted them to see. The Croats called them too, but not domestic reporters, so Yutel was practically banned except in the mixed areas with Muslims, who were very confident in Yutel and were calling us everywhere, which was itself a problem, because you show only Muslim suffering, so you lose credibility. To keep a balance I would take a story from TV Belgrade and another from Croatian TV, so there would be, say, three stories of Muslim suffering, one of Croat suffering, and one of Serb suffering. And it was wrong.

For others, Yutel had already lost its balance by opposing Serb nationalism more than Muslim or Croat nationalism, a view held by Yutel staff members Gordana Šuša and Mirko Pejić (both Serb by nationality). They believe that Milić had tilted in favour of the Croatian cause and that Jevremović brought Yutel a reputation for rudeness by not being 'civilized' to Bosnian Serb and JNA leaders at press conferences in Sarajevo. Jevremović cheerfully admits the fault, without agreeing that she was "not professional". On the contrary, she criticizes herself and Yutel for missing the build-up to war, for example by "ignoring the significance of the JNA withdrawal from Slovenia and Croatia into Bosnia-Hercegovina" during the winter months, and "the fact that Sarajevo was being surrounded by [JNA] artillery emplacements".

Throughout the frantic month of April 1992, as the Serb assault on northern and eastern Bosnia gathered pace and the JNA refused to abandon its barracks in Sarajevo, Yutel and TV Sarajevo newsrooms were sometimes the only forums where political and military leaders could negotiate face to face, or rather voice to voice.

Milić "suspended operations" on 11 May, some five weeks after the onslaught began, "because we lost the second channel of TV Sarajevo", but also because it had become impossible to edit the programme. After 1 May, when Serb forces captured the Vlašić transmitter in central Bosnia,

Yutel was in effect broadcasting just for Sarajevo, a city under siege, because the network of transmitters around the republic had been captured or destroyed. "So what do you do?" asks Milić. "If you have a story ready by 11 a.m., do you keep it for yourself until 9 p.m. or give it to TV Sarajevo? Do you put yourself at the service of defending the government and the people? What do you report in a besieged city? About destroyed houses, people dying, day after day? I don't know. Nobody knows. I didn't know how to solve the problem and I said no, I give up."

Nearly two years on, former Yutel journalists are scattered around former Yugoslavia, working for all kinds of employers, from the United Nations to the Radio Boat.[63] Hardly any work for government-controlled media, which still gloat over Yutel's demise and treat it as a dirty secret in a journalist's past.[64]

Recrimination is active among some ex-Yutel editors, who say unprintable things about each other and especially about Goran Milić, though he has his defenders also.[65] Everyone, however, agrees that Yutel

---

[63] Radio Boat, a radio-station on board a ship in the Adriatic Sea, attempted to do with radio what Yutel had failed to do with television. It is the brainchild of Montenegrin journalist Dragica Ponorac, who persuaded international donors, including the French government, UNESCO and the EC to back the project. A team of 15 journalists from Bosnia, Serbia and Croatia was headed up by editor-in-chief Dževad Sabljaković, formerly of TV Belgrade and Yutel. Radio Boat started on 9 April 1993 to broadcast "for the whole of former Yugoslavia in the Serbo-Croatian language", as Sabljaković put it. However, Radio Boat's signal is not powerful enough to reach much of Yugoslavia. The staple content is news, music, interviews, and "Desperately Seeking", a 'noticeboard' service for refugees and displaced persons. News bulletins draw on information supplied by half a dozen stringers in the capital cities, as well as international agency reports. While Western media gave the station highly favourable coverage, media in Serbia and Croatia were sarcastic at best. *Danas* dismissed Radio Boat as "a sad symbol of a bygone era and of the powerlessness of the Western world to take an efficient attitude to new, post-Cold War problems." In sum, Radio Boat may have come too late; too many people had suffered too much in Croatia and Bosnia to accept being addressed collectively as part of a Yugoslav audience.

[64] This has happened in Bosnia as well as in the other republics. On 27 June 1992, *Oslobodjenje* published an absurd bulletin from the government news agency, BH Press, alleging intimate contact between a former Yutel editor and Radovan Karadžić, leader of the SDS. At least *Oslobodjenje* also published the former editor's dignified reply (on 29 June).

[65] In summer 1992, Milić moved from Sarajevo to Zagreb. Early in 1993, he wrote an accusatory 'open letter' to Serbian journalists. *Vreme* published the text, as well as a reply by its own columnist, Stojan Cerović: "... Milić and Yutel tried to stay neutral and impartial, which turned out to be impossible, but I don't see why he

happened too late to influence events. And as to influence, Pejić rightly insists upon some vital statistics: Yutel had 50 staff, whereas the republican stations employed a total of 24,000.[66]

By most accounts, Yutel's funds were grievously mismanaged. In a typical Yugoslav-federal way, Yutel became a bureaucracy complete with parasites before it was even a product. Milan Gavrović, a board member as well as manager in Zagreb, recalls visiting Yutel's advertising department in Belgrade: it had five employees on the payroll, and no advertisements. "There was a general secretary of Yutel. I still don't know what that meant. There was a director of programming without any programming to direct."

All in all, Gavrović says, Yutel was the worst experience of his professional life. But he adds, "Yutel was fighting for peace, for civil society. It also did that, which was a great thing. You mustn't think the programme was bad, though it made mistakes. Because of that programme, I shall never say I am ashamed I worked for Yutel." Vanessa Vasić Janeković takes a similar view: "When you compare Yutel to what Serbian and Croatian TV did and still do, you see how good it was."

---

regrets it now. He says he had 'illusions about Belgrade democrats', and that 'all of them had the Great Serbian idea in their heads'. I don't want to say they are numerous, but they still exist and obviously they spoil his picture and disturb his conscience. These people did as much as they could against war and criminality ... Goran Milić says that it's nothing but 'cackling and lighting candles', but he should have taken care in the past that he had a right to such moral severity." (*Vreme*, 8 Feb. 1993.)

[66] The figure is corroborated by Nenad Pejić, formerly editor-in-chief at TV Sarajevo, supra note 63 at 19.

Chapter 3

SERBIA SETS THE PACE

Introduction

This report treats Serbia before the other republics because the Serbian media have been the most influential regarding the wars in former Yugoslavia. These wars were begun by Serbia in alliance with Serb forces in Croatia and then in Bosnia, acting under different political constraints but with a single military objective: irreversible territorial control on the basis of the alleged supreme right to national self-determination, a right summarized in the ubiquitous slogan "All Serbs in one state".

In Croatia as well as in Bosnia, onslaughts of 'ethnic cleansing' used terror and slaughter against civilians to create Serb majorities in conquered territory. Remaining non-Serbs were then gradually expelled, while outposts of resistance were surrounded, bombarded and starved.

Once the fighting had begun Croatian forces pursued the same objective, by similar means, against Serbs in parts of Croatia and against Serbs and Muslims in parts of Bosnia. Eventually the Armija Bosne i Hercegovine (ABH, Bosnian Army) also pursued this policy, principally against Croats in central Bosnia.

Apart from its immense military advantage (the JNA[1] sided with the Serb forces), Serbia's leadership could claim to represent the most widely distributed as well as the most numerous of the Yugoslav peoples. This abstract claim could not have been converted into the hard currency of nationalist solidarity without the media. A war launched by Serbs outside Serbia, but instigated by the Serbian government, could only be sustained if a majority within Serbia accepted that Serb forces would be fighting in the name and interest of all Serbs. Croatia's leadership later used the same tactic in Bosnia.

This chapter reveals how the mass media in Serbia were used to convince their audience that the Serbs of Croatia and Bosnia were, above

---

[1] Jugoslovenska Narodna Armija, Yugoslav People's Army.

all, dispersed members of a Serbian 'national entity'. Least of all were they Croatian or Bosnian citizens of a given national or ethnic genealogy, faith or culture.[2] This media task was made immensely easier by the fact that Croatia's own leadership corroborated this definition of Croatian Serbs. The notion that citizenship and its rights should not be determined by national identity did exist in former Yugoslavia.[3] The wars have almost extinguished this concept in the successor states.

In this sense, the propagandists of nationalism in Serbia (and Croatia) had won once the fighting began. The logic of war then ensured the maximum mutual alienation of the peoples represented by the warring sides, confirming the imperative need for national territory, justifying the conflict and even legitimating, retrospectively, the politics which had produced the war.

The national consensus, however, was not easily achieved. It was the fruit of several years' labour by the government, which used its power to marshal media workers who either volunteered for nationalist service (through conviction) or were press-ganged (by economic pressure, fear of professional isolation, reprisals, or ingrained habits of obedience). Journalists who opposed the government faced marginalization or, in government-controlled media, demotion and sacking, while others departed in the face of government pressure.

For the story of media control in Serbia and Croatia is very much a matter of the deployment of nationalism against independence in broadcasting and the press. Serbia's government achieved a head start in this labour. Unlike in Croatia, the main media in Serbia were seized by a

---

[2] According to the 1991 census, 66 per cent of Serbia's population of 9.88 million were Serbs, 17 per cent were Albanians and 3.5 per cent were Hungarians.

[3] The 'evil' of citizenship was identified by Miroslav Toholj, a leading member of the Srpska Demokratska Stranka (SDS, the Serb Democratic Party), the radical party of the Serbs in Bosnia, when he attacked Bosnian government policy, following the 3 March 1992 declaration of independence (on the basis of a referendum which the SDS had boycotted). "The Serb name has finally been taken away from the Serbs," Toholj said, "they have been turned into citizens, which Serbs won't accept". (*Vreme*, 9 March 1992.) This hostility is shared by nationalists in the self-proclaimed 'Croat Republic of Herceg-Bosna'. The keynote article in the official weekly paper *Hrvatski list* of 30 March 1994 (after the cease-fire between Croat and Bosnian-government forces) heaped scorn on Bosnian Muslims who "drivel about the Republic of Bosnia-Hercegovina, indivisible and civil", that is, constituted on the basis of individual rather than national rights.

nationalist regime before multiparty elections. The Milošević government has known how to exploit and keep this advantage.

Background: Kosovo

The Serbian media campaign in the late 1980s had a context: the phenomenon that has been aptly called "the Serbian cultural revolution" of 1986 to 1989.[4]

The Kosovo media campaign became the cornerstone of this revolution, forging a language and style which dissolved the boundaries between political, social, and cultural issues. Its aim was to mobilize a people disenchanted with politics and the political class by convincing them that, as Slobodan Milošević told the executive of the League of Communists of Serbia on returning from Kosovo in 1987, "[w]hat we are discussing here can no longer be called politics, it is a question of our fatherland". The self-image of the subject had to be altered: Ivan Čolović's description "from Working People to Serbian People" encapsulates the intended change.[5] The political agenda had to be revised in the name of a necessity which transcended mere politics.

The new media language avoided moribund socialist terminology in favour of a language of demagogy and headlong irrationality, of rhetorical questions and exclamations, of destiny and mission: a 'celestial people' confronting its fate; a language of menacing ultimatums, of infinite self-pity, of immense accusations backed by no evidence or investigation; of conspiracy-mongering, paranoia, and brazen incitement to violence. It was, in fact, a language of war before war was even conceivable in Yugoslavia.

The Socialist Autonomous Province of Kosovo, about 100 kilometres square, lay in the south-western corner of Serbia, next to Montenegro, Albania and Macedonia. As an autonomous province, Kosovo was a constitutional unit within the Yugoslav federation. It was also, by a deliberate constitutional ambiguity, a unit within the Republic of Serbia.

---

[4] P Garde, *Vie et mort de la Yougoslavie* (Paris: Fayard, 1992), 252.

[5] I Čolović, *Bordel ratnika* (Belgrade: Biblioteka XX vek, 1993), 149.

It was the most densely populated part of Yugoslavia, with the highest unemployment, the lowest average wages, and the highest rates both of students and of illiteracy. The explosive aspect of Kosovo, however, was, and remains, its demography. Its Albanian population, with the highest birthrate in Europe, stands at some 1.7 million, more than 90 per cent of the total. The proportion of Serbs and Montenegrins has shrunk to 7 or 8 per cent from a figure of 28 per cent in 1953.

These demographic and economic facts served to create an inflammatory situation, ignited in the 1980s by the post-Tito power vacuum at the federal centre and by Kosovo's traditional status in Serbian culture. Kosovo is held, by almost all Serbs, to be the sacred site of national history, the fountainhead of national spirit, and the guarantor of national values. The old patriarchate of the Serbian Orthodox Church lies in Kosovo, and the medieval battle which symbolized the fall of the Serbian empire occurred in Kosovo.

Everybody in Kosovo could justly complain about something: poverty, underdevelopment, unemployment, corruption. Both national communities had grounds for grievance. The Albanians, traditionally underdogs in Kosovo, ceased to be so with the reforms of the late 1960s and 1970s, producing resentment and fear among Serbs and Montenegrins, whose emotions found an echo among Serbs throughout Yugoslavia, at all levels of society.[6]

In 1986, Serbia's most prestigious national intellectual forum, the Serbian Academy of Sciences and Arts, drafted its notorious Memorandum upon the perilous plight of the Serb nation. It denounced "the physical, political, legal and cultural genocide" of Serbs in Kosovo, where Albanians were waging "open and total war", and called for the autonomy of the province to be revised. The Memorandum set the tone (at once self-pitying, morbid and vengeful) of nationalist discourse ever since, and it has been widely regarded as the blueprint of the expansionist designs upon Croatia and Bosnia which were revealed in 1991 and 1992. The Serbian Central Committee met and condemned the document. Slobodan Milošević, then leader of the League of Communists in Belgrade, spoke only to insist that the Committee's condemnation be kept secret.

---

[6] Albanians saw Tito as their defender against Serb nationalism. In 1981, a year after Tito's death, Albanian demonstrators demanded a 'Kosovo Republic', to give them equal status with the six so-called constitutive nations of Yugoslavia.

Under Milošević, nationalist emotion was for the first time exploited by senior politicians to win support for an assault on the Federal Constitution and, then, to legitimate themselves as truly national leaders rather than Communist bosses.[7] From being officially taboo, this brand of nationalism became respectable and then obligatory.

It was in 1989 that the ground of the 'revolutionary' struggle for Kosovo shifted from culture to politics. Masses of Serbs had been mobilized behind the leadership's demand that Serbia must be 'reunified' through appeals to cultural particularity (history, myths, language and religion), but also to political rationality; for reunification was presented as the right and proper way to break the post-Tito log-jam in the federal system.

What reunification meant, practically, was the abolition of Serbia's two autonomous provinces (the other was Vojvodina in the north, with a large Hungarian minority). When this was achieved in 1989 and 1990, the Serbian leadership began the political battle against other republics by using its extra weight within federal institutions.

At the famous Eighth Session of the Serbian Central Committee, in the autumn of 1987, Milošević took power in the League of Communists partly by using the Kosovo issue to outflank and discredit his opponents. His accession marked the first victory of a collusion among Serbia's Communist politicians, its bureaucracy, its intellectual class, and its news media.

From this point on, the League's media policy consisted of pressuring or forcing every significant organ of information and opinion to chorus the same litany of complaints and demands. The phrasing varied slightly, according to the source and the intended audience: sometimes the Albanians were characterized as anti-Yugoslav counter-revolutionaries, sometimes as Muslim rapists of nuns. The upshot was always the same: Kosovo must be regained for Serbia; or, as Milošević put it, Serbia will be united or it will not exist.

Venerated novelists, the Orthodox Church, philosophers, the Association of University Professors, party apparatchiks, slogans at public rallies, tabloid newspapers and television news all insisted that Kosovo

---

[7] The summit of injustice and betrayal was alleged to be the 1974 Federal Constitution which, by elevating the two autonomous provinces almost to the level of republics, reduced Serbia's control.

Serbs faced genocide from Albanian "terrorist-separatists", and that mere justice demanded the province be reabsorbed into Serbia, losing its political and constitutional rights.

As a strategy to forge and consolidate public support for an aggressive expansionist project, this campaign had no precedent in post-1945 Europe, perhaps because the conditions had not existed since the 1930s (greater German ambitions toward Austria, Czechoslovakia, and Poland). The Kosovo campaign warrants a place in general studies of mass manipulation and contemporary fascism. For the purposes of this report, it matters above all because it created a media model which was extended to embrace other targets of the Serbian leadership. It was a model which identified and stigmatized a national enemy, homogenized Serbs against this threat, and called for resistance. After the Albanians of Kosovo, the enemies were Slovenes and Slovenia, then Croats and Croatia, then Bosnia and its Muslim population. Sporadic offensives against domestic and foreign targets (the CIA, the Germans, the Vatican, the Masons, the Jews, and the USA) ran concurrently with these.

This model was intact before multiparty elections were a cloud on the Yugoslav horizon. Hence the alleged Serbian national emergency in Kosovo, presented as so dire and extreme that any means of rectification was valid, was a pretext for recentralizing and disciplining the mass media by all the means of pressure and coercion available in a party-state.[8] Kosovo was the issue over which the federal framework of television scheduling was broken.[9] It then served as the pretext for purging Serbian news media of resistance to Milošević, just as the League of Communists was purged of opposition during the Eighth Session of its Central Committee in 1987, which was, significantly, the first such event to be televised.

Between September and November 1987, the first important heads rolled. Among the political casualties was Dragiša Pavlović, chief of the

---

[8] The Kosovo radio and television service, Radio-Television Priština, was taken over by the government on 5 July 1990; the editor-in-chief was replaced and 1,300 staff were dismissed. *Rilindja*, the only Albanian-language newspaper, was closed down the following month, and its 200 journalists lost their jobs. Six Albanian-language local radio stations were also closed. Further dismissals followed with the enactment of the 1991 Law on Public Information. (Human Rights Watch/Helsinki, *Open Wounds: Human Rights Abuses in Kosovo* [New York: March 1993], 100-101.)

[9] See Ch. 1, section on 'The Rise of Television' infra.

Belgrade branch of the League of Communists, abruptly removed after criticizing the burgeoning nationalism of the dailies *Politika* and *Politika ekspres*, and the popular news magazines *Duga* and *Intervju*. All except *Duga* are published by the Politika group, which was a mainstay of the media campaign.[10] Pavlović had told a group of editors:

> [I]f the struggle against Albanian nationalism is accompanied by intolerance and hatred towards the Albanian nationality, which is what we find in some of our press organs, then the struggle departs from socialist principles and comes close to nationalism itself. ... As of today we must criticize Serb nationalism on a daily basis, for the Serbian nationalists are presenting themselves as the saviours of the Serbian cause in Kosovo, when in fact they cannot solve a single social problem.[11]

The Politika group was setting the tone for the political 'nationalization' of Serbia's news media; that the Belgrade party chief could be purged for criticizing it, proves its strategic importance to the government at that time. A few weeks later, Pavlović was followed by Ivan Stojanović, the director-general of the Politika group, and Mirko Djekić, editor of *NIN*, Serbia's leading news magazine (also published by the Politika group); both were sacked for not supporting Milošević. Next to fall was Mihailo Erić, editor-in-chief of news at TV Belgrade (TVB), sacked for "one-sided and untrue reports which constituted crude disinformation and an attempt to politically manipulate the public".[12] Erić's actual 'offence' was to have defended several of his staff against politically motivated attacks by Milošević supporters during the Eighth Session.

Since Kosovo's autonomy was revoked in 1989 the region has remained the government's surest means of legitimizing itself by mustering support which can then be applied to causes other than Kosovo, and to

---

[10] On the Politika group, see section on 'The Politika Paradigm' infra.

[11] B Magaš, *The Destruction of Yugoslavia: Tracking the Break-up 1980-92* (London: 1993), 109.

[12] *The Guardian*, 26 Nov. 1987.

opponents other than Albanians. News about the region is carefully screened and administered. An example of Kosovo's continuing propaganda function occurred on 6 January 1993, when President Milošević publicly consented to Western pleas to persuade the Bosnian Serb leaders to accept the Vance-Owen Peace Plan for Bosnia. That evening, TVB news showed the international peace negotiators David Owen and Cyrus Vance agreeing on this point with the Serbian President at a press conference, all talking English, the international mediators flanking Milošević almost like a police escort. The report then jumped abruptly to later remarks made by Milošević to the domestic media, declaring (in Serbo-Croatian) that Kosovo was part of Serbia, and that there was no question of secession. This was irrelevant as information, since Kosovo's status was not in doubt. This coda to the report was a reassuring dose of national bravado and uplift after the rare glimpse of Milošević in concessionary mode.

Media and the Law

Although a number of Serbian laws restrict press freedom, these laws have only rarely been invoked against journalists since the late 1980s.[13] Laws which could have been invoked to protect media freedom have either been misapplied or ignored. Instead the government has used a variety of non-legal means to control and punish critics.

Both the 1990 Serbian and 1992 Federal Constitutions guarantee "the freedom of ... thought and public expression of opinion" and "freedom of the press and other forms of public dissemination of information".[14] Both also prohibit "censorship of the press and of other forms of public dissemination of information". These guarantees have not, however,

---

[13] Except in Kosovo, which lies outside the scope of this report where individuals and journalists have been prosecuted for speech directed against the Serbian population. The "false information" provision has also been invoked against Muslims in Sandzak.

[14] On 27 April 1992, in support of their claim to inherit the international status of the former Yugoslavia (SFRY, Socialist Federative Republic of Yugoslavia), Serbia and Montenegro proclaimed a new federation: the Federal Republic of Yugoslavia. The new federation's claim to be a successor state has been rejected by the United Nations and the European Union.

prevented the authorities from suppressing media for disseminating information and opinions opposed to the government. Media which have been suppressed have been unable to obtain redress through the courts.

In March 1991 the Public Prosecutor ordered a 36-hour blackout on the transmissions of two independent stations (B92 radio and Studio B television) to prevent broadcast of an opposition demonstration in Belgrade. The Public Prosecutor failed to respond to a challenge against the ban lodged by the two stations.

In some cases, the courts appear reluctant to challenge government decisions, as happened in the case of journalists dismissed from Radio-Televizija Srbije (RTS, Serbian Radio-Television) in January 1993 who prosecuted the organization for illegal dismissal. The court ruled in their favour and ordered their reinstatement.[15] RTS appealed to the Supreme Court which in September overturned the lower court ruling on a technicality, a decision which independent journalists believe was politically motivated.[16]

Government officials are given enhanced protection against criticism of their public functions under the Serbian Penal Code. Article 98 punishes with imprisonment of up to three years:

> public ridicule [of] the Republic of Serbia or another
> Republic within the Federal Republic of Yugoslavia,
> their flag, coat of arms or anthem, their presidencies,
> assemblies or executive councils, the president or the
> members of the presidencies, the president of the
> assembly or the president of the executive council in
> connection with the performance of their office.

The Federal Criminal Code similarly protects the presidents of federal institutions, the Yugoslav Army and federal emblems. Both laws allow limited exemptions for journalists. These provisions run counter to European law which has established that public officials, governments and government institutions must face greater scrutiny of their actions than private individuals. In addition, prison sentences of any length for

---

[15] *Republika*, Sept. 1993.

[16] Journalists are now planning to take individual legal action against RTS to seek redress for their dismissals.

defamation are unacceptable, except in the most extreme circumstances.

The libel clause of the Federal Criminal Code was used against Dragoljub Žarković, *Vreme's* editor-in-chief, in June 1993. Following *Vreme's* publication of a cartoon, Žarković was charged with insulting two Heads of State (Dobrica Ćosić of Yugoslavia and Constantine Mitsotakis of Greece). The Public Prosecutor later dropped the charge.

An August 1993 issue of *Srpska reč*, the magazine of the Srpski Pokret Obnove (SPO, the Serb Movement of Renewal), the opposition party, was seized by the police because it contained a cartoon which portrayed President Milošević in Hitlerian pose. The Public Prosecutor has initiated criminal proceedings against the editor on the basis that the cartoon was "an insult to the person and work" of the President.[17]

Article 133 of the Federal Criminal Code (incriminating "hostile propaganda") was amended in July 1991, partly under pressure from the Council of Europe. The new provision narrows the offence to "incitement to violent attack on the Constitutional Order". Other offences have not been narrowed and potentially restrict the right to freedom of expression, including Article 218 of the Serbian Criminal Code which provides broad powers to punish "false information":

> spreading false information or statements with intent to provoke disquiet among citizens or to threaten public order and peace or to prevent the implementation of government decisions or measures, or to diminish the confidence of citizens in such decisions or measures, shall be punished by imprisonment of up to three years.

Two key media laws were enacted in 1991: the Law on the Basis of Public Information (enacted in March) and the Law on Radio-Television (in July). Article 5 of the 1991 Law on Public Information stipulates that publicly-funded organizations, such as the state-controlled broadcasting service, must state in their founding statutes that their programme is not partisan. Article 13 requires publicly funded media to inform the public impartially and in a timely way. Numerous examples in this chapter show

---

[17] The SPO leader, Vuk Drašković, was a particular target of the government in summer 1993.

that the state-controlled media, especially state television, regularly fail to fulfil these public service obligations, not least in their biased coverage in favour of Slobodan Milošević during the 1992 elections.[18] When journalists and opposition party politicians have sought redress against false and defamatory statements about them in the public service media, they have met with little success.[19]

In September 1993, the Federal Minister of Information proposed an amendment to the Law on Public Information to give the federal parliament the right to veto international aid to media organizations. At a time of economic catastrophe, when the natural audience for many independent media (students and professional people) had fled abroad, and those who remained often could not afford to buy food, let alone newspapers and magazines, such an amendment would have had a crippling effect. It was presumably mooted as a shot across the bows of independent media and their benefactors (mostly international media foundations) and has since been abandoned.

The Serbian Law on Radio-Television controls the allocation of frequencies. (Other provisions of this law are discussed in the section on 'Law on Radio-Television' below.) The Serbian government's seizure of control over electronic frequencies from the federal government began in March 1991, with the Law on Public Information. The Law on Radio-Television confirmed this and provided for a government-appointed commission to oversee the allocation of frequencies. The law contravenes European standards on broadcasting freedom which are based on the principle of pluralism and require that regulation of broadcasting be independent of government.

On 24 October 1991 the Yugoslav Constitutional Court found the appropriation of frequencies to be unconstitutional, a judgment ignored by the Serbian government,which, even before the promised commission had been appointed, dealt with frequencies as it chose.[20] An urban FM radio

---

[18] See section on 'Television' infra.

[19] M Lucić-Čavić, 2 *Voice Bulletin* (Belgrade: Centre for Anti-War Action, April 1992) gives two examples: journalists defamed by the leader of Srpska Radikalna Stranka (SRS, the Serbian Radical Party), Vojislav Šešelj, on 10 April 1992 failed to get RTS to broadcast any response; politicians attacked by the Socialistička Partija Srbije (SPS, the Socialist Party of Serbia) and SRS members during the 1992 election campaign were equally unsuccessful.

[20] Although federal law requires that republican law be in harmony with the

61

station in Belgrade, Radio Ponos, which broadcast nationalist neo-folk music interspersed with gung-ho messages for the troops 24 hours a day, was allowed to begin broadcasting without a licence at the end of 1992. The station was close to the extreme nationalist SRS, led by Vojislav Šešelj.[21] Federal authorities ordered Radio Ponos to close but police refused to implement the order. After Šešelj fell out of favour with the ruling SPS in autumn 1993, the authorities closed down the station. On the other hand, a company owned by Federal Prime Minister Milan Panić, Milošević's main rival in the 1992 Presidential elections, was denied a television frequency.[22] When the privately-owned Studio B television station applied for a second frequency, the government avoided a point-blank refusal by demanding a fee of 500,000 Deutschmarks, a sum which the station could not remotely afford.[23]

The frequencies commission was eventually appointed on 24 November 1993 but all its members are either members of the ruling Socialistička Partija Srbije (SPS, Socialist Party of Serbia) or known sympathizers. Parliament had recessed, so the government's choice of members could not be immediately challenged. Its members are the Deputy-President of the Serbian government, the Minister of Information, the Minister of Transport and Communications, three officials from these two ministries, and two of RTS's own board of directors.

Non-Legal Actions Against the Media

While some of the assaults on media freedom have been carried out by legal means, most of the worst abuses have been accomplished through extra-legal means of control. The most significant of these (which is discussed at length in later sections of this report) is the total and arbitrary

---

Federal Constitution, the Serbian Constitution of 1990 provides in Art. 135 that the Republic may pass laws to protect its interests if they are deemed to be threatened by federal laws.

[21] Vojislav Šešelj, *četnik vojvoda*, or 'duke', and subsequently leader of the Serbian Radical Party. He has boasted of his followers' role in committing atrocities.

[22] Lučić-Čavić, supra note 19.

[23] L'Organisation Internationale des Journalistes, *Reporters and Media in Ex-Yugoslavia* (Paris: Les Cahiers de l'Organisation Internationale des Journalistes, Jan. 1993), 59.

control of editorial, personnel and other essential decisions in the government-controlled media.

Occasionally, government forces have been responsible for physical attacks on journalists. Police harassed, intimidated and assaulted 17 journalists as they covered a demonstration in Belgrade on 1 June 1993. Helsinki Watch found that at least three of the 17 were badly beaten after identifying themselves as journalists.[24] Journalist Dušan Reljić from the independent weekly, *Vreme*, was kidnapped on 21 September 1993 and held two days for questioning. His kidnappers identified themselves as military intelligence agents.

There have also been armed attacks against the media. In January 1993, NTV Studio B staff travelling in a truck containing broadcasting equipment for the station were threatened by armed men who then set fire to the truck and equipment. The previous month, equipment destined for the station was stolen near the same border crossing. In May 1992, armed men broke into the bureau office of *Oslobodjenje* and Radio-Televizija Sarajevo (RTVSA, Sarajevo Radio-Television). The attackers changed the locks on the office doors and threatened to kill the bureau chief Branislav Boškov.[25]

The Press

The press in Serbia has a richer history than anywhere else in former Yugoslavia. This includes a liberal tradition, which tenuously survives in the federal daily *Borba*, the weekly magazine *Vreme*, and a fringe of other publications with tiny sales figures.[26]

This history also includes a tradition of service to warmongering governments. "Due to the highly developed political life, journalism plays a very important role", wrote Leon Trotsky, who worked as a Belgrade correspondent before and during the Balkan Wars of 1912-1913.

---

[24] Helsinki Watch, *Belgrade Demonstrations: Excessive Use of Force and Beatings in Detention* (New York: Aug. 1993).

[25] *Oslobodjenje*, 27 May 1992.

[26] See Ch. 2 supra for discussion of *Borba*.

In both Serbia and Bulgaria the press was one of the
key factors in the creation of the psychological
preconditions for war. ... The single, unified political
slogan of Belgrade's independent politically oriented
press became "Agitation for war, never mind against
whom, whether it be Austria, Bulgaria, Turkey or
even the entire European community."[27]

After 1987 the press again became a key factor in mobilizing the
country behind an expansionist plan. While electronic media are the main
sources of information for a growing majority, the press was probably
crucial in cultivating educated, urban opinion, whose non-cooperation
would be most dangerous to the government, and for intimidating those
who could not be coerced, by demonstrating how outnumbered they were
and by denying them a hearing.[28]

There has always been a great volume of newsprint in Serbia. By
the outbreak of war in 1991, there were some 300 news publications in all,
"from party papers that are sold on the streets in just a few hundred
copies, to those published by large institutions".[29] Only a few marginal
publications have been forced to close by the economic crisis. The range
includes an extreme nationalist press represented by *Pogledi*, a monarchist
magazine from Kragujevac, and the neo-fascist *Nove ideje*, across the
spectrum to the fortnightly *Republika* and the bimonthly *Pacifik*, both
explicitly anti-nationalist and anti-war.

Three national daily papers and several news magazines dominate
the market, although people also rely upon regional and local publications
for information. It is the national dailies, above all the two Politika group
titles, *Politika* and *Politika ekspres*, that project and reflect political power.

The third daily paper, *Večernje novosti*, is even more
pro-government than the Politika titles. In the late 1980s, it was the

---

[27] L Trotsky, quoted in M Malešić, (ed.), *The Role of Mass Media in the
Serbian-Croatian Conflict*, Psykologist Försvar Report 164 (Stockholm: 1993), 57 and
62.

[28] Two surveys since October 1992 indicate that television or radio are the most
frequently used sources of information for 66-76 per cent of respondents. Only 14 per
cent chose newspapers or magazines. (Information supplied by the Institute of Social
Sciences, University of Belgrade.)

[29] Malešić, supra note 27 at 40.

biggest-selling daily in Yugoslavia, selling over 300,000 copies. By August 1993, consumer poverty and the paper shortage, due to trade sanctions, had reduced the print run to 27,000.[30] *Večernje novosti* belonged to the Serbian branch of the Socialist Alliance of Working People (SAWP), which merged with the League of Communists to form the SPS before the 1990 elections.[31] The government has ensured that the process of nominal privatization into a joint-stock company has steered a controlling share of the paper into government supporters' hands. Little more will be said about *Večernje novosti* in this chapter, because its coverage of the war was the same in all key respects as that of the Politika press, but even more extreme.

Printing and Distribution

There are three printing houses with the capacity to produce daily newspapers: Politika (belonging to the Politika group) and Borba Publishing, both based in Belgrade; and Forum, based in Novi Sad. Opposition and politically independent magazines are mostly printed by Forum.

Newsprint is manufactured in Serbia and Montenegro by only one company, Matroz, a state-owned business. International trade sanctions since 1992 have caused severe problems for Matroz; in March 1994, for example, shortage of oil forced the plant to close.

However, Matroz's customers have fared worse: sanctions left the media with no alternative to Matroz except the black market or, for independent papers (such as *Borba, Vreme, Republika*), occasional donations from international media organizations. There are complaints that Matroz favours the Politika newspapers, only selling elsewhere whatever is surplus to their requirements. Stevan Nikšić of *NIN* magazine alleges that *Politika*, for example, has received "special donations of paper from State reserves" as a consequence of its political loyalty to the government.[32] Branislav Milošević, deputy manager of *Borba*, says that

---

[30] *Vjesnik*, 17 Aug. 1993.

[31] On the SAWP, see Glossary.

[32] From an article by S Nikšić of *NIN* weekly magazine, distributed by the AIM Network, Jan. 1994.

Borba has to pay three times as much for Matroz's product as a government-controlled paper like *Večernje novosti*.

There is no simple monopoly of distribution which can be abused by government to suppress unwanted media, as has happened in Croatia.[33] There are four companies in Serbia: Politika, Borba Plasman, Štampa, and Forum. The Politika distribution house belongs to the Politika group; Borba Plasman separated from the *Borba* newspaper in the late 1980s. These two distributors operate throughout the republic, and own about 800 kiosks each. Štampa has about 250 kiosks, all in Belgrade. Forum operates in the Vojvodina region. There is also a handful of independently-owned kiosks in Belgrade.

This means that two companies, one of whom is emphatically pro-government, control press distribution in central and southern Serbia. This, the heartland of support for the ruling party, is the region of the country which cannot receive privately-owned radio and television stations (Studio B, TV Politika and Radio B92).

Sanctions have further limited press penetration of the area. At times in 1993, Borba Plasman could not afford enough motor oil and truck tyres to cover more than the "bigger towns".[34] The result is that independent printed media, like their electronic counterparts, are generally restricted to Belgrade and its surroundings, and large towns in Vojvodina (Novi Sad and Subotica).

There is a further effect of the economic crisis to which sanctions have so greatly added. The distributors take at least a month to pay their customers. With inflation running at over 1,000 per cent per month during 1993, media were making a gross loss on kiosk sales: a powerful disincentive to publish. *Vreme* responded by employing a team of 50 street-vendors, who sell some 6-7,000 copies. These sales, along with the 5,000 copies sold for hard currency abroad, subsidize the 8,000 or so copies which sell through kiosks.

---

[33] For the case of *Danas* magazine, see section on 'News Magazines' infra.

[34] B Milošević, deputy manager of *Borba*, to author, 7 Oct. 1993.

The Politika Paradigm

Two of the three national dailies, *Politika* and *Politika ekspres*, are owned by the Politika group which has a place to itself in the history of Serbian media. Nearly 70 per cent of regular newspaper readers in Serbia buy one of these two papers.[35]

Historically, *Politika* (founded in 1904) is the authoritative national daily and is still the most widely read and most trusted newspaper.[36] *Politika ekspres* (founded in 1970) has a more sensational format, with short articles and big headlines. Like *Večernje novosti*, it is pitched at less educated readers. *Politika ekspres*'s editor-in-chief since 1986, Slobodan Jovanović, has been a staunch supporter of Milošević.

"*Politika* is much more in this country than a newspaper. It is an institution", says Aleksandar Nenadović, a former editor-in-chief. *Politika* merits special attention in this chapter because it was exceptionally influential, and also because it was typical of Serbian media at the end of the 1980s in two key respects: the way in which the Communist leadership influenced its editorial policy without ever owning it, and the style of the paper's support for the Communist leadership. What *Politika* did in print, TVB did on screen.

As a veteran liberal, Nenadović finds it painful to discuss the paper's vanguard role in Serbia's nationalist revival of the late 1980s. As a journalist with four decades of loyalty to the paper, he cannot help extenuating that role:

> The explosion of nationalism was something so authentic, so Serbian. Communism was relatively thin, imported, new. And *Politika* was at the heart of this thing. The regime took out everything that was good about us, and made the paper a launching pad for the nationalist offensive. They killed its liberal soul.[37]

---

[35] S Antonić, "Fighting for the Truth", *East European Reporter* (July-Aug. 1992).

[36] Research in summer 1993 by the Public Opinion and Marketing Centre at the Institute for Political Studies, Belgrade.

[37] A Nenadovic to author, 8 Oct. 1993.

The ownership status of *Politika* and its parent company, the Politika group, the biggest media organization in the Balkans, with 20 publications (including two daily newspapers), a radio station and a television channel, was formally independent within the Yugoslav socialist system. It was defined as 'social property', nominally controlled by the staff, who were responsible to the republic branch of the SAWP. This situation was basically unchanged after the republican SAWP merged with the League of Communists to form the SPS, before the 1990 multiparty elections. Although there are no formal links between the Politika group and the SPS, the Politika group has always been too important in Serbian life for the republican League of Communists not to decide the key executive and editorial appointments. Editors-in-chief were installed and removed by the League's leadership of the day. Nenadović himself was ousted in 1972, following the purge by Tito of Serbia's reformist leadership. In 1983, editor-in-chief Dragoljub Trailović was forced to resign "amid charges of Serbian nationalism".[38] When Milošević defeated his rival, Ivan Stambolić, the Politika group's director-general and the editor-in-chief of the weekly *NIN* (which had not supported the Milošević faction) were soon replaced.

Significantly, the issue which provoked internal dissatisfaction with the Politika group's orientation was unrelated to the national question. Following protests against biased coverage by *Politika* and *NIN* of an opposition rally in Belgrade in June 1990, a group of journalists from these media signed a petition criticizing the coverage.[39] Later that year, journalists formed the Independent Trade Union of Politika. The new union came to the fore after the March 1991 demonstrations in Belgrade, when it called for the resignation of Živorad Minović, director-general of the Politika group since November 1987 (as well as editor-in-chief of *Politika*), and of the editors-in-chief of the group's other political publications.

---

[38] P Ramet, "The Role of the Press in Yugoslavia", in P Ramet (ed.), *Yugoslavia in the 1980s* (Boulder, Colorado: Westview Press, 1985), 421. The real reason for Trailović's effective dismissal may have had more to do with his criticism of the federal government's refusal to reveal the amount of Yugoslavia's foreign debt. Thus, straight political repression was disguised as anti-nationalism. (Ramet, at 119).

[39] Some journalists were dismissed from these papers for refusing to report incorrect information about the rally. Committee to Protect Journalists, *Attacks on the Press 1990* (New York: 1990).

It was Minović who had committed *Politika* to endorse Milošević and his faction in the struggle for power within the League of Communists of Serbia, which climaxed with Milošević's victory at the 1987 session of the League's Central Committee. Following that victory, Minović had replaced Ivan Stojanović as the group's director-general; he then oversaw the transformation of *Politika* and the rest of the group's news publications into ideological weapons of the Serbian government. In April 1990, Minović reduced the salaries of 40 *Politika* journalists and advised them to seek alternative employment because of their opposition to the Serbian leadership.[40]

From 1987, *Politika* was swiftly monopolized by hate- and fear-mongering articles about a growing roster of internal and external enemies (the Albanians of Kosovo and, later, the Croats, the Slovenians, the Bosnian Muslims, the Vatican, and the CIA). The back pages of the paper, meanwhile, were "given over to interminable obsessive features on Serbia's past: its battles, its dynasties, its unique sufferings".[41]

Under union pressure, Minović resigned his editorial position in March 1991 but remained as director-general of the group. The question of editorial policy was swallowed up by the increasingly open threat of war with Croatia; the paper's continuing loyalty to the Milošević government could be disguised as solidarity with the imperilled nation.

Discontent grew among *Politika*'s staff, and, in 1992, they tried to buy out the paper under the Federal Law of 1989, the only existing privatization law. The government responded with a bill to take direct control of the group. When the group's entire staff of 4,000 took action (with the first official strike in the paper's 88-year history), and other media showed active solidarity, President Milošević decided to reject the bill as unconstitutional. He has been rewarded with the newspaper's continuing loyalty on the only all-important subjects: the Serbian national question, and the war in Bosnia.

The buy-out proceeded: staff own 51 per cent of the company, on paper. In reality, control lies with the board of directors led by Živorad Minović, who still heads the group. He has continued to prove his resourcefulness since 1992, cleaving close to the government without

---

[40] Id.

[41] A description of *Politika*'s back pages in the spring of 1988, in Magaš, supra note 11 at 120.

submitting to it. He threatened to resign over the nationalization bill, denouncing the government's "real intention [of] subjecting *Politika* to its total control".[42] In the aftermath of the bill's rejection, *Politika* printed some unwonted pieces, such as interviews with opposition leaders and other critics of the SPS. In mid-1993, Minović's board of directors illegally abolished the workers' councils in *Politika* and its sister paper *Politika ekspres*, which represented staff interests at management level. Without them, the directors are unaccountable, so the hidden hand of government can continue its manipulation, above all in screening and replacing personnel. In the words of a senior *Politika* journalist, "[o]ur 51 per cent is meaningless".

Coverage of Serb Rebellion in Croatia

The Politika papers' account of national relations inside Croatia before the outbreak of war in summer 1991, and of the main political challenge to Milošević's rule, are presented below in a good deal of detail, for two reasons: Politika's coverage was typical of reportage in the government-controlled media at the time; and, also, the media's work was in a crucial sense complete when war got under way. The mere logic of events then did much to substantiate the fantasies of national beleaguerment and solidarity which the media had been conjuring.

In April 1990, open elections brought Franjo Tudjman and his Hrvatska Demokratska Zajednica (HDZ, the Croatian Democratic Community) to power in Croatia, with the aim of gaining sovereignty for Croatia within a reformed Yugoslavia, or independently. Radicals among Croatia's 580,000 Serbs (12 per cent of Croatia's population) agitated against the new government, seeking to mobilize the minority behind the first of what became a series of escalating demands: for cultural autonomy, for political autonomy, for territorial sovereignty, and then for unification with Serbia and Serb-controlled parts of Bosnia.

The main agitator was Srpska Demokratska Stranka (SDS, the Serb Democratic Party), led by Jovan Rašković. At an open-air meeting on 25 July 1990, Rašković proclaimed the autonomy of Croatian Serbs. The

---

[42] Quoted in European Institute for the Media (EIM), *The 1992 Federal and Republican Elections in Serbia and Montenegro: Coverage by Press, Radio and Television*, A Report by the Media Monitoring Unit (Manchester & Dusseldorf: Jan. 1993), 56.

proclamation was, of course, not recognized by the Croatian government. The following day, *Politika* carried a long report of the meeting, with excerpts of speeches, under the headline "Serbs in Croatia proclaim autonomy". Related headlines were: "We shall have Serbian TV", "The spirituality of the Serbian people", "Rašković: I won't negotiate with *ustaše*", and "This is an uprising".[43] Elsewhere in the issue were articles about *ustaše* crimes and death camps from the Second World War;[44] and a satirical report about the Croatian parliamentary session the day before to approve 12 constitutional amendments, one of which 'derecognized' Cyrillic script (which had enjoyed parity with Latin script) except in Serb-majority municipalities.[45]

President Tudjman's claim, in his speech to parliament, that the Serbs wanted to destabilize Croatia to the point where the JNA would intervene, was reported in *Politika ekspres* on 26 July, with a malicious commentary. The simultaneous meeting of Croatian Serbs, by contrast, was reported in a poetic and celebratory tone. The same issue included a feature about the Jasenovac concentration camp.[46]

Next day *Politika ekspres* reported Croatian Serbs' fears of the militia and the *šahovnica*, Croatia's national emblem, which, because of its resemblance to the flag of the Second World War Croat fascist regime, reminded them of the SS and Hitler Youth.[47]

---

[43] See Ch. 4, section on 'Profile of Journalists' infra for Croatian television's coverage of this speech, which continued "but an uprising without weapons".

[44] In summer 1990, five or six pages of *Politika* were devoted to articles about *ustaše* crimes. (P Tašić, *Kako je ubijena druga Jugoslavija* (Skopje: AI, 1994), 193.) Tašić also mentioned that *Politika* organized a speleological expedition to some caves, in order to prove that the bones therein had belonged to Serbs killed by *ustaše* in the Second World War, not — as the Croatian press maintained — to Croat victims of the Partisans.

[45] The Cyrillic script is traditional in Serbia. Although it was not used by the majority of Croatian Serbs, 'derecognition' was widely felt, and was intended to be felt, as a form of discrimination.

[46] At Jasenovac the *ustaša* regime killed as many as 150,000 Serbs, Jews, Gypsies and political enemies in 1941-1945. For *ustaša* see Glossary.

[47] The *šahovnica* is a red and white checked shield and the centrepiece of the new Croatian flag. While the emblem is some 500 years old, and also featured in Croatia's Communist heraldry, its prime association for Serbs is with the Croat fascist regime, led by the *ustaša* movement, which ruled the Nazi-puppet Nezavisna Država Hrvatska (NDH, Independent State of Croatia) in 1941-1945, and was responsible for the murders of several hundred thousand people.

On 30 September, a radical Serb faction in Knin, the centre of rebellion against Zagreb, founded its own 'parliament', the Serbian People's Council. The following day, this body declared full autonomy on the basis of a referendum held on 2 September in territory where the SDS was strong.[48]

That same day, *Politika* went into overdrive with article upon article stressing the Croatian threat, typified by recent raids by Croatian militia searching Serb areas for weapons. Headlines included: "Serb children as hostages", "Attack on the Serb people", "A voice against *ustašism*", "'We are not fascists, we are *ustaše*'", "Croatian leadership again shames the Croatian people". A report from Petrinja declared, "scenes from fifty years ago were repeated, when Croatian *ustaše* attacked the Serb people".

The following day's headlines included: "The whole Serb people is attacked", "1941 started with same methods", and "All means to resist terror of *ustašoid* government", and "Dramatic situation in Croatia: autonomy proclaimed by Serbs". Headlines on 3 October included: "Genocide mustn't happen", "Mad policies of Croatian government", "*Ustaše* are destroying Yugoslavia and making Serbs responsible", and "Croatian Specials speak Albanian",[49] a fine example of a favourite technique: assimilating Serbia's enemies to one another, epitomizing them as a vast collective driven by a self-evident metaphysical purpose: to sow dissension among the Serbs before killing as many of them as possible.

Politika ekspres, meanwhile, described the referendum results and the proclamation as part of the "natural course of things". Unarmed Serbs are defending themselves from the *ustaše* by proclaiming autonomy, the

---

[48] "A strange referendum! No legal authority had decided to organize it. No precise question was posed, the voting paper bore only the words 'Vote to decide on Serb autonomy - For - Against'. The juridical consequences of a vote 'for' were not explained. There were no electoral registers, anyone who wanted to vote could do so: not Croats, but Serbs from the area, including those who had not lived there for a long time, and others who were passing through. The vote was 99.2 per cent 'for'. Instead of dismissing this spectacle, the Croatian government declared that it would prevent it. This it was incapable of doing. The Serbs' anxieties grew, the authority of the government shrank." (Garde, supra note 3 at 285.)

[49] 'Specials' were special police units organized by the Croatian Ministry of the Interior for use in high-risk situations. In April 1991 the Specials were absorbed into the National Guard, a proto-army, organized by the Ministry of Defence and renamed the Croatian Army in September 1991.

paper continued, rounding off that such "political means ... obviously will not suffice". The paper carried photographs of well-armed Special Police captioned "Ready to attack Knin" (there was never an attack on Knin). Other headlines included: "Serb People's Council calls on the Serb people to resist the terror of the *ustašoid* government", "Genocide mustn't be repeated", "The ghost of Jasenovac threatens", "Response to terror", and "Protecting Serbs from vampirical *ustaše*".

Coverage of Internal Opposition

On 9 March 1991, a crowd of around 30-100,000 demonstrated in central Belgrade against President Milošević and TVB. The demonstration, organized by the opposition SPO party, was directed against government control of the state media, but it swiftly escalated into a general protest against President Milošević's authoritarian rule and the economic chaos in Serbia. When riot police were deployed, the demonstration turned violent. One policeman died in clashes, and a student was killed by a police bullet.

The President and his government were briefly stunned: Serbs were marching against their leaders. The pro-government media, with the Politika press and state-controlled television in the lead, could not blame a non-Serbian enemy. Instead they focused on an internal political enemy, the strongly nationalist SPO party with its charismatic leader Vuk Drašković, and accused them of undermining democracy; for Milošević and his party were the nation's choice, so marching against them was marching against the nation.

Under its 10 March front-page headline, "Milošević says Serbia must fight the forces of chaos and frenzy", *Politika* reported "great and aggressive destruction", "great violence, destruction and vandalism", and "an attempt to realize the scenario of destroying the legitimate Serbian authorities legally elected in multiparty elections". "Yesterday a betrayal of the Serbian people was witnessed"; "confusion and disorder", and "destroying the constitutional order" were the goals; "armed members of the SPO started the 'peaceful demonstration' in which 'dozens of militia men were wounded'".

Readers learned that "Studio B encouraged the rebellion", that "Vuk Drašković had informed the Albanian secessionist leaders about the scenario under preparation", because the SPO wanted what the *ustaše* and

Albanian separatists wanted.[50] It was a preposterous allegation, as the SPO's record shows; it was not meant to provoke an intellectual reaction, but to forge a link in readers' minds between the demonstration (which was still shocking, raw, and not yet defined) and those other undoubted mortal enemies of each Serb.

On 11 March, *Politika* readers were greeted with the headline "Rugova prepared a celebration dinner" (after the demonstration, so gleeful was he).[51] Under another headline, "Militiaman killed defending peace and democracy from the forces of darkness", the dead man's brother was quoted: "it would be much easier for me if he had been killed in Kosovo". Under "Script-writers of madness", the "Drašković-Rugova axis" was analyzed, alleging that the United States Ambassador was involved in the plot. Also, it transpires, "the scenario was known to certain Western journalists and television networks". Another headline mentions "The smell of foreign political kitchens". Headlines on the 12 March included: "Paid traitors to their own people", "Traitors to Serbia sow seeds of division", and "Attacking their own people".

Politika ekspres was less subtle. On 10 March under the headline "With stones against militia", it described "the *četnik* hordes from the SPO" and their motivation:

> It is obvious that a Bastille did fall yesterday, but it was the Bastille led by Vuk Drašković, who was consumed by the flames of his own hatred for Serbia.[52] ... The demonstrations weren't aimed at the leadership and the leadership of TV, rather they were directly destructive against Serbia.

Under "The *šiptars* are watching and waiting", readers learned that "leaders of *šiptar* secessionism knew the whole scenario two days before the demonstration".[53] These unnamed leaders allegedly claimed that

---

[50] On the independent television station Studio B, see section on 'Other Television News' infra.

[51] Ibrahim Rugova is president of the Democratic League of Kosovo, the largest organization of Kosovo Albanians.

[52] The TVB building in Belgrade is known satirically as the 'Bastille'.

[53] On *šiptars*, see Glossary.

Drašković had given them more help toward their separatist goals than President Tudjman, President of Slovenia Milan Kučan, and their foreign supporters.

Politika ekspres maintained its theme; on 11 March, under "Disorder planned in detail", it revealed that "Belgrade's 9 March was planned to the last detail, and the planning took three months. From very good sources, we have learned that the SPO informed its collaborators in advance that it would destroy the legal government in Serbia." The United States Ambassador was implicated: he had promised help to Drašković if he rebelled, the paper alleged. The "Drašković-Rugova axis" was aired once more. Under the headline "It was *šiptars* and Croats who demonstrated", *Politika ekspres* reported witnesses' statements that the demonstrators were heard speaking Croatian words with Albanian pronunciation. Another article told how 150 Albanians had travelled by bus from Slovenia to join the demonstration.

Anecdotal evidence suggests that the official version of the 9 March demonstration was not very influential; people who swallowed other disinformation and propaganda baulked at this, perhaps because the alleged involvement of outsiders was too slender and far-fetched. Public opinion was much less suggestible when the targets of propaganda were Serbians, let alone Serbians whose boundless patriotism was known to all, indeed still ringing in everyone's ears from the election campaign in 1990. It is notable that the papers did not know how to characterize the students and other Belgraders at the demonstration, who were far more numerous than the SPO activists or *četniks*. It would have been risky to stigmatize ordinary citizens, so the papers almost ignored them, further damaging the plausibility of their interpretation of events and causes.

Coverage of Plitvice

The next step toward full-blown conflict was taken at the end of March 1991, when Croatian militia tried to regain control of the Plitvice National Park, in central Croatia, from Serb rebels who had annexed the area to their 'Autonomous Region of Krajina'. The Croatians were ill prepared; their bus was ambushed and two men died. On 1 April, *Politika* spoke of the "defenders of the National Park of Plitvice", and published

Radio Knin's appeal to citizens to come with their weapons.[54] Next day's headlines included "Krajina decides to join Serbia", "The Army must secure peace for all citizens", "Krajina must defend itself", and "Serb people - protection from genocide".

Politika ekspres on 1 April reported from Knin, using local sources such as police chief Milan Martić. Headlines included: "We shall resist", "Attack on whole Serbian people", "Volunteers from Knin go to Korenica" (a town near Plitvice), and "Protecting the Serbian people". Below the headline "Under one flag", the paper reported an appeal for volunteers by Postojbina, a Serb organization in Kosovo. On page 6, however, the paper did mention the Croatian version of events.[55]

On 2 April, under the headline "Fragile peace", *Politika ekspres* described how Croatian police "mercilessly conquered the territory of the National Park of Plitvice, to put it under the sovereignty of the *šahovnica*". A follow-up report, "Specials like tourists", alleged that Specials had infiltrated a group of 250 Italian tourists staying at Plitvice. A third article, "Plitvice affair — part of strategy to revive NDH: Plitvice as training ground", revealed how the Croatian action "was prepared in *ustaše* dens in their training grounds all around the world. *Ustaše* are training special soldiers who are infiltrating Serb villages in Croatia. The goal is to revive NDH. ....". Other stories included: "Krajina with Serbia", "Planning a bloody Catholic Easter", "Ghost of fascism awakens", "Serbian unity — saving Krajina", and "Army attacked with weapons".

Reporting Borovo Selo

On 4 April 1991, under the headline "Sparking the conflict", *Politika ekspres* carried news of Serbian volunteers arriving in Borovo Selo, an obscure village in eastern Croatia which would very soon make the headlines. The reporter mentioned Šešelj's *četniki* arriving in Borovo Selo; two of them were pictured, brandishing guns. The caption identified one as Boro Poljković, whose name will shortly recur.

---

[54] Radio Knin, a station in the Croatian Radio network, had been taken over by the Serb rebels.

[55] For the Croatian version, see Ch. 4, section on 'Profile of Television Journalists' infra.

On 2 May, an unknown number of Croatian police, Serb paramilitaries, and villagers were killed in Borovo Selo, near Vukovar in eastern Croatia. According to the Croats, two police patrol cars were ambushed at night in Borovo Selo by Serbs, including volunteers from Serbia proper. One car escaped, leaving two wounded men behind. Next morning, the Serb commander invited the Croats to collect the two men; the bus-full of police who fell for the decoy were then ambushed. Twelve police and three Serbs were killed.

According to the Serb side, the two patrol cars had opened fire upon entering the village. The villagers (no outside volunteers) fired back, wounded two of the Croats, and sent them to hospital for treatment. Next day, a short convoy of police vehicles raced into Borovo Selo and 300 Specials poured out. In the ensuing shoot-out, 25 Specials and one unarmed Serb who had been guarding the infirmary were killed.[56]

Under "Tragic events in Borovo Selo near Vukovar, several dead and wounded in clashes", *Politika* carried a short front-page report on 3 May, quoting Serb witnesses. On 4 May, the paper described how "peace has been taken away from Serb villages and Serbs are threatened in the Vukovar district".

Politika ekspres, blunter as usual, reported that Specials had "raided" Borovo Selo; its late edition on 3 May carried a report from the village. "Several tens of Specials were killed", said the reporter, adding that the Yugoslav flag was flying on the Serb political headquarters; that the Specials, shooting "madly at everything that moved", had killed Vojislav Milić, a Serb from Nova Pazova, as he guarded the headquarters "barehanded".[57] The reporter claimed Serbs had swiftly arrested more than 70 Specials — the arrival of the JNA had saved their lives. In conclusion, the Serb people were not going to give up; even unarmed people were ready to fight barehanded against the armed forces of "the most democratic country in the world" (a sarcastic reference to President Tudjman's style of rhetoric).

Next day, the paper reported President Tudjman's speech about Borovo Selo on the front page, "The 'Ban' Calls for War".[58] (In fact, the

---

[56] B Hall, *The Impossible Country. A Journey Through the Last Days of Yugoslavia* (London: Secker & Warburg, 1994), 97-98.

[57] See also Ch. 2, section on *'Borba'* supra.

[58] The 'Ban' was the Governor of the Austro-Hungarian provinces of Croatia

President had said the killing marked the "beginning of open war" against Croatia.) Another article was headlined incitingly, "Let's go and protect our people". Boro Poljković (see above) was named among the victims of the Croatian action, as a "wounded civilian", not a gun-toting *četnik* as shown in the paper a month before.

Reporting Slovenia's and Croatia's Independence

On 25 June 1991, Croatia and Slovenia declared their sovereignty and independence. Next day *Politika* reacted apprehensively: "Dramatic moments for Yugoslavia", "Croatia proclaims itself a sovereign state", "Danger for Europe", "Yugoslavia's most dramatic week", "Yugoslavia's collapse begins". Further into the paper, the articles sharpened: "We can't accept Croatia keeping these borders", "Protecting Yugoslavia with the Army", "Secession — a criminal act", "No negotiations with Slovenia", "Victory of evil", "Krajina in same state with Serbia, Montenegro and Bosnia-Hercegovina", and "Slavonia, Baranja and Western Srem proclaim autonomy".

Among all this, one article about Slovenia's declaration provided a factual and objective report from Ljubljana, confirming by its very tone that Slovenia's declaration, no less momentous than Croatia's from the angle of Yugoslav federal unity, was of little concern to *Politika*. Over the next four days, as the world was riveted by the fighting in Slovenia, *Politika* kept up the polemic and threats against Croatia: "We shall defend Krajina and the whole Serb ethnic territory", "We are ready in case of attack", "Aggression against Krajina is aggression against whole Serb people", "Kalashnikov democracy in Croatia", "Jasenovac mustn't be forgotten", "People flee as special militia surround villages", and "*'Knindžas'* defending Krajina".[59] *Politika ekspres* followed *Politika's*

---

and Slavonia.

[59] In 1991, the Politika house published a comic book called *The Demons Return*, featuring the "*Knindžas*", Serb warrior-heroes who practise their martial arts against the Croats. Their name puns on ninja and Knin, the town in southern Croatia which was the stronghold of Serb rebellion against the Croatian government in 1990 and 1991. Croatia too had its comic-strip heroes. The adventures of "Superhrvoje" ran in the Croatian daily *Slobodna Dalmacija* in 1992. The eponymous hero returns from Germany, where he lives, to defend his 'Holy Land' in Dalmatia from the *četniki*. (Čolović, supra note 4 at 136-139.)

line, with a neutral report from Slovenia on 25 June, beside other articles entitled "HDZ on the path of hatred" and "Sowers of hatred".

Supporting the Drive for Volunteers

The Politika papers, along with other media, played a role in the drive to muster paramilitary volunteers as the military campaign against Croatia was getting under way. While the JNA and the Serbian government were negotiating peace with the European Community (EC), the Belgrade press was painting a very different, more accurate, picture of their intentions.

On 5 June 1991 *Politika ekspres* ran a piece titled "Serbs must get weapons", about the self-proclaimed Serbian National Council for Slavonia, Baranja and Western Srem demanding weapons so that "the people" could defend themselves from "*ustašism*". On 9 June, under "Time for unity", the paper profiled a nationalist demand for the Krajina leaders in Croatia to "give everything, even military help, to fight the Croatian *ustaša* government". There was the latest news of armed volunteers going to Krajina, and of the formation of the Homeland Front of Banja Luka, a Bosnian Serb organization to support Krajina.

On 2 July, the day JNA Chief of Staff Blagoje Adžić went on TVB to threaten full-scale war against Slovenia, *Politika ekspres* reported the formation of a new volunteer guard "to defend Serbia and Serbian citizens". Another article reported Šešelj's statement at a press conference that voluntary brigades of his *četniki* were fighting in Borovo Selo. Next day Jovan Marjanović, vice-president of the opposition SPO (the 'traitors' of the March demonstrations in Belgrade) was quoted prominently: "The [Yugoslav] Army must come into Croatia and occupy the line Benkovac-Karlovac-Pakrac-Baranja." (In other words, the JNA should carve out a Greater Serbia.)

On 7 July the EC brokered the Brioni Accords, and *Politika ekspres* carried an interview with Knin Police Chief Martić, about training the special units of *Knindžas* and other matters, under the headline "We can defend ourselves". The interviewer asked who had helped him to get equipment and troops. "The most important help came from the government of Serbia, in almost all ways", Martić replied. The interviewer then asked if he would co-ordinate actions with the JNA in the event of fighting against the Croatian armed forces. "Co-ordination already exists. We and the JNA have a mutual enemy", responded Martić.

On 8 July, *Politika ekspres* carried "The war without war", a report about journalists visiting a JNA brigade in Western Srem (inside Croatian territory already claimed by Serb rebels). A photograph showed a multiple rocket launcher in a field. A local Serb spokesman claimed that Romanians, Kurds, Tamils, and Albanians were on the other side. "The reservists are impatient: 'How long are Serbs going to keep waiting for a peaceful solution while the others are killing them?'." The journalist quoted a JNA colonel: "People are just waiting for the order. The reservists' morale is boosted incredibly when I give them ammunition. They want to go into action, to finish it for ever. Our goal is to put units between the two sides in the war. The missile systems are ready to raze the enemy to the ground." These last three sentences, combined as if there was no contradiction among them, was typical of the JNA's blatantly duplicit rhetoric in 1991.

On 9 July, *Politika ekspres* reported that "They're demanding a Serbian army", a reference to an SPO gimmick: enrolling military volunteers on Belgrade's main square. The same day, *Politika* declared "Rebellion is the only possible way of resisting". This referred to the Serb 'War Council' in Glina, Croatia, proclaiming a rebellion in the Banija region. The Council was forming volunteer units: "We are ready to solve once and for all the question of the status of the Serb people in Croatia."

On 10 July, *Politika* ran a story from Bosnia: "State of emergency to be proclaimed in Banja Luka". The self-constituted 'Council for People's Defence' had proclaimed a State of Emergency and was mobilizing volunteers for Krajina. (Banja Luka was the headquarters of the SDS, which led the political, and later armed, resistance to the government of Bosnia.) On 13 July, under the headline "City of men", a Serb leader in Borovo Selo boasted that 70,000 armed men in the region could be mobilized within 20 minutes. Another article, "Volunteers are getting ready", reported that the nationalist parties in Serbia, including Drašković's SPO, Šešelj's SRS, and the ruling SPS had all agreed upon the formation of volunteer units.

The War in Bosnia

The Politika press reports of the war in Bosnia supported the war effort from the outset. As in Croatia, the papers gave every possible credit, and the benefit of every doubt, to the Serb side without argument or examination. Throughout May 1992, *Politika* reprinted a series of First

World War propaganda posters: "Serbia Needs Your Help" (1917), "Save Serbia Our Ally" and "La journée Serbe" (1916).

With their pages unsullied by any effort to present or analyze the Bosnian government's arguments, the Politika press at best tagged behind the military onslaught as loyal camp-followers. At worst, their coverage was part and parcel of the onslaught, actively helping to brew the fog of fear, ignorance and hatred that blinded so many Serbs, while pacifying or ridiculing the doubters.

Zvornik

The district of Zvornik (81,000 people in 1991, 59 per cent Muslim, 38 per cent Serb) lay in the path of the initial onslaught against eastern Bosnia. According to the UNCHR Special Rapporteur, most of the town was captured by the JNA and Serb irregular forces on 8 April 1992.[60] Resistance mustered around Zvornik's medieval fortress of Kula Grad above the town, which held out for 20 days. Survivors have described terror, torture and killing of Muslims on a massive scale, as well as wholesale plunder of Muslims' property. During the week after Kula Grad fell, the Red Cross counted 12,000 refugees from the area.

Politika first mentions the town on 6 April: Serbs were packing and leaving, due to the "tensions in the Zvornik area". On 9 April, *Politika* reported "no peace", because Muslim extremists had attacked "the Serb municipality of Zvornik", terms which wholly assent to the radical Bosnian Serb definition of the conflict.

Next day, *Politika*'s front page bore the headline "Serb forces in control of Zvornik". On page 6, under "Zvornik liberated", was the news that "[a]ll vital buildings in the town have been taken and the customary cleansing of the town is under way". Instead of accepting the ultimatum to surrender, reports correspondent D Pejak, the other side "fired on members of the Territorial Defence of the Serb municipality of Zvornik. ... Green Berets are, by tried and tested means, keeping defenceless people hostage."[61] (The word used for defenceless people was *nejač*, a folklore

---

[60] United Nations Commission on Human Rights (UNCHR), Report by Special Rapporteur Tadeusz Mazowiecki, 10 Feb. 1993.

[61] The Green Berets were a militia force organized by the main Muslim party in Bosnia; they later merged with the Bosnian Army.

archaism connoting epic travails under the Ottoman empire.) *Večernje novosti* on this date likewise reported the liberation of Zvornik, and added the detail that the liberators played 'The March to the Drina' from the minaret loudspeakers.[62]

On 11 June, Pejak denied reports in Sarajevo media that Zvornik had been devastated. "There is no reliable information about casualties", he insisted. Tanjug was quoted, citing a Yugoslav Ministry of Defence denial that the Muslims of Zvornik had been persecuted. (On 12 June, *Večernje novosti* reported "superhuman efforts" by Serbian Territorials to drive the more numerous and better armed Green Berets out of Kula Grad. The only damage in Zvornik was broken glass.) On 21 April, *Politika* reported that "Muslim forces are still shooting at peace".

Then a brief item appeared on 26 April, "All quiet in Zvornik", information belied next day when, under the headline "The stronghold of Muslim extremists in Zvornik has fallen", readers learned that Yugoslav and Serbian flags now fly from Kula Grad above Zvornik. "Relief [was felt] on both sides of the River Drina" (the border between Serbia and Bosnia). The extremists had rejected all the Territorial Defence's appeals to surrender; calls for peace were met with bullets. Prisoners revealed that "Alija's army" includes Bangladeshis and *šiptars*, and that Bosnian Muslims from Sarajevo and Bihać had been in command.

On 28 June, Pejak reported that Muslim paramilitaries had retreated from Kula Grad to a nearby village and opened fire from there. By the following afternoon, Pejak continued, the Yugoslav flag was flying over the village and the Serb forces were trying to release defenceless Muslims (*nejač* again) from the cellars where they were hiding from their own oppressors (*zulum*, another heroic folklore word).

So much for the fate of Zvornik. In the pages of Serbia's most prestigious daily, the seizure and genocidal devastation of this town never happened. After provocations and tensions, the Muslim extremist forces had lost fair and square; their dastardly plans to enslave the local Serbs

---

[62] 'The March to the Drina' is a famous old Serbian military song. During the 1992 pre-election campaign, the ruling SPS used this song as the soundtrack for its key promotional spot on television, a 17-second film with the caption "This is Serbia". (S Milivojević and J Matić, *Ekranizacija izbora. TV prezentacija izborne kampanje 92. u Srbiji* [Belgrade: Vreme knjige, 1993], 88.) The River Drina marks Serbia's historic western border with Bosnia; however, any Serb who marched to the Drina in 1992 was going not to defend that border, but to extend it.

were foiled. *Politika*'s reporting of Foča, Srebrenica, Bijeljina, Višegrad, and Prijedor (all attacked in a similar way) repeated the pattern.

The Bread-Queue Massacre

Politika's biggest challenge occurred on 27 May 1992 with the bread-queue massacre in Sarajevo, when 17 people were killed by mortar shells as they queued in a narrow pedestrian street. Film of blood-soaked and mutilated victims, strewn around, shocked a global audience.

How to deny with any plausibility the overwhelming likelihood that the Serb side had perpetrated this atrocity? The answer took a day to locate, maybe because it was so obvious; the enemy's advantage had to be turned on its head. How could the Bosnian TV cameraman have filmed the effect of the mortar blasts unless the atrocity had been planned? *Politika*, on 28 May, led with top-level JNA and Bosnian Serb denials of Serb responsibility; no Bosnian government source or opinion was quoted. By the next day, however, the pro-government press had found its feet again. "Has the governor's palace affair been repeated?", the paper asked rhetorically, referring to the 7 October 1991 explosion in the Croatian President's Zagreb offices (as if there was no doubt that the Croats had staged that attack to frame the Yugoslav air force). That favoured assimilation technique was to the fore again.

"SRNA has concluded that the massacre was stage-managed by Muslim militia and paramilitary units", the article continued.[63] "Most of the victims were Serbs", moreover, but in order to maximize the propaganda, Serb corpses were swiftly swapped for Croats and Muslims wounded earlier elsewhere in the city. (*Večernje novosti* on 29 April offered a blunter front-page variant on this conspiracy theory: the "horrible massacre in Sarajevo was used for politicking purposes by means of cunning TV marketing".)

On 30 May, *Politika* went further: "There is evidence that the Serb side was not responsible" for the massacre. No evidence was, however, presented. The paper demanded an international inquiry.

---

[63] SRNA (Srpska Republika Novinska Agencija) is the news agency of the 'Serb Republic of Bosnia-Hercegovina'.

Television

Introduction

Radio-Televizija Srbije (RTS, Serbian Radio-Television) is the most important news medium in the country and holds a monopoly on state-wide broadcasting. It consists of three channels, the most important of which is Channel 1, the main news and information service, which broadcasts in 96 per cent of Serbia as well as in parts of Croatia and Bosnia. (The other two channels cover slightly less territory and do not try to compete in news and current affairs broadcasting.)[64] The state service is made up of three stations, Radio-Televizija Beograd (RTB, Belgrade Radio-Television), Radio-Televizija Novi Sad (RTNS, Novi Sad Radio-Television), and Radio-Televizija Priština (RTP, Priština Radio-Television).

RTB is the senior station among the three; RTNS and RTP were established in the 1970s as part of the empowerment of the two autonomous provinces of Vojvodina and Kosovo, respectively. When Serbia gained political control over the provinces in 1989, RTNS and RTP also lost their independence from RTB. This change was ratified by the 1991 Law on Radio-Television, which placed all three stations under a new umbrella, RTS, and reduced RTNS and RTP to the status of regional studios. While the regional stations no longer enjoy editorial independence, they still produce some news programmes.

The single most important news programme is *Dnevnik 2*, the evening news, which is shown by all RTS stations, as well as by the television studios in Serb-controlled Croatia (TV Knin and TV Beli Manastir) and Bosnia (TV Banja Luka and TV Pale), using captured transmitters as well as their access to the EBU's satellite facility. *Dnevnik 2* is the news flagship of RTS, setting the national tone, reflecting the ruling party's pressure most directly, and reaching by far the most people.

According to RTS the average audience for the evening news in October 1990 was 2.5 million people in Serbia (excluding Vojvodina and Kosovo).[65] By October 1991, the figure had climbed to 3 million; more

---

[64] EIM, supra note 42 at 6.

[65] In summer 1991, a special supplement was regularly appended to the 7.30

than 60 per cent of the population over 10 years of age. Including Vojvodina (whose population is 54 per cent Serb) the figure reaches 3.5 million.[66]

Meanwhile the circulation of printed media has plummeted. Serbia's newspapers sold 1.1 million copies daily in 1990; by 1993 the figure was estimated at 300,000.[67] Surveys indicate that television is used as a source of news five to six times more than newspapers, the second favourite source along with "family, friends and colleagues".[68]

In addition there are two privately-owned stations which broadcast in Belgrade and the surrounding areas, reaching about a quarter of Serbia's population. The existence of NTV Studio B and TV Politika increases the pressure upon RTS to respond to events and stories which it might otherwise ignore. The Institute of Social Science surveys found that the two privately-owned stations are trusted by a higher proportion of their audiences than RTS but since RTS' audiences are so much higher, its supremacy is not threatened.[69]

There is also satellite and cable television but no estimates of viewers are available. According to one source cited by the European Institute for the Media (EIM), there were about 100,000 satellite dishes in the former Yugoslavia.[70] The EIM found no evidence that foreign broadcasts exercised a significant influence during its monitoring of the 1992 elections, but pointed out that foreign broadcasts were an important

---

p.m. news, spinning out the war coverage to an hour and more each night.

[66] S Antonić, *Vreme*, 25 May 1992, and in *East European Reporter* (July-Aug. 1992).

[67] According to the 1991 census figures the overall illiteracy figure is about 10 per cent, rising to 30 per cent outside large towns. Twenty-nine point eight per cent of people did not complete elementary school and a further 24.5 per cent have only elementary school education. The rate of illiteracy in Croatia in 1991 was 3 per cent; estimates for Bosnia range from 15 to 20 per cent.

[68] Surveys conducted across Serbia, except Kosovo, in October 1992 and April/May 1993 by the Institute of Social Sciences, University of Belgrade. RTS surveys indicate that trust in State television has fallen; in 1989, 39.1 per cent of respondents trusted RTV "very much", by 1991 the figure was 28.6 per cent. (EIM, supra note 42 at 7.) A July 1993 survey by the Institute of Political Studies found that only 8.4 per cent of viewers said that RTS kept them "well" informed against 43.5 per cent who said "badly".

[69] Id.

[70] EIM, supra note 42 at 11.

source of information for journalists and opinion leaders. Their use by independent media as sources of information, as well as the limited effect of foreign broadcasts (when they are rebroadcast by local broadcasters) in forcing the government to reveal information, is noted at different points throughout this chapter.

The government has not been unduly worried about its image abroad and its vilification of foreign media, which it has accused of lies and distortion, has probably lessened the impact such broadcasts may have in the country. In April 1994, the government announced that it was withdrawing the credentials of a number of foreign news teams from Serbia for, according to the Federal Minister of Information Slobodan Ignjatović, "waging an obsessed media warfare against Yugoslavia from its soil".[71] This may indicate that the government is concerned about the impact of these broadcasts within Serbia, but was more likely meant to 'remind' Serbs of the world conspiracy against them at a moment when the UN and NATO were acting with new-found resolution against the Serb forces in Bosnia.

Serbian Radio-Television (RTS)

President Milošević's government keeps RTS in an iron grip, lending prima facie support to the view of Ivan Djurić, leader of the tiny Serbian Reform Party:

> Milošević has surely never read Marshall McLuhan
> but he has grasped better than anyone the function of
> the mass media and of television in particular: he
> well knows that there is nothing except national TV,
> and that on national TV there is nothing except the
> 7.30 evening news. It is there that the consensus of
> public opinion is formed.[72]

---

[71] The self-proclaimed 'government of the Serb Republic of Bosnia-Hercegovina' followed suit by banning anyone working for American news organisations in Serb-held areas.

[72] Interviewed in 6 *L'Indice*, (Italy: June 1993).

The government treats RTS as a party-state resource like the police and the army. The director-general of RTS, Milorad Vučelić, also sits on the executive committee of the ruling SPS. Staff are suspended and removed without a pretence of legality. Before the 1992 Federal and Republican elections, when Milošević stood for re-election as President, RTS television and radio openly sided with the incumbent and his party against his principal rival, Milan Panić, the Federal Premier. A team from the European Institute for the Media, which monitored the elections at the request of the Council of Ministers of the European Union, found "substantial evidence of bias in favour of" the SPS. The team cited four examples:

a) The coverage given in news broadcasts of allegedly non-electoral activities of Mr Slobodan Milošević far exceeds that justified by his performance of his duties as the President of Serbia.

b) Serbian State Television operates a policy of minimal coverage in the news of the activities of other presidential candidates.

c) In the case of Mr Milan Panić, Serbian State Television has broadcast statements in which he is accused of treason and is called a criminal. By doing so Serbian State Television has failed to treat Mr Milan Panić as duly nominated opposition candidate.

d) Serbian State Television has refused to transmit certain advertisements of the opposition parties.[73]

A monitoring mission from the Conference on Security and Cooperation in Europe (CSCE) expressed the same conclusions, more outspokenly:

The pre-electoral campaign was tainted by shameless propaganda in the state-run media, especially

---

[73] EIM, supra note 42 at 33.

television, that exclusively supported the governing party and either ignored or distorted the message of the opposition.[74]

A third team, of British parliamentary observers, pointed out that "coverage of the elections by RTS ... has been consistently and blatantly in contravention of those articles of the Federal Election Law which regulated pre-election coverage". The British observers drew attention to a final statement by the Supervisory Committee which had been appointed, under the Federal Election Law, by the Federal parliament to oversee the elections. Issued four days before polling day, the Committee statement concludes:

> that through the selection of information to be broadcast, and through commentating on events and personalities, ... RTS has openly sided with one of the parties in the election campaign. ... [B]y pursuing such an editorial policy, RTS has called in question the regularity of the forthcoming elections at all levels ... .[75]

Calls for Reform at RTS

The nationalist manipulation of TV news got under way with the mass rallies of solidarity with Kosovo Serbs, the so-called 'meetings of truth', organized around Serbia in 1988. According to Branka Mihajlović, a former news editor,[76] these meetings received special coverage in the news; crowd sizes were exaggerated, Milošević's heroic status and popularity were stressed, and "nationalist emblems unacceptable to most viewers (*četnik* badges and old Serbian flags) were not shown".[77]

---

[74] Id., at 70.

[75] As quoted by the British parliamentary observers. Id., at 74.

[76] In countries of the former Yugoslavia, the news editor (who is responsible for writing the news script) is also the presenter.

[77] B Mihajlović to author, 30 Sept. 1993.

The first ripples of internal dissatisfaction came, not from the news department, but from technical staff and cultural journalists. In January 1989, some 15 television engineers wrote an open letter to President Milošević, querying the recent appointment of Dušan Mitević as director-general of RTB. In June 1990, journalists who refused to broadcast biased information about an opposition rally in Belgrade were suspended. Later that year, journalists whose concern at falling standards was spurred to action by Mitević's political interference in an esteemed arts programme, *Cinema Eye*, joined together to form the Independent Trade Union of Belgrade Radio-Television, which claims to be the first independent trade union in Serbia.[78]

Within a few months, some 800 of RTB's 4,076 employees had joined the union. As part of its struggle for "free and objective coverage and professional rights of the employed", the union drew up a code of conduct to regulate television treatment of political parties during the election campaign at the end of the year. All parties signed except the SPS and its key ally, the SRS, with the result that it was utterly ignored.

According to Isidora Sekulić, a founder member of the union, up to half of the staff at TVB's news department joined the union. These people were, she says, "delicately backgrounded. Their reports were filtered out until they weren't working at all." They were finally dismissed in January 1993 as part of a huge purge, when 14 of the 17-strong union executive were removed and banned from the television centre.

The demand for RTS to be democratized has been a rallying cry of the political opposition in Serbia. It was this cry which mobilized the most effective challenge Milošević has yet faced. In March 1991, students and opposition groupings responded to a call by the main opposition party to join a protest against the government's abuse of television. Some 20,000 people marched past the RTB building, known as the 'Bastille', walking with eyes closed and holding their noses.[79] The protest triggered a wider demonstration against Milošević and his government, which drew in all the main opposition parties and electrified the city for several days.

---

[78] Nezavisni sindikat RTB, *Čistke u RTB, Purges in Belgrade Radio-Television: januar '93* (Belgrade: 1993), 86.

[79] EIM, supra note 42 at 9. For the press response to the demonstrations, see section on 'Coverage of Internal Opposition' supra.

The government met the demonstrators' demand that senior officials at RTB, especially director-general Dušan Mitević, be replaced. Four senior staff, including Mitević, were replaced and a small number of journalists and editors who had been shelved for political reasons were given work again:

> For a moment the ruling structures stepped back: assessing the contents of the programme of RTB during 1990, they admitted that the SPS had been privileged on TV.[80]

Behind the ostensible compromises, however, the government's will to control and manipulate the electronic media was steeled by the protests. The effort to convince Serbs that no alternative existed to full-scale confrontation with Croatia, cost what it must, was infused with fresh urgency. Miloš Vasić of *Vreme* magazine later pointed out that the media campaign and the military offensive were a single strategy:

> On 15 March, Milošević summoned all the mayors of Serbia to a meeting [and] outlined a strategy for provoking ethnic conflict in Croatia. ... A massive media campaign convinced the Serbs in Croatia that they were in danger of a "new genocide". ... The initiative was now in Milošević's hands, and on 1 April the first fighting began at Plitvice National Park.[81]

The thaw at the 'Bastille' was shallow and brief. A new law on radio and television had been in preparation for months; its passage on 31 July 1991 was problem-free, as the opposition was boycotting parliament at that time.

---

[80] P Plavšić, M Radojković & R. Veljanovski, *Toward Democratic Broadcasting* Media-01 (Belgrade: Soros Yugoslavia Foundation, 1993), 22.

[81] 2 *Yugofax*, 14 Sept. 1991. For press coverage of the Plitvice incident, see section on 'Coverage of Plitvice' supra.

Law on Radio-Television

The July 1991 Law on Radio-Television preserved RTS as a 'public company', but transferred parliamentary powers over radio and television to the government. The government henceforth appointed the director-general of RTS and the 17-member RTS governing board, including the five members drawn from inside RTS. It also appointed the RTS Supervisory Committee which reports to government. The programme councils, vestigial organs of self-management socialism which could have been reformed and given a public service role, were swept away. The Law also ratified the government's seizure of control of electronic frequencies from the Federal Broadcasting Authority.[82]

Ominously, the Law was not based on the existing March 1991 Law on the Basis of Public Information which defined the public service nature of broadcasting and would have limited government interference. However, the Law does contain a public service commitment by which its performance can be judged: it defines the activity of RTS as "the creation and production of radio and television programmes for citizens of the republic".

RTS Purges Since 1991

The first decision made following the introduction of the 1991 Law on Radio-Television was the suspension of the management of RTS, "that is, of those in RTS who held responsible positions and were favourably assessed in parliament after March 9".[83] Vučelić, the new director-general, has proved as loyal to the government as Mitević had been.

The editorial team at TVB news was changed, member by member. The new editor-in-chief of news was Krste Bijelić, a Croatian Serb and hard-line nationalist, who had reported for TVB from Slovenia and Croatia before the war. Bijelić has since been replaced by another hard-line nationalist, Dragoljub Milanović, a newspaper journalist from *Politika*

---

[82] See also section on 'Media and the Law' supra.

[83] Plavšić et al, supra note 80 at 22-23.

ekspres newspaper, with one year's experience of television.[84] The new team recruited new reporters, "people with no relevant experience" according to a former TVB news journalist. (All former RTB journalists contacted by ARTICLE 19 echoed this verdict.) The turbulence of war and the trade embargo have since made it all the easier to shelve politically unsuitable reporters, under the guise of economic rationalization, and replace them with pro-government staff.[85]

RTS's methods of ridding itself of unwanted staff are harsh and insidious. Prior to the 1993 purge, journalists were rarely sacked; they were removed from the public eye, demoted, discredited, demoralized, ignored by their commissioning editors, sent on compulsory 'paid leave' (receiving only 10-30 per cent of their salary), and eventually banned from the television building.

The business of discrediting can be savage; a key figure involved, in 1992-1993, was Vojislav Šešelj, the member of parliament and *četnik* leader, who heads the SRS. As Milošević's key parliamentary ally until September 1993, Šešelj was used to denigrate the government's targets in the media. Thus, on 10 April 1992, he attacked RTS journalists by name on the TV news:

> ... Maja Vlahović, a big Serb-hater and daughter of a
> *Vjesnik*-commentator, Ana Kotevski, pro-Bulgarian
> and married to a reformist, Djordje Malavražić, a
> great dogmatist and Communist ... .[86]

This performance, probably timed as a distraction from the horrors then newly under way in Bosnia, was a warning to the public that traitors were about, and to journalists that they must tread with special care.

Šešelj was deployed again on 6 January 1993. He called for a "cleansing" of "undisciplined and party-tainted journalists" at RTS "to put things in complete order". About 30 per cent of RTS journalists should be

---

[84] The news editor-in-chief is a key position; Mihailo Erić was sacked from TVB for his lack of enthusiasm for Milošević's brand of reform in 1987. (EIM, supra note 42 at 18.)

[85] Vlado Slijepčević can stand as an example of the new breed of RTS television war reporter. See section on 'How RTS Presented Serb Territorial Conquest in Bosnia' infra.

[86] *Borba*, 11-12 April 1992. *Vjesnik* is the leading Croatian daily.

sacked, he said.[87] A youth leader of the ruling SPS followed suit on 9 January, explaining that people "who do not think like us" cannot work in state institutions.[88]

Two days later, about one third of RTB's broadcasting staff, some 200 journalists, including the most experienced and respected, were dismissed.[89] Over 1,000 staff were removed from RTS in the January purge which was justified as a "necessary rationalization" due to UN economic sanctions.[90] On arrival at the TV centre, the targeted staff found the entrance hall filled with armed police; sharpshooters were visible at upper windows. Their pass cards were taken and torn up, they were told that from this moment they were on "compulsory holiday" and were banned from the RTB premises. Journalists challenged their dismissal in the courts but, in September 1993, the Supreme Court overruled, on a technicality, a lower court judgment ordering their reinstatement. The Independent Union of Journalists has announced its intention of supporting individual legal challenges by sacked workers against RTS in a continuing effort to gain redress for dismissed staff.

The Format of the News

The introduction to RTS Channel 1 news features a graphic resembling a burnished astrolabe; its gleaming rings are stamped with the names of Serbian cities in Cyrillic letters, somehow suggesting a Serbo-centric cosmos. These names pass reverently across the screen to the sound of a fanfare. Then the main stories are headlined, before a commercial break. After the break, the editor appears behind a desk, greets the "respected viewers", and launches into the lead story. There is a supporting cast of other readers and sometimes a commentator. "The order of items simply reflects political priorities. If Milošević wants a peace plan

---

[87] *Borba*, 7 Jan. 1993.

[88] Nezavisni sindikat RTB, supra note 78 at 9.

[89] Id. at 84.

[90] *Index on Censorship*, April 1993.

at Geneva to go ahead, war footage goes to the back; if not, then atrocities move to the front", explains Branka Mihajlović, a former news editor.[91]

Visually and verbally, the programme is turgid and confusing, notably more so than Croatian or Bosnian television news. Political speeches are relayed for many minutes on end. Newscasters are often switched in mid-report, jarring the narrative. Foreign reports are given as voice-overs to a technicolour postcard image of the relevant capital city. War reports are accompanied by fresh footage which may be unrelated to the words, by archive footage (rarely identified as such) or, often, by a map showing the area in question.

The news scripts are straightforward, if the subject is uncontroversial. Otherwise they tend to be incoherent and stuffed with red herrings: rhetorical questions, prejudicial metaphors, innuendo, exhortations, warnings, and bizarre analogies.

Perhaps the most unusual feature, to foreign eyes and ears, are the 'commentaries' — editorials delivered to camera by one of the news journalists. These seem intended as a gloss upon the rest of the programme, uttering the political subtext of the news reports. Rare nuggets of information are distorted and lost amid convolutions of rhetorical sarcasm, special pleas, and paranoid non-sequiturs. Following is a typical example of TVB editorials. From *Dnevnik 2*, it is a piece by Nebojša Janković delivered on 10 May 1992, hollowly intoning the standard falsehoods about the West and Bosnia as if these were self-evident truths, hoping perhaps to inoculate his audience against the EC's imminent decision (it was announced the following day) to withdraw ambassadors from Belgrade:

> If we agree with the assessment that political pressure
> on Serbia in international forums reached an apex last
> week, at the end of that same week we must ask
> ourselves what are the real political motives of these
> pressures and if they conceal intentions that are
> difficult to fathom at the moment. ... The first

---

[91] The best known editor of *Dnevik 2* in 1993 was Milorad Komrakov who summarized his opinion of the programme's obligations: "Every station has its own editorial policy, and ours certainly isn't tendentious. However, on this television nothing gets through which insults or is against the state or the President". *Vreme*, 15 Nov. 1993.

suspicion is provoked by the American proposal for Yugoslavia's suspension from the CSCE. Even modified, the European variant of this proposal is *contradictio in adjecto*: Serbia is accused of bearing all the blame for the war in Bosnia, but is at the same time suspended from the decision-making process for the settlement of the crisis there.

Even more suspicion is provoked by the total absence of official reactions from Europe and America to the numerous moves which the government in Belgrade has made towards meeting their demands. ... The declaration issued at the proclamation of the Federal Republic of Yugoslavia [by Serbia and Montenegro on 27 April] recognizes de facto the inviolability of the borders of former Yugoslav republics. Movements by all paramilitaries across the river Drina [between Serbia and Bosnia] are banned. Army reservists from Serbia and Montenegro are ordered back into these two republics. On the internal plane, dialogue is being offered to the minorities on a level of autonomy which would not jeopardize the territorial integrity of the State, with which even the West finds no fault. [92] ...

Dnevnik 2 ends with the weather forecast. Even this portion of the programme is not without an element of disinformation. The weather report features a map of the territory of former Yugoslavia, but with only Serbia and Montenegro (the new Yugoslavia) highlighted. When that area's forecast is finished, the 'Serb Krajinas' — territory captured in Croatia and Bosnia — lights up too, and the voiceover delivers a quick forecast for these areas. This meteorological vision of Greater Serbia includes land which Serb forces never captured in Croatia: the northern half of UN Protected Area 'West' and most of the coast between Zadar and Split.

---

[92] Tanjug, 11 May 1992.

Television and the President

Unlike his Croatian counterpart, Milošević is not a garrulous leader. When he does speak, he usually reiterates a few tough telegraphic messages: that all Serbs have the right to live together in one state; that Serbs outside Serbia are defending themselves from fascists and religious extremists; that Serbia is not waging war against Croatia; that Serbia is not involved in the Bosnian civil war; that Serbia wants peace but peace with justice for Serbs outside Serbia; that international sanctions are the unjust price which must be paid for supporting Serbs outside Serbia; that justice will prevail if the Serbs stand together. He keeps his plans to himself, and very rarely criticizes his opponents. Everyone in Serbia talks compulsively about Milošević; Milošević, as a rule, talks about no one.

Thus RTS news gives more insight into policy at any moment than the President's own statements. When, for instance, Milošević wanted to attack Yugoslav President Dobrica Ćosić, it was Vojislav Šešelj, not a member of the ruling SPS, who gave a ranting press conference, which featured prominently on the evening news, with no opportunity for Ćosić's side to reply.[93]

Coverage of the President's Volte-face on the Vance-Owen Plan

The correlation between President Milošević's policies and television coverage is most acutely revealed when there is little time to perform the usual distancing tactics, as happened when Milošević performed an about-face on Bosnian Serb acceptance of the Vance-Owen Plan. At the end of March 1993, viewers of the main evening news were being advised that the Vance-Owen Plan would open the door to "ethnic cleansing" of Serbs in Bosnia, and agreement would be tantamount to national suicide: the Serbs would have to convert to Catholicism or Islam, or emigrate. On 4 April 1993, viewers learned that Belgrade peace activists

---

[93] An example is given in section on 'How Negative Information Was Omitted and Obscured' infra.

were "Alija's followers".[94] Later in April and May, the news treatment both of the Vance-Owen Plan and the priority of peace revealed more clearly than any policy statements that Milošević was convinced for the first time that Western military intervention would follow if the Bosnian Serbs rejected the international Peace Plan for Bosnia.

Bosnian Serbs interviewed on 3 and 4 May, before their leaders voted on the Vance-Owen Plan on 5 May, were exclusively in its favour. On 11 May, four days before the Bosnian Serbs voted in a referendum on the plan, the news carried a pregnant message from Milošević. The screen showed the President's face while the newsreader announced that President Milošević had met President Bulatović of Montenegro and 'President' Hadžić of the 'Serb Republic of Krajina' (Serb-controlled territory in Croatia), and the three had agreed that Serbs outside Serbia could no longer be Serbia's prime concern. The coded message to Bosnian Serbs could not have been plainer.

Elena Popović of the Centre for Anti-War Action in Belgrade monitored most of the news bulletins on RTS Channel 3, known as 3K, between 23 April and 5 May 1993, the date when the so-called Bosnian Serb Assembly spurned the plan, sugaring the flat rejection by calling a referendum on the issue for 15 and 16 May, to let Bosnia's Serbs decide for themselves: as predicted, they overwhelmingly rejected the plan.[95]

Before the 1990 elections, 3K was the innovative channel of RTS; for instance it carried the first television interview with veteran dissident Milovan Djilas. Now it is chiefly an entertainment channel, including music video spots, magazine programmes and a resident astrologist.[96] It can be seen throughout the republic. Its news service consists of almost hourly bulletins from a studio editor (with no correspondents' reports)

---

[94] 'Otvoreni dnevnik', *Borba*, 2 April 1993 and 5 April 1993. 'Otvoreni dnevik' was an analysis of the evening news on TVB, published in *Borba* two or three times weekly over ten months in 1992 and 1993. The authors were two former newsdesk journalists, Branka Mihajlović and Milica Pešić. Their work was an invaluable resource in preparing this chapter.

[95] The referendum effectively killed the Vance-Owen Plan, and it was buried by the 13-point 'action plan' for Bosnia unveiled on 22 May by the USA, Russia, the UK, France and Spain.

[96] In one memorable programme, the resident astrologer warned about the vampires threatening Serbia. When asked how to recognize these vampires, she replied: "Just watch the TV news and you will see all those people who come here from the West, with their vampirical pointed ears." (*Globus*, 5 Nov. 1993.)

from noon until 11 p.m. There is a longer programme at 11 p.m., which is dropped if it clashes with a movie or another feature. The frequency and almost subliminal brevity of these bulletins make them ideal research material for media monitors.

On 24 April 1993, as talks continued in Belgrade between Lord Owen and the Bosnian Serb leadership, these bulletins were cautious and undecided, using only Serbian sources and passing references to world reactions. At 11 p.m., however, a whole range of different sources was quoted from Tanjug to the BBC via Hrvatska Televizija (HTV, Croatian Television).

Two days later, the Bosnian Serb leaders met and rejected Vance-Owen. At noon, 3K news broadcast the meeting's message to Bosnian Serbs "to persevere in their struggle to the end", ahead of reports of the letter by Milošević, Ćosić and Bulatović (Presidents of Serbia, Yugoslavia and Montenegro respectively) calling on the Bosnian Serbs to sign the plan, terming it "an honourable peace" that would ensure "equality and freedom". By 3 p.m., however, the letter took prime position, bolstered by comments, foreign news agency reactions, and Lord Owen's and the JNA's responses. In the following days, foreign politicians supporting the Plan were quoted in detail, and Owen's "praise" for the Yugoslav leaders' efforts to pressurize the Bosnian Serbs was cited.

"Almost at the same moment," Popović notes, "battlefield reports [from Bosnia] also changed. While on 24, 25 and 27 April these reports were based, as usual, on Serb sources or without any named source at all, on 28 April information was taken from UNPROFOR and Tanjug for the first time." The 'urgent public health situation' in Belgrade began to feature prominently in bulletins, with a revised order of causes: first, now, was the war, and second, was sanctions, although the latter had previously been presented as the source of every difficulty in Yugoslavia. (The third cause named was "the shortages" [sic]; fourth was the great number of refugees.)

When the negotiations moved from Belgrade to Athens, 3K's bulletins included "world reactions", emphasizing the breadth of support for Yugoslavia's leadership. The news that Karadžić had signed the Vance-Owen Plan, on 2 May, was described by 3K as "beautiful". Karadžić's key precondition for signing (that the Plan still had to be ratified by his 'Assembly') was mentioned only in passing, omitted through the afternoon, then mentioned briefly again in the evening: reflecting the government's wish to downplay the significance of

Karadžić's caveat. The 7 p.m. bulletin commented, apropos the continuing battles in Bosnia, "On paper, peace. On the ground, war!" The war reports still blamed Muslim forces for provocations and attacks, but without the usual abusive terminology.

Throughout the following days, 3K's bulletins stressed positive international assessments of the Athens summit. When the 'Bosnian Serb Assembly' turned down the Peace Plan on 5 May, 3K bulletins were "obviously trying to shift the responsibility from the Yugoslav and Serbian government to the Bosnian Serb leaders", says Popović. Ćosić's condemnation of the vote was quoted. The Assembly President's appeasing denial that Vance-Owen had been definitely rejected, was not mentioned; so "the condemnation of the Assembly was open and unqualified", says Popović.[97]

Hazards of Reporting the War in Croatia

Among the RTS journalists purged in January 1993 was Vlado Mareš, who had worked extensively from Croatia in 1991. Between April and August, and again between October and December, he reported from Knin, Slavonia, Banija, areas where the Serb rebellion was brewing and which then ignited. He was thus in a good position to assess television's coverage against the reality on the ground.

"The war started for television viewers before it began for people actually on the spot", he says, citing the example of a murder in Zadar in Spring 1991, committed by one man against his business partner. TVB reported this as a sectarian murder, and offered no correction when nationalist motives turned out to have played no part. By such means, Mareš believes, viewers were persuaded that "war had broken out long before serious conflict had really begun". An idiom of war came gradually into use, launched by politicians, not journalists, though very quickly adopted by some of the latter.

Mareš tried to meet Croats who had refused to leave their homes inside rebel-controlled territory in Bratuškovac:

---

[97] Information supplied by E Popović, Oct. 1993.

> A group of Serbian journalists tried to cross into this Croat-held village. The Serbs let us through after failing to dissuade us. The Croats repelled us, stoned us and beat some of us. The police came to our protection, took us away to Šibenik [a large coastal town nearby], questioned us and released us.

He said that Croatian television reporters had similar experiences trying to get into Knin, the Serb stronghold.

According to Mareš, the rebels treated TVB reporters proprietorially. Their tactic from the outset with visiting Serbian journalists was to urge them against trying to cross the line to see both sides and check different versions of the crisis against each other; they risked being killed, and so on. Such warnings fell on open ears: "Belgrade journalists were nervous. There were lots of guns around, and journalists were already being beaten up." As for the occasional Croatian journalists, Mareš said that at that time the rebels tried to scare them away without harming them.

Generally, Mareš did not try to report from Croatian towns for the significant reason that "I knew TVB wouldn't be interested." When he did visit Zagreb as late as July, and "could report freely", TVB "didn't want such material". In the autumn he spent a month around Pakrac, in Serb-controlled Slavonia, investigating Šešelj's *četniks*. "Eventually I got the story. They described their killing methods to me. TVB didn't show it, but because I sent it to Belgrade on the link via Sarajevo, Yutel and HTV picked it up and showed it." Mareš believes that this report was one reason why his career soon ground to a halt: a few months later, his editor-in-chief called him in to tell him he would get no more work.

From August 1991, when the fighting intensified, any remaining trust between the two nationalities in the war areas disintegrated, and journalists' access was ever more tightly controlled by the military. Also, there seems no doubt that journalists were routinely targeted by the Serb-JNA side and sometimes by the Croatian side, both to prevent unpleasant truths emerging and to 'prove' that the conflict really was escalating into a deadly war; no one was safe.

As the war progressed sources from the other side dried up completely, posing difficult ethical questions for journalists wanting to report the truth. The mere possibility of balanced reporting vanished, as Vlado Mareš learned in August 1991 when Gordan Lederer, an HTV cameraman, was fatally wounded by rebels in the Banija region (the JNA refused to evacuate him by helicopter). Mareš went to the village of Ćukur, near Kostajnica, to cover the event for TVB. He interviewed a Serb who had been involved in the shooting, because, he says, there were no other witnesses he could talk to, or who would talk to him. When the report appeared, Mareš was accused in Croatia of giving publicity to a *četnik* murderer. "In that situation," he says, "objectivity is impossible. Journalistic principles go out of the window. I did the only thing I could do."[98]

Coverage of the War in Bosnia

Since the onslaught against Bosnia in March and April 1992, the RTS Channel 1 television evening news has been monitored intermittently in Belgrade by journalists at *Borba* and *Vreme*, by the Centre for Anti-War Action, by a group of researchers at the Agency for Applied Sociological and Political Research, and by two academics (Snježana Milivojević and Jovanka Matić).

RTS has covered the war at great length; even during the six weeks of the 1992 pre-election campaign, the war was the subject of 22 per cent of the evening news, scarcely less than the elections themselves with 25.6 per cent. The two analysts who noted these proportions also observed that only one-sixth of RTS's coverage featured actual footage from the war; the rest of the time, the editor or a reporter was speaking to camera, a map was shown on screen, a 'still' of a scene in Bosnia was shown, or a clip of archive film, often of Sarajevo before the war. Even that sixth part was, say the analysts, "of very bleak semantic value: the mountainous Bosnian setting was more prominent than the people and their actions in that setting. The horrors of the war, which could be seen in the reports on foreign TV stations, were conspicuously absent."[99]

---

[98] V Mareš to author, 7 Oct. 1993. Television coverage of the war in Croatia has not been monitored by any group. ARTICLE 19 tried without success to get access to TVB's news archives.

[99] S Milivojević & J Matić, supra note 62.

Language and Tone

The emphasis in RTS coverage was on the defensive nature of Serb activity; the Serbs were "fighting for freedom", "defending" and "guarding", protecting their "native soil" from "the Muslims", who were waging a religious war, and wanted to force Serbs to belong to an Islamic state, and from "the Croats", who wanted to unite with Croatia, and whose anti-Serb fascism was already known. The RTS journalists' terms for these enemies were manifold; Snježana Milivojević and Jovanka Matić noted "evil-doers", "cut-throats", "*ustaše*", "Islamic *ustaše*", "*mujahedin*", "*jihad* warriors", "commando-terrorist groups" and "Muslim extremists".[100]

Radivoje Gutić, reporting from Hercegovina for RTS, said, "Croatian and Muslim forces want to destroy everything Serbian in these areas. Terror, fanatical hatred, and physical and spiritual genocide against Serbs in Hercegovina are the basis of their political and military effort, and permanent aggression against Serbian territories." Ranko Elez, in a single report from Foča on 17 August 1992, spoke of "Alija's wanton hordes", "*ustaša* chauvinists", "Islamic chauvinists", and "Islamic fundamentalists".[101]

RTS news about Bosnia invariably supported the Bosnian Serb leadership's version of reality, even at moments when that leadership's relations with the Serbian government in Belgrade were strained.[102] Bosnia is always qualified as "former"; the ABH is never named as such, but at best as "Muslim forces", "green berets" or, in the early days, "forces loyal to the Muslim-Croat Presidency" (there were still Serb members of the collective Presidency, but not SDS Serbs, hence not recognized as Serbs by RTS). The President of the Bosnian Presidency was just "the Muslim leader"; Foreign Minister Haris Silajdžić was qualified as "the Muslim". Croatian forces were commonly "extremists", "HOS", "*ustaša* forces", until fighting between them and the ABH got underway in 1993.[103]

---

[100] Id. at 35-36.

[101] 'Otvoreni dnevnik', *Borba*, 19 Aug. 1992.

[102] See section on 'Coverage of the President's Volte-face on the Vance Owen Plan' supra.

[103] The HOS (Hrvatske Oružane Snage, Croatian Defence Forces) is the armed wing of an extreme nationalist party in Croatia, the Hrvatska Stranka Prava.

The Serbian side never attacks; it responds to enemy provocations, assaults, crimes or genocide. At the beginning, Serb forces were often "unarmed defenders of centuries-old hearths"; this was shortened to "defenders" and, often simultaneously, "liberators" of towns and territory. Sarajevo was a site of conflict, but the daily bombardment of the city by Serb forces was not mentioned for two months. The fact of a siege was not denied, it was turned inside out: "The Muslim authorities are holding Sarajevo under siege from within", said reporter Rada Djokić, adding, "The Serbs continue to defend their centuries-old hills around Sarajevo."[104] According to Petar Luković of *Vreme* magazine, it was not until 31 May, four days after the bread-queue massacre in Sarajevo, that Serbian television first revealed that Serb forces were bombarding Sarajevo:

> It was only at 6 p.m. on 31 May, two hours before the beginning of the session of the United Nations Security Council (devoted to the imposition of sanctions against Serbia) that Serbian Television — in a desperate effort to forestall the blockade — broadcast the statement of the Serbian government denouncing the 'bombardment of Sarajevo by the Serbian forces'.[105]

An important point is that, given the structure of the news programmes, RTS depended very heavily on its reporters and editors on screen to present its version of the war. Interviews with Serb soldiers, politicians and civilians slotted into a context created by the editors and reporters, who editorialized continually about the Serbs' "struggles for freedom and self-determination"; affirmed repeatedly that this was "a crucial moment in history" for the entire nation, and "nobody can stop Serbia helping its people in Bosnia"; and denounced the "hysterical", "methodical" campaign by foreign media to "satanize" Serbia and Slobodan Milošević.[106]

---

[104] 'Otvoreni dnevnik', *Borba*, 28 Dec. 1992.

[105] P Luković, "Media and War", in S Biserko (ed.), *Yugoslavia Collapse: War Crimes* (Belgrade: Centre for Anti-War Action, 1993).

[106] Milivojević & Matić, supra note 62 at 37.

How RTS Presented Serb Territorial Conquest in Bosnia

The two major Serb gains in autumn 1992 were the towns of Bosanski Brod in northern Bosnia, captured on 6 October, and Jajce in central Bosnia, taken on 29 October.

On 6 October 1992, TVB reported from Bosanski Brod that, under very heavy shelling from the Croatian Army, Serb forces pushed back the aggressors, who burned houses and a petrol refinery as they retreated. This was followed by a filmed report which claimed to show Serb houses near Zvornik destroyed by a Muslim offensive.[107] Ten minutes into the next night's *Dnevnik 2* news programme, viewers learned from the newscaster that "Serb forces have been in control of Bosanski Brod since last night. Bosanski Brod was the last stronghold of Croat and Muslim forces in northern Bosnia." Then followed a crackly report from TVB's reporter on the spot, Vlado Slijepčević: "... Instead of the *šahovnica* and green flags with half moons, you can see the Serb flag and hear Serb songs ... Croat aggressors [are] fleeing in panic".[108] Slijepčević wound up with "Croat-Muslim forces suffered great losses, although the Serb liberators had enabled them to cross the bridge to Slavonski Brod." He added, "Because Croat forces blew up the bridge, Alija Izetbegović's fighters couldn't cross over to '*lijepa nasa*'." (*Lijepa nasa* are the first words of the Croatian anthem, "Our beautiful homeland".)

These words were spoken over film of Bosanski Brod, showing a dusky townscape devoid of people and traffic. A solitary ambulance moved through the streets. In the distance, a building blazed. No shooting. No casualties. The total effect is to distance the fighting, rendering it unreal, unhuman — like a movie. Slijepčević showed his mettle with that final sarcastic touch, sketching a cartoon of the buffoonish ABH racing absurdly toward the vanished bridge, unaware that their supposed allies had so literally let them down.

Vlado Slijepčević is a Bosnian Serb journalist with experience at Croatian newspapers and in local radio in northern Bosnia. When he began

---

[107] M Pešić & B Mihajlović, *Republika*, 1-15 Dec. 1992.

[108] A standard oxymoron, by TVB's standards; the news on 17 Aug. 1992, for example, carried Vlado Tršić's report from the Majevica front, admitting enemy casualties while insisting the Serb side "didn't do anything". *Borba*'s monitors tartly asked if mass suicides were the explanation (19 Aug. 1992).

to work for TVB in summer 1991 he was a JNA reservist, in uniform (a notable example of TVB's wartime recruiting policy). *Dnevnik 2* on 29 October 1992 carried a piece by Slijepčević, from Jajce, accompanying Serb forces attacking the town. The film showed artillery fire from the Serb side directed towards the town, while Slijepčević mentioned only shells from the Croat and Muslim forces within the town.[109] "Krajina liberators are breaking the strongest *ustaša* and *jihad* fanatics' citadel in occupied Jajce", he confided, and went on to explain contradictorily, "The Muslims and Croats are trying to threaten the positions of the Serb Army. The Serb Army has already reached the outlying houses."[110]

Next day, *Dnevnik 2* began with sundry items of domestic news before a report from Slijepčević, crackling through the static, announced that Serb forces now controlled Jajce. Spliced in at this point was a long item about *mujahedin* aggressors in Bosnia, setting the tone for the remainder of the Jajce report. "As of yesterday evening a Serb flag flies on the castle of Jajce. ... Breaking the last pockets of enemy resistance", Serb soldiers had "liberated Jajce". At the ensuing press conference, Slijepčević explained, an officer declared there was room in Jajce for all honest and well-intentioned citizens, be they Serb, Croat or Muslim. No mention of the huge column of refugees fleeing to Travnik. The film, meanwhile, showed several soldiers advancing untroubled though domestic gardens to the town gates. Then, as at Brod, the camera panned over silent and deserted streets.

How Negative Information was Omitted and Obscured

Some negative and unwanted news was merely omitted by *Dnevnik 2*; there was nothing in mid-August 1992 about the 28,000 Muslims 'ethnically cleansed' from western Bosnia.[111] Other information omitted was: the disclosure by the Special Rapporteur of the UN Commission on Human Rights that a mass grave had been found at Ovčara, near Vukovar (on 22 October 1992); the US Secretary of State's naming of Milošević and other Serbian leaders as candidates for a "second Nuremburg" tribunal (on 16 December); Serb forces blocking a UN relief convoy to Cerska (on

---

[109] 'Otvoreni dnevnik', *Borba*, 31 Oct. - 1 Nov. 1992.

[110] Pešić & Mihajlović, supra note 107.

[111] 'Otvoreni dnevnik', *Borba*, 14 Aug. 1992.

14 January 1993); and, 18 Sarajevans killed while queuing for water (on 16 January). A different kind of negative news was omitted on 8 February 1993: the military call-up of all male Croatian Serbs aged 18 to 65 in Serbia and Montenegro, on pain of forcible conscription, prosecution, and loss of property.[112]

Elementary editing can remove minor irritations. Serbian opposition parties' demand, on 6 November 1992, for radical changes at RTS were omitted from its report of these parties' conditions for participating in elections. Yugoslav President Dobrica Ćosić's disagreements with Milošević likewise vanished on several occasions in sharp contrast to Vojislav Šešelj's attack on Ćosić, quoted at length on 7 January 1993 (and timed to counteract Ćosić's expression of support for the Vance-Owen Plan the previous day). When a BBC radio report about possible US aid to "the Muslims" was used on 2 October 1992, the BBC reporter's conclusion (that the likelihood of a US military commitment in former Yugoslavia was smaller than ever) was omitted.[113] When General Morillon of UNPROFOR visited the Serb-besieged eastern Bosnian town of Srebrenica, in March 1993, an early report that he was being kept against his will by the desperate people was soon corrected by Morillon himself and by the French government. *Dnevnik 2* only ran the first report, not any of the corrections.[114]

When a story cannot be ignored or re-edited, perhaps because foreign coverage has been so vociferous that a response is necessary, RTS has three basic damage limitation tactics used separately or in tandem. A denial can be issued, usually without citing the report in contention, so viewers hear the denial of guilt simultaneously with, or even a fraction before, the accusation. The effect of the story can be pre-empted by careful preparation and presentation. The story can be smothered or spoiled by moving it to the end of the programme or by running a mirror-image story on the same subject.

*   The bread-queue massacre in Sarajevo on 27 May 1992 could not be ignored — it was headline news around the world. According to Branka Mihajlović, RTS delayed showing news footage of the blood-soaked

---

[112] 'Otvoreni dnevnik', *Borba*, 10 Feb. 1993.

[113] 'Otvoreni dnevnik', *Borba*, 5 Oct. 1992.

[114] 'Otvoreni dnevnik', *Borba*, 15 and 17 March 1993.

Sarajevo street until the official line was broadcast: that the Sarajevo government perpetrated the atrocity themselves to win international sympathy and hasten military intervention by the West. (See section on 'The War in Bosnia' above for the Politika press coverage of the massacre.)

* The CSCE suspended Yugoslavia (Serbia and Montenegro) for three months, on 8 July 1992, accusing it of aggression against its neighbours. This was leading news "for the whole world but not for TVB. It was mentioned in the 58th minute, when most people would have turned over to watch the football match on the second channel, thinking the important news was over."[115]

* The shooting by sniper of two orphans on a refugee bus departing Sarajevo on 2 August was not mentioned, until a denial that Serb soldiers were involved was broadcast on the evening of 4 August.[116] When shells exploded in the cemetery during the infants' funeral, TVB news editor Rada Djokić explained why the Muslim side was almost certainly responsible; what was it but "the tested scenario" of perpetrating a crime in order to blame the Serb side?[117] Nor was there mention of the mortar attack on the Hotel Evropa in Sarajevo which killed five refugees; instead, an unintelligible denial by Tanjug was read out.[118]

* On 8 September 1992, the news reported that an explosion had killed four people in Sarajevo. Without any attempt to investigate the story, editor Lidija Duvančić immediately accused "the Muslims" of causing the explosion, "continuing with [their] well-known scenario of satanizing the Bosnian Serbs in order to bring international military intervention."

* An example of parallel reports to detract from the authentic news occurred with Vlado Slijepčević's reports from the camps, or 'centres', in

---

[115] B Mihajlović, in *Druga Srbija* (Belgrade: Plato-Beogradski krug-Borba, 1992).

[116] 'Otvoreni dnevnik', *Borba*, 5 Aug. 1992.

[117] 'Otvoreni dnevnik', *Borba*, 6 Aug. 1992.

[118] 'Otvoreni dnevnik', *Borba*, 20 Aug. 1992.

Bosnian Serb-controlled territory on 8 August 1992. His purpose was to show how exaggerated were the reports of concentration-camps, which had burst upon the world's attention on 5 August with reports by UK Independent Television News (ITN) and other foreign press teams. Slijepčević duly visited Omarska, where he met well-fed prisoners who looked very different from the ones filmed by ITN.[119]

*   On 22 October 1992, 17 Serbian Muslim civilians were abducted by armed, uniformed men on the road between Sjeverin and Priboj, in the Sandžak area, close to the border with Bosnia. TVB first mentioned the matter at the end of the news on 24 October, in the form of a neutral government statement. Reports on 26, 27 and 28 October interviewed only local officials but not witnesses, relatives of the victims, or neighbours.[120] However, *Borba* cited Serbian military sources to report that the 17 Muslims were killed by Serb forces near Višegrad, in Bosnia, on the day of their abduction.[121]

According to the bulletin of the Centre for Anti-War Action, in Belgrade, which draws on witnesses' accounts, the 16 men and one woman were taken directly to Višegrad, in eastern Bosnia, to be exchanged for 28 Serb paramilitaries captured by the ABH. When the ABH refused the exchange, the Muslim hostages were killed.

However, the abductions must also be seen as part of a campaign of terror against Sandžak Muslims, through the autumn and winter of 1992-1993. This campaign, in which RTS collaborated by the ostentatious partiality of its reporting — when it reported at all, has achieved extensive 'ethnic cleansing'. By March 1993, the Muslim population of Sjeverin alone had fallen from 700 households to three.[122]

*   On 12 November 1992, Muslim refugees from Han Pijesak in Serb-controlled Bosnia were interviewed in Belgrade. No one had expelled

---

[119] 'Otvoreni dnevnik', *Borba*, 10 Aug. 1992.

[120] 'Otvoreni dnevnik', *Borba*, 26 Oct. 1992 - 4 Nov. 1993.

[121] Amnesty International, *Amnesty International Report 1993* (London: 1993), 71-72.

[122] 2 *Voice Bulletin*, April 1993, Centre for Anti-War Action, Belgrade. This issue also details other incidents in the campaign against Sandžak Muslims, such as the arson at the village of Kukurovići on 18 February, and the abduction of 19 Muslims from the Belgrade-to-Bar train later the same month.

them, they said; they had left voluntarily. The reporter didn't ask the glaring next question: why, then, did you flee your homes?[123]

* On 8 January 1993 the Deputy-Premier of Bosnia, Hakija Turajlić, was travelling in a French UN armoured personnel carrier from Sarajevo airport to the city centre, when the vehicle was stopped by Serb forces. The French commanding officer parleyed with the Serbs and, contrary to UN regulations, consented to open the door of the carrier, revealing the passenger's identity. One of the Serbs shot Turajlić, who died shortly after.

The same day saw publication of an EC official investigation into rapes in Bosnia, which estimated that 20,000 Muslim women had been raped by Serb soldiers as part of their campaign of terror. RTS news that evening made no mention of either event; however, it did feature an EC official saying that military intervention was now practically out of the question.

The next night on RTS, Turajlić's murder was broached early in a sombre, diplomatic comment by the Danish Foreign Minister (then President of the European Council of Ministers), as he emerged from talks with Milošević who added his own token condemnation "of all hostilities". A detailed report of the murder followed. Turajlić "was killed" near Sarajevo airport, said the newscaster, mispronouncing the Bosnian's name. She then read out a long statement by "the general staff of the Army of the Serb Republic": when the UN convoy was stopped for a "routine control" between the airport and the city centre, Turajlić began to insult "our soldiers", showing "a high degree of hatred". One soldier, distraught because his family had recently been massacred by Muslims, opened fire, wounding Turajlić, who "unfortunately" later died in the care of French doctors.

This version has little in common with the point-blank shooting described by foreign media and the UNPROFOR report. The Serb forces' action was not routine, and Turajlić passed no comment on his captors before they shot him.

The next item that evening took Bosnian Serb rape-victims as its subject. Again, the EC investigation of rapes of Muslim women in Bosnia was not mentioned.

---

[123] Pešić & Mihajlović, supra note 107.

The news on 10 January carried an item seemingly designed to counteract any effect of the Turajlić murder; part of a pre-war interview with President Izetbegović was shown, implying that he was a treacherous fundamentalist.

*   On 14 January 1993, when EC Foreign Ministers told the Bosnian Serbs to accept the Vance-Owen Plan or suffer complete economic and diplomatic isolation, the news began with a Russian delegation visiting Milošević. Viewers learned that "The Russian and Serbian peoples have sincere and warm feelings for each other." Ten minutes later, Radovan Karadžić answered an interviewer's question about "the seven-day ultimatum"; neither explained what it was, whence it came, or its implications.

*   Another example of parallel reports came in February 1993. The expulsion of hundreds of Muslims from the Serb-controlled town of Trebinje was mentioned in the Serbian press on 5 February, but not on RTS news. Instead, it carried a report about Serb refugees from the town of Mostar, controlled by the HVO and ABH. On 10 February, when RTS eventually reported the 4,000 refugees around Trebinje, it interviewed the regional SDS leader, Božidar Vučurević, who duly said that President Izetbegović and his party, the SDA were responsible for the exodus.[124] No refugees were interviewed; nor was there any reference to an EC monitors' report, published on 9 February, holding the Serb authorities responsible for 'ethnic cleansing' which had left only 800 Muslims in Trebinje from a pre-war total of 5,000.[125]

RTS's masterpiece of omission, however, is more than the sum of its parts. It has constructed a version of reality in which Serb forces never attacked Bosnia, never slaughtered scores of thousands of its people and displaced scores of thousands more, never besieged its cities and towns, and never laid waste its villages. "Not once has TVB shown a war map of Bosnia-Hercegovina to show which armies possess what, and what the

---

[124] Stranka Demokratske Akcije (SDA, Party of Democratic Action), the Muslim party in Bosnia.

[125] 'Otvoreni dnevnik', *Borba*, 8 Feb. 1992 and 12 Feb. 1992.

strategic goals are. There has been no word about destruction wrought by Serb forces. Only Serb victims are described or shown."[126]

RTS Coverage of Attacks Against Serbs

On 16 January 1993, the ABH fired shells across the River Drina into Serbia, for the first and only time. The settlements of Bajina Bašta and Skeleni were hit. It was the lead story that evening: "Muslim forces" had attacked "the territory of the Federal Republic of Yugoslavia." Unusually casualties were shown: a dead child and a wounded man. The news editor explained that RTS offered its report of the attack to foreign networks, and "not a single television station in Europe took it. This isn't the first time," she said, "that the world media haven't wanted to hear the other, Serbian side."

Six days later the Croatian Army attacked rebel-held territory in northern Dalmatia, recapturing a few kilometres of ground. It was the first significant Croatian breach of the January 1992 cease-fire. "Croatian armed forces have attacked the territory of the Serbian Krajina Republic" was RTS's mantra, repeated over and again by the studio newscaster and the reporter on the spot. The reporter was more outspoken, however, referring three times to "*ustaša* forces". He interviewed a local commander, "We trusted Vance and Owen," said the furious soldier, "and even if an *ustaša* is dead and buried, don't turn your back because he'll stab you." The report rounded off with the detail that the paramilitary leader Željko Ražnatović, known as Arkan, had appealed for volunteers to go to Krajina's aid. Thus three key axioms were deftly rehearsed: Serbs suffer aggression at home and betrayal abroad; Croats are *ustaše*, with everything that entails; and Serbs must be ever-vigilant, willing to mobilize for self-defence.

Selection of Studio Guests

Programme guests are often presented without explaining who they are and what they represent. On 5 November 1992, a Russian general was given the chance to avow that Russian officers were ready to intervene militarily on the side of their Orthodox brothers; not mentioned was the

---

[126] M Pešić & B Mihajlović, supra note 107.

111

fact that the general was retired and represented only himself. (He featured again the following evening, this time as the guest at a Radical Party public meeting.)

During the first year of war in Bosnia, say Pešić and Mihajlović, TVB had three favourite foreign guests. The first, John Kennedy, an enigmatic character, possibly of Serb extraction, raised by an adoptive family in Britain, had stood (and failed) as a parliamentary candidate for the Conservative Party in the UK. ("British parliamentary candidate" was his billing on TVB.) In 1992 he became an informal spokesman for Radovan Karadžić and the Serb Democratic Party.

However, Kennedy was soon overshadowed in this role by the second of the trio: John Zametica, also from Britain. A researcher who was employed and published by the prestigious International Institute for Strategic Studies and partly-funded by the University of Westminster,[127] Zametica defended the Bosnian Serbs in the British press.[128] Zametica served the Bosnian Serb team as an adviser during the London Conference in August 1992. TVB presented him as an oracle of inside knowledge about Western geopolitics and diplomacy. When he eventually lost his position at the University, Zametica decamped to the 'Serb Republic of Bosnia-Hercegovina' where he currently serves as a senior adviser.

The third favourite foreigner was Eduard Limonov, a Russian literary self-publicist who took up the Bosnian Serb cause, apparently, for its shock-value.

Other Television News

Among the several television channels in Serbia outside direct government control, only NTV Studio B and TV Politika carry news. They broadcast in and around the Belgrade area, reaching an estimated one-third of Serbia's inhabitants.

Studio B (as it is commonly known) was founded as a radio station in 1970 by the newspaper *Borba*, and became an independent company in

---

[127] J Zametica, *The Yugoslav Conflict*, Adelphi Paper no. 270 (London: Brassey's for the IISS, 1992).

[128] For example, *The Guardian*, 11 May 1993.

1972, the first of its kind in Yugoslavia. Staff now own 86 per cent of the station.

After years of planning and setbacks, it finally launched its television channel in March 1990. Its signal was blocked after 70 minutes by the Federal Broadcasting Authority. Milorad Roganović, Studio B's director of programming, believes that the Authority was acting under pressure from the Serbian authorities. After a campaign against the Authority's action, Studio B was granted a 10-year licence in November 1990. The new Serbian Law on Public Information of March 1991 transferred control of frequencies to the Serbian government and the 1991 Serbian Law on Radio-Television, enacted a few months later, required that Studio B's federal licence be approved by the Serbian authorities. Although Studio B has not received this approval, the courts have ruled that the station is entitled to continue to broadcast. Despite this, however, the Serbian authorities claim they can legally revoke the licence at any time.

The station relies on advertising revenue and commercial sponsorship for income. Employing around 180 full-time personnel, the radio and television stations blend news, current affairs and entertainment with talk shows, foreign movies, children's and youth programmes, and documentaries; a daily average of 14 hours' broadcasting.

The station has a policy of training newcomers to television rather than recruiting from other stations. "Nobody here is a professional TV journalist. Everybody does everything", was the youngest recruit's description.[129] The drawback of this policy is a nagging lack of method and clarity. The freshness and enthusiasm, however, are also evident; Studio B is altogether more attractive than the state television news.

In view of its audience and its slender resources, Studio B specializes in Belgrade politics, opposition politics mainly. Its live coverage of the March 1991 anti-Milošević demonstrations exposed the falsehoods and omissions on TVB. A police raid followed and transmission was blocked by order of the Public Prosecutor for 36 hours.

The declared concept of Studio B news is to furnish as much original information as possible, from a range of sources, and without "comment" (referring to the manipulative editorializing which RTS has mastered). "We leave the comments to the viewers", says Roganović. The

---

[129] J Gec to author, 5 Oct. 1993.

news programme has a high reputation in Belgrade. "If you want to know what's happening now, watch Studio B", advised a member of the Centre for Anti-War Action; but he continued, "If you want to know what will happen next in state policy, watch the state TV news." People can do both, for Studio B news ends at 7.30, when the RTS news begins.

Surveys indicate that Studio B's information is trusted by a higher proportion of its audience than that of other stations.[130] Nevertheless, people commonly describe Studio B as a committed opposition channel with special links to the SPO party. However, this judgement was not borne out by a comparative analysis of Serbian television coverage of the 1992 election campaign.[131] Probably it is a perception which reflects, firstly, the fact of the station's outsider status (Milošević and his circle do not accept Studio B's invitations, and it has had difficulty obtaining information about top-level political events, such as visits by foreign envoys to Milošević); and, secondly, the lack of experience of independent broadcasting, even among urban circles which know very well why the government impugns Studio B.

Milorad Roganović explains, "NTV Studio B was never biased in favour of the opposition; it has always been equally critical of the authorities and the opposition, but the side which gives more reasons for criticism has obviously more reasons for dissatisfaction."[132] What people perceive, though, or think they perceive, is a station campaigning for an opposition cause in the sense that RTS campaigns for the government and the ruling party.

On 19 December 1992, two truckloads of equipment destined for Studio B, valued at $236,000 and supplied by the International Media Fund, were stolen soon after crossing the border from Hungary. The authorities deny the equipment ever entered the country, and for that reason have refused to investigate the theft. A month later, in January 1993, three Studio B staff, including its director, were harassed and threatened at the same border point by four armed men, who then set fire to the journalists' truckload of equipment for the station.

Elections were scheduled for 20 December 1992 and the UN Sanctions Committee had responded to pressure from bodies such as the

---

[130] Surveys by the Institute of Social Sciences, supra note 68.

[131] EIM, supra note 42 at 21.

[132] EIM, supra note 42 at 9.

International Media Fund by lifting the embargo on equipment for independent media in Serbia. This move triggered a campaign by RTS to discredit those media.[133]

It was notable that such smears and pressure were repeated during the campaign before the December 1993 elections. The then Serbian Minister of Information, Milivoj Pavlović, chose 13 December 1993 to tell Studio B that its access to three transmitters, granted in 1992, would be cancelled, owing to the station's failure to apply in time for an extension of its licence.[134] Their access was cut off and the station is challenging the Minister's decision in the Supreme Court. Studio B's signal was jammed again in December 1993 to block transmission of footage of an opposition party rally and people queuing for food hand-outs.[135] This pattern of harassment shows that Studio B is obstructed at crucial political moments. At other times, its independence is tolerated.

Studio B's approach to Bosnia has been markedly different from that of government-controlled television. Independent analysts who monitored both stations' news in November and December 1992 found that Studio B's output about Bosnia "was structured around the problem of a solution to the conflict, and especially the possibility of foreign armed intervention". Whereas fully half of RTS news in this period was devoted to the sufferings of the Serbs in Bosnia, Studio B gave little space to this theme. While some reports mentioned the defensive posture of the Serb forces and the offensive aims of the other two sides, others stated that the Serbs were the "most aggressive" side in the war, that Serbs "were carrying on the barbaric practice of ethnic cleansing", and "maltreating women and torturing civilians".

The reports themselves were highly factual but visually poor. Their terminology was relatively objective: "the Serb side", "the Muslim side", "the Serb Republic army", "the Bosnian Army", "the HVO". Overall, the analysts noted 25 'positive' references to Serbs in Bosnia, against 16 'negative'. On RTS during the same period, the ratio was 73:11. Regarding

---

[133] Pešić & Mihajlović, supra note 107.

[134] *Borba*, 14 Dec. 1993.

[135] *The Guardian*, 18 Dec. 1993, and *Radio Free Europe/Radio Liberty Research Report*, 4 Feb. 1994.

Muslim ethnic groups, the neutral and positive references almost equalled negative references on Studio B, while the ratio on RTS was 73:3.[136]

Lack of funds prevents Studio B from sending teams outside Belgrade regularly. A reporter has twice been sent to the Bosnian Serb headquarters at Pale; otherwise Studio B uses Tanjug and Agence France Presse (AFP) wire services, draws on neighbouring republics' radio and television reports (always naming the source), and uses footage from Reuters and World Television News. The station also quotes SRNA but mostly in a sceptical fashion. In addition it shows extracts from other foreign stations' footage in a nightly anthology programme called *Around the World*.

TV Politika began broadcasting on 28 June 1990 in the Belgrade area and includes a general mixture of news, current affairs and entertainment to the greater Belgrade area. It also specializes in covering aspects of Belgrade political and social life which are not shown on RTS. TV Politika also claims that its evening news programme is watched by at least 60 per cent of a potential audience of 3.5 million.[137]

Unlike Studio B, TV Politika's independence is a matter of debate. Along with Radio Politika, the TV station became formally separate within the Politika group in 1993, in preparation for joint-stock conversion.[138] The conversion, however, left control of TV Politika with RTV Politika's board through their own share, plus the 25 per cent of stock sold to government-controlled companies. The managing director of RTV Politika, Dragan Tomić, is also a director of Jugopetrol, the state oil and petrol giant, and is considered a Milošević supporter.

TV Politika's main news runs at 10 p.m. for 12 minutes, followed by *What Others Watch*, a quarter-hour of clips from foreign networks' reports from former Yugoslavia. Newsroom staff claim their station pioneered this kind of anthology format in Serbia, imitated by TVB (*24 Hours in a Day*) and Studio B (*Around the World*).

TV Politika never uses terms such as *četniki*, *ustaše*, bandits, or *mujahedin*. Yet according to newsroom staff there is no house style; the Bosnian Army is called by that name, or "Muslim forces", depending upon which editor is on duty. Tanjug reports are broadcast intact.

---

[136] Milivojević & Matić, supra note 62 at 35-38 and 103.

[137] EIM, supra note 42 at 9.

[138] *Republika*, Sept. 1993.

Like Studio B, TV Politika relayed TV Sarajevo's live coverage of the first days of violence in Sarajevo. The station has no one stationed in Bosnia, and has sent a reporter to Serb-controlled territory on a few occasions. Vesna Popović, a reporter who has cultivated the station's contacts in Bosnia, believes, revealingly, that "good relations" with Bosnian Serb leaders dispenses with the need for reporters on the spot. The example she gave was from 10 October 1993, when a number of Belgian UN troops were beaten by Serb forces in Serb-controlled eastern Croatia. Thanks to these contacts, Popović said, TV Politika broke the story. She talks with UNPROFOR also, by phone, and the newsroom receives Bosnian and Croatian television by satellite.[139]

Radio

Radio Belgrade, along with TVB, was a chief victim of the 1991 Law on Radio-Television. Its management had steered a tactful course some distance from the government media excesses. In the wake of the March 1991 demonstrations, "Radio Belgrade was praised both by the ruling party and the opposition parties represented in the parliament."[140] The managers took a keen interest in the upcoming Law but were not consulted in its drafting. The Secretariat for Public Information ignored their request to participate, as it later ignored written criticisms of the drafts from other professional quarters, including a working group from RTB itself. After the Law's enactment, the radio management was changed and the news service brought into line with the television.[141] Independent-minded current affairs shows have been cancelled or purged, and a large number of radio staff were dismissed in the January 1993 purge of RTS.

The most influential and popular station of Radio Belgrade is Channel 1, which concentrates on news and current affairs. Channel 2 is a popular music station and Channel 3 broadcasts educational and cultural

---

[139] V Popović to author, 13 Oct. 1993.

[140] Plavšić et al, supra note 80 at 22-24.

[141] M Dragičević-Šešic, 'Media War and Hate. The role of media in preparation of conflicts', a conference paper delivered in October 1992 and made available to ARTICLE 19.

programmes. As with television, audience research shows that the credibility of state radio has fallen sharply since 1989.[142] Research in Belgrade in 1991 found that 40 per cent of people over the age of 10 listened to Channel 1 "almost every day".[143]

According to Slobodan Stupar, a Radio Belgrade editor who was dismissed in January 1993:

> Channel 1 and its programmes sailed unharmed through the first major storms of multiparty parliamentarianism in Serbia. While battles were fought for control over television, radio stuck to its professionalism, its reporting unbiased and comprehensive, allowing listeners to reach their own conclusions and form their own opinions. And so until the summer of 1991 ... The new editor-in-chief came from the recently deceased *Komunist* magazine; others followed. It was the beginning of the end.[144]

The largest private radio station in Belgrade is Studio B which broadcasts to about one-third of the country. Like the television station, it is mostly staff-owned and funded by advertising. It carries hourly news bulletins and an hour-long news programme in the evening. Its editorial concept is the same as NTV Studio B.

The Politika group also launched a radio station for the Belgrade area, in 1991. By its own account, Radio Politika carries "no political or current affairs comments, only agency news [mostly from Tanjug] and reports from *Politika* and *Politika ekspres* war correspondents".[145]

The alternative news on the airwaves is Radio B92. Launched in 1989 by the former staff of student radio programmes, it is financed from advertising and donations, including from international media foundations. It started transmitting without a frequency licence, and its applications for

---

[142] Surveys by the Institute of Social Sciences, supra note 68.

[143] EIM, supra note 42 at 7.

[144] *Republika*, Sept. 1993. *Komunist* was the organ of the League of Communists; it had a print run of half a million copies, and was distributed free to League members.

[145] Id.

a licence have repeatedly been refused. The Federal Broadcasting Authority informed B92 in July 1993 that it would be deprived of its frequency.[146] After international protests and a "telephone campaign" directed at the Authority, the threat of closure was withdrawn but it demonstrates how the authorities can use the station's vulnerability as a weapon of intimidation. B92 has been refused permission to use a more powerful transmitter and is limited to a potential audience of about 2 million in the Belgrade area.

Since 1991, B92 has acted as a rallying point for anti-war activity in the capital, co-ordinating with the handful of peace groups around the country, hosting rallies and publishing books. It has encouraged young Serbs to dodge the draft, and has collected food and medicine for Sarajevo. It has seven full-time employees, aged 19-31, and a network of some 80 stringers. The station has received bomb threats, and staff suffer intimidation and worse. Two staff members were beaten by unknown assailants at the station, and one was attacked at his home.[147] Like Studio B, B92's coverage of the March 1991 demonstrations was blocked by the government.

The station aims to allow the broadest spectrum of minority groups to be represented; it "claims to be a voice for all minorities, enabling ethnic minorities, poor people, homosexuals, addicts and even gang leaders to appear. Thus Albanians who would not have an outlet in the official media are regularly able to contribute."[148] "[B92's] interview shows make a feature of phone-in programmes between listeners of opposing views. The announcer's only task is to cut callers off if they get out of control."[149]

In April 1992 the station had a correspondent in Sarajevo and three stringers in other parts of Bosnia (Mostar, Doboj and Banja Luka). The man in Sarajevo was wounded ("we're trying to get him out"), the man in Mostar fell silent in July 1992 ("he may be working for Bosnia-Hercegovina radio-television, we don't know"), and the man in

---

[146] *The Guardian*, 28 July 1993.

[147] *New York Times International*, 28 Aug. 1993.

[148] EIM, supra note 42 at 11.

[149] *The Guardian*, 16 Feb. 1993.

Doboj, in Serb-controlled northern Bosnia, has been mobilized. The stringer in Banja Luka continues to work.[150]

"For [coverage of] the rest we have done what we can", says journalist Aleksandar Vasović. "When a story breaks, if we don't have anyone on the spot we use agencies and international networks: AFP, BBC, Reuters, Sky, AP. We always name our sources, for instance as 'Serb military sources'. We have to use Tanjug, there's no alternative — the sheer volume of bulletins, all in the Serbian language. So we try to extract the bald facts, for instance that there have been 'combat activities' in an area."

The house style for terminology is to use the different sides' names for themselves and their officials, providing these sides have been legitimated by international diplomacy. The 'Serb Krajina Republic' in Croatia remained "so-called" on B92, says Vasović, until its negotiating team was invited to the international peace conference on former Yugoslavia. Likewise with the 'Serb Republic' and the Croat 'Herceg-Bosna' in Bosnia.

Vasović maintains that B92 and *Vreme* are the Serbian news sources most quoted by foreign journalists in Belgrade. The station's international profile may be its best defence against political interference, but without a licence to use its new transmitter, which would cover an 180 kilometre radius, its influence is in any case limited. As things stand, Vasović estimates that "95 per cent of people in inner Serbia haven't heard of us". To counter this virtual blockade on their wider access, B92 has organized a programme exchange network among a small group of local independent radio stations in Serbia. It also exchanges programmes with two independent stations in Bosnia, Radio Zid and Radio 99.

Local Radio

The RTS network includes 32 local stations but the ownership status of many of these is contentious. Many are publicly owned and some are controlled by local municipalities, major enterprises or have an educational or student involvement, and their political affiliation varies

---

[150] A Vasović to author, 8 Oct. 1993.

accordingly.[151] Radio Kragujevac, for instance, appears to act as a clearing-house for statements by the Bosnian Serb leaders, which are then quoted on the RTS evening news. On the other hand, two local radio stations, Radio Pančevo and Radio Smederevo, have become thorns in the flesh of local SPS and SRS party activists.

Radio Pančevo was accused of anti-Serbism and anti-patriotism following its reports of disarray in the JNA during the war in eastern Croatia, and because it persisted in broadcasting Croatian rock music (the only station in the country to do so, except B92).[152] It ran into trouble again for carrying objective reports about the bombardment of Sarajevo.

Radio Pančevo was able to carry this material because reform-minded municipal authorities in Pančevo had allowed the station to begin the process of privatizing itself back in 1989. This process was completed only in 1992, but it put the station beyond reach of the SPS-SRS coalition which won the local elections in 1992. The first decision of the newly-elected municipal assembly, however, "was to wrest control of the founding rights over all local media, giving them unlimited potential to influence editorial policy".[153] In November 1993 the radio staff went on strike to defend their independence and, by March 1994, it had still not been resolved.

The case of Radio Smederevo, down the Danube from Belgrade, is equally revealing. Since the staff succeeded in buying out the station with a controlling share of the capital, there is no straightforward way for the municipal authorities to curb its output. The station has had threats of closure, however, and its personnel have suffered reprisals as a result of some of its broadcasts. According to Svetozar Polić, former editor-in-chief of Radio Smederevo:

> Towards the end of August 1991, some 700 JNA reservists from Smederevo refused to be taken from a still peaceful Bosnia to the war zone in Croatia (the same would happen again in October). The patriotic

---

[151] EIM, supra note 42 at 8.

[152] Anica Nonveiller, music editor at Radio Belgrade, was demoted for playing Croatian rock songs about the war and interpreting them as anti-war. (B Milinković, "The Role of Mass Media in the Serbian-Croatian Conflict", in Malešić, supra note 27.

[153] *Republika*, Sept. 1993.

souls of local bosses were greatly humiliated, and even the reservists explained themselves by appealing to nationalism and patriotism. ... not that they had much choice in the prevalent warmongering atmosphere.

Instead of branding them as traitors, which would have pleased the authorities, Radio Smederevo gave them 90 minutes of prime time. Following this broadcast, the local committee of the SPS issued a statement that 'Radio Smederevo is guilty of incitement to desertion'. ... Constant threats of closure or of personal reprisals against staff became a reality in September. Many journalists and contributors were called up. ... Yet the editorial policy remained unchanged, and so did the station's attitude to war.[154]

News Magazines

At a time of plummeting sales and general crisis, the actual influence of news magazines is probably very slender. The leading examples, *Duga* (owned by the Belgrade publishing conglomerate, BIGZ) the weekly *NIN* (part of the Politika group until it became independent in 1994), and the independent weekly *Vreme*, do have symbolic significance, however, in different ways. The recent career of the first two titles confirms the hegemony of pro-government nationalist publications; the third title confirms the great difficulty of opposing this hegemony.

NIN dates back to 1935; after a respectable career in Tito's era, in the late 1980s it went the way of all Politika publications. Disaffected journalists left in 1988 and 1989, some of whom went on to found the weekly *Vreme*. By 1992, circulation had plunged from 70,000 in 1990 to around 20,000, and the staff tried to buy themselves out of the Politika group. The group could not deny the legality of the staff's balloted decision; but when the staff vetoed the sale of the magazine to the Karić

---

[154] *Republika*, Sept. 1993.

Bank (privately owned, but closely linked with the government), the group evicted *NIN*'s staff from their premises. Their demand for a due portion of investments and properties (even of the property which the magazine originally brought into the Politika group in 1959) was rejected. As from 1 January 1994, *NIN* has been independent, but unprotected by the Politika group against Serbia's economic chaos, the magazine's prospects are not good.

Duga is pitched at a less literate readership. With lots of political gossip, celebrity interviews, colour features, and a lightly-clad model on the cover, *Duga* combines the standard nationalism with neo-fascist and anti-Semitic items, leavened, since 1993, with occasional criticism of the government and the nationalist ethos.

Vreme, modelled on American news weeklies, is the leading news medium in Serbia in terms of wider international reputation. Launched in 1990 by Srdja Popović, a human rights lawyer, and disaffected *NIN* journalists, *Vreme* billed itself as "a magazine without lies, hatred or prejudice". Its start-up capital came from private sources.[155] It sells an average of 25,000 copies, including 5,000 in the USA and Western Europe. To its sympathizers, it is an emblem of non-partisan, liberal Belgrade and of independent journalism. To others, including a majority of the population, it is what the government says it is: a platform for national traitors, subsidized by Serbia's enemies. (*Vreme*, along with *Oslobodjenje* in Sarajevo, is a most favoured recipient of Western donations to ex-Yugoslav media.)

Vreme analyzed lucidly and scathingly the background to the war, such as the JNA's disorientation, the iniquities of the Milošević government, and the pomposity and threatening posture of the Tudjman government. When fighting started, however, *Vreme*'s view of the Croat side hardened, although it never used stereotypical terms which were standard in other media (*ustaša*, secessionists, 'Specials').

The magazine's coverage of the war in Croatia was analyzed by Marjan Malešić of the Defence Research Centre in Slovenia. He found that *Vreme* called a plague on both houses; it "accused leaders on both sides of pushing their peoples into war. When the war did begin to spread, it decided that the war was a civil war, a total, dirty and aggressive war in which hostilities were bound to escalate." It was "much more critical of the

---

[155] *Borba*, 23 Oct. 1990.

Croatian state and the Croat people than its attitude towards the war might suggest".[156]

Vreme published information about the war in Bosnia which no other Serbian news media would touch, and it never chorused the standard anti-Muslim and anti-Bosnian justifications of the war. Its tone when it cited such justifications was roundly sarcastic. However, the sarcasm bespoke a deeper resignation; for *Vreme* gave up the struggle to contest those justifications. Perhaps this reflected a pragmatic decision not to waste energy by vainly defending Bosnian integrity; or it may have reflected political disagreement among the magazine's editors. On 9 March 1992, its cover warned of "Civil war in Bosnia", whereas on 13 April the cover headline was "War against Bosnia". Over the next two years, the magazine often appeared to veer between these different interpretations of the conflict.

Reportage was very difficult to obtain because *Vreme*'s reputation made it dangerously unpopular in Serb-occupied territory. It lost its own Sarajevo correspondents quite early, through the circumstances of war. Nevertheless the magazine's analyses are often more searching and informative than anything else available in Serbia or Croatia. While journalists and others in Sarajevo express regret that *Vreme* (which had a strong following in Bosnia before the war) did not seek more contributions from Bosnian writers, there is no doubt that the magazine was a beacon of independence and sane resistance to the nationalist 'logic' of war.

Conclusions

*   The premise of the government's attitude to the media is that only four of them really matter: Serbian Radio-Television (RTS) and, to a lesser extent, the three daily national newspapers. RTS is government-controlled; so is one of the papers, *Večernje novosti*. The other papers, *Politika* and *Politika ekspres*, are controlled indirectly, via the collaboration of the directorship of the Politika group.

Outside this quartet of giants, the government and the ruling SPS does not systematically suppress critical voices. The regional media are

---

[156] Malesić, supra note 27 at 60 and 62.

liable to all kinds of harassment and obstruction by municipal authorities and branches of the SPS or the SRS, but the independent media in Belgrade are generally able to say what they want — though they may be raided by the police at any moment, or have their licence to broadcast revoked.

As a result, the capital city became the media equivalent of a safari park. International visitors would notice the exotic fauna, often without grasping how marginal they were to the everyday life of the two-thirds of the population outside the invisible fence.[157] In terms of independent media, Belgrade stands to Serbia much as Speakers' Corner in Hyde Park stands to London. Anyone can say whatever they wish, and it makes no difference to anything.[158]

* The "Serbian cultural revolution" of 1986 to 1989 was a mass movement as well as a Communist strategy. Journalists were under political pressure to support the nationalism of the Milošević government; they were also under social pressure to join the patriotic euphoria. Those who resisted were demoted or dismissed .

The political content of their publications could not be changed, however, without changing the ownership structures. Transformation of ownership is legally possible but the government's influence in the economy and the judicial system is so strong that important media companies can easily be prevented from falling into unsuitable hands. War conditions and the international trade embargo have facilitated this method of control. The independence of the Politika group is a fig-leaf. The magazine *NIN* has succeeded in extricating itself from the group, but its solitary prospects are bleak in Serbia's unfree market.

Meanwhile, the government protects RTS's primacy by preventing existing independent radio and television stations from enlarging their audiences, and preventing new rivals from starting up.

* Direct government control operates in partnership with modes of influence and indirect control. The legal system, for example, is

---

[157] According to some estimates, as much as 90 per cent of all newspaper sales are in Belgrade. (P Luković, *Vreme*, 7 Jan. 1993).

[158] The Hyde Park analogy was mentioned by D Puvačić, quoted by D Velikić, *Vreme*, 15 Nov. 1993.

compromised. The judiciary have ignored government violations of legal or constitutional guarantees for the media. The banking system is another area of decisive influence (see the example of the Karić Bank, in section on 'News Magazines' above). These malpractices are the true legacy of the Yugoslav Communist system of self-management socialism, which disguised one-party power by devolving it among a range of apparently independent institutions. In this sense the SPS continues the cynical work of its former self, the League of Communists of Serbia.

However, another part of the background, or rather, another mode of indirect control, is the broad public consensus that 'the national question' was the only all-important issue for Serbs. The media played an essential role in forging this consensus, which in turn was the foundation of the SPS's election successes in 1990, 1992 and 1993.

* As a result of the government's direct and indirect control, journalists in the key media, above all, those in the news departments, had little option but to collaborate or resign. As the experience of Vlado Mareš shows there was no scope for improving the quality of the RTS news from inside; the same was true of the other three 'giants'. Naturally, few opted to resign. An exception who proved the rule was Drago Marić, *Politika*'s correspondent in Mostar (the capital town of Hercegovina). On 31 May 1992, Marić read his letter of resignation on Bosnian radio:

> Aghast at the [Serb] crimes in Sarajevo and embittered by the pitiless destruction of Mostar and the bloody aggression against Bosnia [by Serb forces], I hereby submit my resignation as *Politika*'s correspondent and *Politika*'s collaborator in treachery against Hercegovina. This is my moral duty as a citizen of Bosnia-Hercegovina to all the innocent victims, to the shattered history of Mostar, Sarajevo and many other towns in the independent state of Bosnia-Hercegovina.[159]

Marić's moral stand did not alter *Politika*'s coverage from Bosnia.

---

[159] Printed in *Vreme*, 8 June 1992.

*   Opinion poll surveys can be cited to support claims that Serbia's mass media exert an extraordinary hold on public opinion and knowledge. A pair of poll results in April 1993, by the MEDIUM agency in Belgrade, were widely quoted in this regard. The first poll, on 9 April 1993, showed that 70 per cent of Serbs in Serbia opposed the Vance-Owen Plan for Bosnia. The second, identical poll on 27 April (after the government's about-turn on the issue, faithfully reflected in the controlled media) showed only 20 per cent against the Plan and 39 per cent in favour.[160]

As for knowledge: a July 1992 survey by the Institute for Political Studies (IPS) in Belgrade asked 1,380 respondents who had bombarded Sarajevo from the surrounding hills during May and June. No fewer than 38.4 per cent answered "Muslim-Croat forces", nearly twice as many as those who admitted they didn't know (22.5 per cent) or who thought Serb forces were responsible (20.5 per cent).

However, a more thorough set of surveys than those by the MEDIUM agency cited above, found that basic views of the rights and wrongs of war in Bosnia did not shift significantly through the crucial weeks of April and May 1993, despite the government's about-turn. The "don't knows" increased, while the number fell of those who believed the Serb forces should keep everything they controlled. But the number who thought the Serbs should not give up all the land demanded under the Vance-Owen plan, barely wavered. Another question asked respondents what they would think if a relative had to go and fight in Bosnia or Croatia; the number of respondents who would oppose the move slightly decreased during these weeks, while those who would accept it as a "patriotic duty" increased.[161]

The July 1992 survey by the IPS also asked respondents what they thought of RTS as a medium of information, compared with (unspecified) "independent media". Only 8.4 per cent replied that RTS kept them "well" informed, against 43.5 per cent who replied "badly". The figures for independent media were 42.9 and 12.9 per cent, respectively.

These results spur several reflections. Firstly, people's bedrock attitudes toward the wars in Croatia and Bosnia are not created by the state

---

[160] *The Economist*, 15 May 1993, 53. See also section on 'Coverage of the President's Volte-face on the Vance-Owen Plan, *supra*, for discussion of the turnaround regarding the Plan.

[161] Surveys conducted in April and May 1993 by the Institute of Social Sciences, University of Belgrade.

media; rather, the media play variations upon those attitudes, which derive from other sources (national history, family background, education, oral culture). Media did not inject their audiences with anti-Muslim prejudice or exploitable fear of Croatian nationalism. The prejudice and fear were widespread, latently at least; there was a predisposition to believe 'news' which elicited and exploited the prejudice. Media could not produce a nationalist society; without the media, however, Serbia's leaders could not have obtained public consent and approval of its extreme nationalist politics.

Secondly, having used the media to obtain public approval of extreme nationalist politics, Serbia's leaders found in April 1992 that they could not use the same media to switch people's opinions within a few weeks. The government was apparently, for this brief period, a prisoner of the prejudices which it had worked so hard to inflame.

Thirdly, if a large number of Serbia's citizens watch and listen to RTS news broadcasts, and are strongly influenced without being deceived about the quality of information which is influencing them, the reason may be precisely that RTS is the voice of political power.[162] In a society unaccustomed to any independence in the media, many people may not *want* independent information (especially given that independence in this context is associated so strongly with 'treachery').

* If this is so, the independent media are doubly victims of the situation they oppose. RTS news not only enjoys every practical advantage: it is 'sexier' than its rivals because it matters so much more than they do. The rivals, standing outside 'the Bastille', offer conjectural weather reports about the storm of Serbian politics; RTS sits in the citadel beside the divinities who shape the weather. The point is that RTS reflects the reality of power. The political narratives which are related to the nation by means of this mirror have immeasurably helped to create a total context, affecting all public information in Serbia, that neutralizes countervailing messages *a priori*.

---

[162] Vuk Drašković, leader of the opposition SPO party, tells a story from the election trail in rural Serbia. He was explaining to a peasant farmer why Milošević and the SPS were disastrous for Serbia. The farmer nodded. "So, can I count on your vote?" asked Drašković. "No." "But you agree with all my arguments?" "I do," said the farmer, "and I'll vote for you too, when you're in power." (With thanks to Dessa Trevisan, Balkan correspondent of *The Times*.)

Back in May 1992, Stojan Cerovic of *Vreme* wrote that the director-general of Serbian Radio-Television (RTS), Milorad Vučelić,

> can now calmly invite the opposition to say whatever it wants on television, because he knows that ... anybody who explains the truth can do so only at his own cost. Reality sounds like the blackest anti-Serbian propaganda, and anyone who describes it will frighten people and turn them against him.[163]

During the two year since this was written, the situation appears to have deteriorated even further.

---

[163] *Vreme,* 11 May 1992.

Chapter 4

CROATIA CATCHES UP

Background

April and May 1990 witnessed epoch-making events in Croatia: the first multiparty elections went off smoothly and the Communists lost, departing without resistance.

The victorious party was the Hrvatska Demokratska Zajednica (HDZ, Croatian Democratic Community) led by Franjo Tudjman. Croatia's electoral system meant that, with 42 per cent of the vote, Tudjman's party gained an absolute majority in the parliament, which subsequently elected him as President of the Presidency.[1] The new Constitution, promulgated in December 1990, was of the 'Gaullist' kind, concentrating vast power in the President's hands.[2]

In their ambitions for Croatia and their intentions toward Yugoslavia, Tudjman and the HDZ were radical, even revolutionary. Their rhetoric and programme were anti-Communist, while their conception and practice of power were modelled upon the former Communist system, in which Tudjman himself had served as a general in the Jugoslovenska Narodna Armija (JNA, Yugoslav People's Army). Following the HDZ's triumph, the ruling ideology changed name. Now it was nationalism, of the toxic 'born again' variety, and the party set out to replace the closed system of socialism with a closed system of nationalism.[3]

---

[1] In 1990, the parliament had three chambers, according to the Yugoslav Communist system, with a total of 356 seats. The HDZ won 205 of these; the leading opposition party was the Party of Democratic Change (formerly the League of Communists of Croatia) with 73 seats. The parliament has since been reorganized into two chambers, the Chamber of Representatives and the Chamber of Municipalities. The President of the Republic is now directly elected as Head of State.

[2] *East European Constitutional Review* (Chicago: Fall 1993/Winter 1994), 79-80.

[3] According to the 1991 census figures, the population of Croatia was 4.76 million. Croats were 77.9 per cent of the population; Serbs were 12.2 per cent; Yugoslavs were 2.2 per cent; and Muslims were 1 per cent.

The HDZ was as determined to control the media as its predecessors: unlike those predecessors, who had a functioning state, the HDZ took office when post-Communist disorder was magnified by the Yugoslav context of imploding federalism and the threat to Croatia posed very plainly by Serbia and, imminently, by the JNA. For Serbia was gripped by nationalist frenzy and led by Slobodan Milošević, a man whose non-negotiable position was known: either Serbia would dominate Yugoslavia, or Greater Serbia would be ripped from the territory of Croatia and Bosnia.

Before the 1990 elections, the most important episode in post-1945 Croatia (and the biggest internal challenge to Tito's Yugoslavia since the break with Stalin in 1948) was the 'Croatian Spring'. Beginning in 1967, and gathering pace until it was crushed at the end of 1971, this was a reform movement that was partly cultural in inspiration, and partly driven by impatience for economic reform. It was both right-wing revanchist and left-reformist, both nationalist and democratic, sometimes led by the Croatian Communists and sometimes driving them on. Tito seemed to approve the movement until the JNA and the party old guard persuaded him that Yugoslavia's integrity and one-party rule were threatened. The ensuing 'normalization' of Croatia, including the persecution of the real or alleged supporters of the 'Spring' and its reforms, affected tens of thousands of people in all walks of educated life. This process has been likened to Czechoslovakia's fate after Soviet intervention in 1968.

It has been said that during the Croatian Spring, "the intensity of debate and freedom of expression in the press was unprecedented in postwar Yugoslavia".[4] Reversing this liberalization meant returning to dogmatic definitions of media responsibility and political engagement. In the 1980s, however, the buried seeds began to sprout again, through the generation that was breaking taboos at student radio stations and youth magazines throughout Yugoslavia. The Croatian Communists' sheer lack of popular legitimacy since 1971 meant that, when the political system disintegrated at the end of the Eighties, media organizations had more opportunity to reform themselves along professional lines. TV Zagreb, to take the prime example, covered the 1990 elections impartially.

---

[4] P Ramet, "The Yugoslav Press in Flux", in P Ramet (ed.), *Yugoslavia in the 1980s* (Boulder, Colorado: Westview Press, 1985), 113.

Regionalism is a special factor in Croatian politics. History and geography have made Croatia an aggregate of regions with highly developed identities and relatively weak bonds to the capital. Yugoslavia's devolved version of Communism built on this legacy which has always irked Croatian nationalists, who, like nationalists everywhere, are centralizers. Regional media were prolific in Croatia and, by 1990, sometimes of high professional standards. They stood right in the path of the party's centralizing drive and, consequently, were a prime target for the government's repressive tactics.

Media and Government Control

The situation of the media in spring 1990 was promising. Taboos had shattered; censorship laws lay idle on the statute books. A federal law on privatization was in place thanks to the Federal Premier Ante Marković, whose success in stabilizing the Yugoslav currency had stimulated investment. Croatian television coverage of the election campaign was widely assessed as a model of its kind. There was a lively second television station in Zagreb and private stations were under way in Rijeka and Split. The news magazine *Danas* was noted as the most independent in the country, and regional press and radio had grown bolder. A culture of independent-minded journalism seemed to be taking root in Zagreb.

Like other parties before the election, the HDZ had promised complete freedom of speech and a free press in democratic Croatia.[5] Once in power, with a secure majority, the party showed no inclination to honour its promise. There was increasing evidence that the government wanted to run Croatia as its Communist predecessors had done: as a party-state, but with the difference that policy was now directed by the President. Means of controlling and disciplining the media have included:

---

[5] Civic Initiative for Freedom of Expression (CIFE), *Information on Media Situation in Republic of Croatia and its Social and Political Context* (Zagreb: October 1992). The CIFE was formed in March 1992 by a group of journalists, writers, lawyers, university teachers and others concerned at the deterioration in Croatian media. ARTICLE 19 is much indebted to their fine work.

* Replacing media personnel by HDZ faithful, including those in charge of television, radio, HINA (the new state news agency)[6], and *Vjesnik*, the main national daily newspaper.[7]

* Establishing a framework to define ownership and oversee privatization which allows the government to steer publicly-owned companies (including media companies) either into state ownership ('nationalization') or into the hands of chosen entrepreneurs. The *de facto* result is media ownership by the state or HDZ party officials.

* Reversing privatization achieved under federal law, when its results were unacceptable to the authorities, and repeating the privatization process under the government-controlled framework.

* Preserving a virtual monopoly of the airwaves by withholding long-promised legislation to allow private electronic media.

* Selectively suppressing existing private electronic media, depending on their political profile.

* Exploiting catch-all clauses in laws affecting the media, in order to restrict free speech and intimidate the media.

* Issuing presidential decrees to limit media freedom under conditions of emergency which the President defines at his discretion.

* Using government-controlled media to attack, slander and demoralize journalists and media outside government control.

* Instigating or tolerating paramilitary means to intimidate journalists and gain control of the media.

---

[6] Hrvatska Izvještajna Novinska Agencija (HINA, the Croatian News Reporting Agency).

[7] J Kuzmanović, "The Inevitable First Victim", *East European Reporter*, (July-Aug. 1992).

Media, War and the Political Leaders

The government wanted its version of the war's origins, course, and purpose to be uncontested; it was impatient with agnostics and critics who, in turn, were pressurized more acutely to back the authorities for the sake of the people and the country.

Like most governments in wartime, President Tudjman and his party seized the chance offered by the aggression to discredit their critics as unpatriotic and self-serving. By assuming a monopoly of the Croatian national interest, the HDZ cynically used the war as the ultimate pretext to bridle independent media.

By the time Serbia and its proxies launched war in Bosnia in April 1992, the major Croatian media were tightly controlled: 'unreliable' journalists and editors had been removed. When Croatian forces began their undisguised land-grab in Hercegovina and central Bosnia, and the 'ethnic cleansing' of Muslim areas, in January 1993, the only truly independent medium with a nationwide audience was *Slobodna Dalmacija* newspaper, which was seized by the government a few weeks later.

It is worth noting that Viktor Ivančić, whose views command wide respect among Croatian journalists, believes that open war propaganda in Croatia began in summer 1991 with an action by army commander Branimir Glavaš to "destroy Serb terrorists" in a suburb of Osijek. Glavaš called some 20 domestic and foreign journalists to observe the action. His forces blasted a house with heavy and light weapons; they killed an old man and wounded his wife who was hiding in the cellar. Foreign journalists were appalled by the action, says Ivančić. Domestic journalists, however, filed respectful reports, with the sole exception of a cynical report in *Slobodna Dalmacija* ten days later.[8]

The tone of news information from Bosnia has been extremist, and has been set by the governing élite. For example, media often used the very loaded term '*mujahedin*' for the Armija Bosne i Hercegovine (ABH, Army of Bosnia-Hercegovina) (regardless of whether actual *mujahedin*, several hundred of whom have been active in Bosnia, were involved in the particular action). President Tudjman himself has not scrupled to call Alija Izetbegović, President of Bosnia (a state officially recognized by Croatia)

---

[8] The wounded wife fled to Belgrade, where TVB recorded her plight in a harrowing interview. (V Ivančić, *1 Erasmus* [Zagreb: 1993]).

"the *mujahedin* Alija". When the President used the phrase during a demagogic speech on 15 August 1993, Hrvatska Televizija (HTV, Croatian Television) news included it, and so did the top-selling, government-controlled paper *Večernji list* the following day.[9] Media were merely exploiting the President's own lexicon of racist slang.

At the same time, politicians reiterated the essential message that Croats in Bosnia were only defending themselves; they were victims, pursuing the only course consistent with Croat national interest. Indeed, until mid-1993, when Croatia's Roman Catholic Primate, Cardinal Kuharić, made public his reservations about Croatian policy in Bosnia, no contrary messages were disseminated by voices of political or cultural authority.

Even when news began to pour out of central Bosnia that Croat forces were on the offensive, HDZ politicians denied it axiomatically: Dalibor Brozović, an HDZ member of parliament (MP) and the director of the prestigious Lexicographical Institute, insisted that "the conflict has been staged and somebody was responsible. Certainly not Croats or Croatia. Perhaps the 'omnipotent' Yugoslav security services did it", he added.[10]

Šime Djodan, another senior HDZ member of parliament, a hero of the Croatian Spring and former Minister of Defence, speaking about the village of Ahmići (where at least 89 Muslims civilians were massacred on 16 April 1993 by Hrvatsko Vijeće Obrane [HVO, the Croat Defence Council] according to the Special Rapporteur of the United Nations Commission on Human Rights) said that "an English officer, a provocateur and spy" had led the attack, and the results were filmed by "other British officers in order to show the whole world".[11]

Josip Manolić, President of the upper chamber of parliament, was asked in September 1993 about the recently-opened prison camps for Muslims in Croat-controlled Hercegovina. Unlike Djodan, Manolić is not a radical nationalist, but he had to exonerate the HVO. After commenting, perhaps uniquely for an HDZ luminary, that the camps were "catastrophic

---

[9] The dailies *Vjesnik* and *Slobodna Dalmacija* did not, however, though they are also government-controlled, directly in the former's case and indirectly in the latter's. Presumably the discreet cut reflected these papers' editorial judgement that their readers (typically better educated than *Večernji list*'s) were more likely to be offended by Tudjman's epithet than stirred or amused by it.

[10] D Brozović interviewed in *Globus*, 5 March 1993.

[11] Š Djodan interviewed in *Slobodna Dalmacija*, 4 Sept. 1993.

for Croatia, for the entire Croatian national interest", he added "[y]et the West is losing sight of the evolution of the war in Bosnia, losing sight of the obvious fact that only the Serbs are aggressors in Bosnia".[12]

Journalists and War

Journalists in Croatia enjoyed an interregnum of liberalization between the end of strong Communism and the triumph of strong nationalism. After the 1990 elections, they faced a dilemma. Danko Plevnik, a respected figure in Croatian journalism, proposes an initial classification: "Journalists divided into journalist-dissidents, to whom democracy was more important than the Croatian state, and journalist-converts to whom a state, this time Croatian, was ultimately once again more important than democracy."[13]

The choice was not only a personal matter or a question of convictions. Given the ownership structure of the media, it became an urgent matter of career and even of survival: how to be a 'journalist-dissident', who puts professionalism first, if employers want 'journalist-converts'? The most ardent 'converts' to Croatian nationalism were among the most dogmatic supporters of Yugoslav communism, which was anti-nationalist. Notable cases are Milan Puljiz of Hrvatski Radio (HR, Croatian Radio) and Josip Jović of *Slobodna Dalmacija*, who fiercely defend the HDZ government against its critics.

Through 1990 and 1991, journalists came under intense pressure not to criticize or even question the government. This pressure came from the ruling party, both openly and behind the scenes, and also from other journalists. Venomous attacks on "disoriented", "unpatriotic", "Yugo-nostalgic" journalists became standard in the government-controlled media.

War intensified the career risks and rewards of journalists most acutely in television, the most influential medium. As in Serbia, young reporters were swiftly promoted; by the end of 1991, several had become household names as the exclusive 'live' arbiters of the conflict for most of the population. One HTV source in the newsroom says that most news

---

[12] J Manolić interviewed in *Globus*, 10 Sept. 1993.

[13] D Plevnik, *Hrvatski obrat* (Zagreb: Durieux, 1993), 16.

journalists wanted to work at the front, but many were not allowed to go "because we use our heads. Instead they sent people with a year or two's experience in TV, or none at all." Another journalist, formerly in the newsroom, concurs: "The new young intake were stringers before the war. Their first real TV work has been two years of crammed, extreme experience."

These reporters don't try to verify allegations or to report the other side's view. Their output suggests that they cannot distinguish a news story from a jumble of hearsay narrated excitedly over a string of almost random images of artillery firing, rubble smouldering, refugees weeping, and soldiers taking aim through a smashed window-frame or dashing through the undergrowth. Their disinformation is the more effective for being apparently fresh-faced and ingenuous. The war in Bosnia brought more of the same onto the screen and the radio airwaves, especially after the fighting between the HVO and the ABH got under way in 1993. Since other televised accounts of the war were not available, HTV's violation of its public service obligation to provide accurate and impartial information is all the more serious.

HTV's star war reporter is Silvana Menduší. Menduší came of age in the post-Communist crisis and exploited its career potential. She has said that she fights for Croatia with microphone in hand. Viktor Ivančić, editor-in-chief of the independent weekly *Feral Tribune*, has described Menduší's report from the Zadar hinterland, in January 1993, with a dead Serb soldier behind her, lying in a pool of blood. She said nothing about the corpse: it was decor; or "a message", as Ivančić commented, signifying a war trophy. Ivančić also mentions a print journalist, Dunja Ujević of *Večernji list*, a hard-line nationalist who declared in her column that she would lie for the sake of the homeland. That is her personal choice, Ivančić adds; the problem in Croatia now is that anyone "who doesn't want to lie for the homeland is a traitor and an enemy!"[14]

---

[14] Ivančić, supra note 8.

Media and Law

> The problem is that foreigners read Croatia's media
> legislation, and when you read it, it is fine, even
> idyllic. By law, we do have freedom of the press and
> of expression. In practice, we don't.

Tomislav Jakić's dry remark holds for the Constitution as well as the laws.[15] Promulgated at the end of 1990, eight months after the election, the Croatian Constitution prohibits censorship and enshrines the right to freedom of expression, freedom of "the press and other media", and the right of access to information for journalists. Article 16 states that the rights and freedoms guaranteed in the Constitution may only be restricted by law to protect the rights and freedoms of others, public order, morality and health.

Article 49 of the Constitution prohibits monopolies. On the basis of this article, the Civic Initiative for Freedom of Expression (CIFE) challenged the televisual monopoly of the state-controlled HRT, which possesses all three existing television frequencies in Croatia (while only using two).[16] The Constitutional Court has yet to respond.

Among the sweeping Presidential prerogatives granted by the Constitution are two with ominous relevance to media freedom. Article 17 allows the President to restrict constitutional rights and guarantees "during a state of war or an immediate danger to the independence and unity of the republic". Article 101 authorizes the President "to pass decrees with the force of law ... in the event of a state of war". The latter article was used in 1991 to enact decrees granting powers to restrict the media. The decrees contained provisions allowing for the replacement of media editors and managers in wartime and for the punishment of journalists and the banning of media (without right of appeal) for violating very strict conditions on reporting of military affairs or from war areas. Although they were

---

[15] Tomislav Jakić, formerly the editor-in-chief of news programmes at HTV, speaking at a conference on developing a legal framework for a free press, held in Zagreb on 25-26 Nov. 1993. It was organized by the Croatian Journalists' Association, the Croatian Helsinki Committee for Human Rights, the Fédération Internationale des Editeurs de Journaux, and the International Federation of Journalists, and sponsored by the Council of Europe.

[16] Hrvatska Radio-Televizija (HRT, Croatian Radio-Television).

invoked only once before their repeal (to prevent a right of appeal against the banning of an issue of the weekly *Slobodi tijednik* newspaper), CIFE noted that they had a chilling effect on editors and directors who feared that they might be dismissed for offending the government.[17]

The decrees were repealed in 1992 for a number of reasons. The war was at a virtual halt and control of the media had been successfully accomplished by other means, namely the state-controlled mechanism to reallocate ownership of media. In addition, the decrees were criticized by local and international groups, not least because of their potential conflict with the Constitution, since a state of war or emergency had not formally been declared in Croatia.

Prior to the promulgation of the Constitution, the parliament had adopted four documents of the Council of Europe, obliging all future legislation to respect certain criteria of media freedom.[18] This was the background to the Law on Public Information, enacted in April 1992, which affirms that "every individual or corporate body shall be free to publish printed matter, broadcast radio and television programmes, and produce other mass media in accordance with the law".

The government presented this law as being intended to ensure "a free and editorially independent press in the public and private sectors and to guarantee freedom of information for the people".[19] However, although the Law contains some positive provisions, in practice it has been used to limit media freedom. The Law covers broadcasting but stopped short of legislating for private broadcasters to acquire frequencies, allowing HRT to retain its monopoly.[20] Article 8 requires the state to support, including

---

[17] For more on this case, see section on 'The Weekly Press' infra.

[18] The documents are Resolution 428 (1970), which emphasizes the independence of the media from political control, along with the Declaration on the means of public communication and human rights; Recommendation 834 of the parliamentary assembly (1978), which emphasizes the danger which press concentrations pose for media diversity and pluralism; and the Declaration on the freedom of expression and information (1982), proclaiming the duty of all states to guard against infringements of this freedom. Croatia is also bound by the International Covenant on Civil and Political Rights, Article 19 of which guarantees the right to freedom of expression.

[19] Information Department of the Ministry of Foreign Affairs, *Facts about the Media in Croatia* (Zagreb: 1993).

[20] Draft legislation on the allocation of frequencies was finally presented to parliament in Nov. 1993, after months of delay. See section on 'Croatian Radio-

financially, a diversity of media and opinion. Despite this provision, the government has not reversed its policy of supporting state control in the media. Six months after the Law's enactment, for example, the government-controlled privatization agency moved against one of the few remaining independent publications in Croatia, *Slobodna Dalmacija*, giving majority share-holding first to state-controlled institutions and later selling it to an HDZ member.[21]

The Law specifies in Article 16 that editors-in-chief must be Croatian citizens and must not have immunity from prosecution. Article 7 states that "media must respect the privacy, dignity, reputation and honour of citizens" although Article 6 recognizes that public figures cannot invoke their right to privacy concerning "their public activity". Extensive sections of the Law define the mechanisms for the right of correction for "public and officials whose dignity, honour, rights or interests have been violated by inaccurate, incomplete or defamatory information".

In continuity with former Communist legislation, the Law sets out a framework to establish rules and responsibilities of journalists which potentially restrict their right to freedom of expression. A Council of Europe mission team which investigated media law in Croatia in 1993 noted in their report that

> [T]he ... Law contains an extensive list of 'do's and don'ts', the precise legal ramifications of which are not always clear. [The team] also notes that the scope of potential restrictions on media freedoms, arising from the wide-sweeping formulation of several provisions, would appear to be broad. It feels that some of the provisions of the Law would sit more comfortably in the framework of professional codes of conduct rather than being inscribed in legislation.[22]

Television Law' infra.

[21] See section on '*Slobodna Dalmacija*' infra.

[22] Council of Europe, *Report of the mission of the Council of Europe team of experts to consider the legislative, regulatory and administrative framework for the media in Croatia, 9-12 May 1993* (Strasbourg: June 1993), 8.

Similarly, the Law provides for the establishment of a statutory body to regulate the media, a role which, because of its potential to limit media freedom, is best left to the media profession itself. The Council for the Protection of Public Information is mandated to consider complaints and act as a mediator between a number of interest groups: journalists, editors, journalist associations, media proprietors, public authorities and the government. It has a potentially conflicting role: to "protect freedom of information ... especially the rights of citizens to receive accurate and complete information ... [and] to create conditions for responsible behaviour in the public information sphere". This seven-member body, which was not constituted until December 1993, would be nominated by journalists' unions, literary and legal associations, and the Chamber of the Economy, with a chairperson appointed by the parliament.

Positive provisions include the right of journalists to information, including about the legislature, judiciary, police and other public bodies, and a firm recognition of the right of journalists to protect their sources. Article 11 states that journalists cannot be dismissed for the expression of their opinions and Article 7 provides that public figures cannot invoke their right to privacy concerning "their public activity".

Provisions of the Law which would have restricted government control of the media have in practice been ignored. The stipulation that editors-in-chief cannot be "any person with immunity from prosecution" did not prevent Božidar Petrač becoming editor-in-chief of *Vjesnik* in 1992-1993 while enjoying parliamentary immunity as a member of parliament for the HDZ. HRT's director-general, Antun Vrdoljak, has used his parliamentary immunity to escape prosecution for slandering a journalist whom he then prosecuted for slander. The court ruled against Vrdoljak.

Those who have tried to enforce their constitutional right of correction to inaccurate or defamatory statements in the state-run media have met with little success. Željko Žutelija, a columnist with the then-independent Split daily *Slobodna Dalmacija*, cited Article 39 in vain, after HTV news attacked him on 9 March 1993. Slobodan P Novak, president of Croatian PEN, followed suit when he had a similar experience on 6 October 1993. Again to no avail. The Croatian branch of the Stranka Demokratske Akcije (SDA, Party of Democratic Action), the main Bosnian Muslim party, protested when, on 17 August 1993, HTV news showed one of its party leaders during a report alleging that Islamic humanitarian organizations in Croatia were involved with terrorism. The SDA's correction was read out on HTV but without a key sentence, so changing the tone completely.[23]

The Law on Public Information contains broad defamation provisions. Article 30 states that the publisher of a medium is responsible for content which harms a person's honour, dignity and reputation. The Council of Europe mission team noted that provisions giving defences against defamation actions are ambiguous and expressed concern that they may not adequately protect press freedom. The ambiguities in the Law have produced a flurry of defamation prosecutions against the media. Zvonimir Hodak, a Zagreb lawyer well known for his work in defending freedom of expression, told ARTICLE 19 that Article 30 of the Media Law is now the most dangerous piece of legislation for the media in Croatia. One notable defamation case concerns the publication of a leaked Ministry of the Interior document alleging criminal activity in 1991 on the part of forces led by Tomislav Merčep, now an advisor to the Ministry. The document was published in *Globus* newspaper, which is now being sued by Merčep for damages of 800,000 Deutschmarks.

During 1993, the State Prosecutor and the Ministry of Culture prepared an amendment to Article 30 of the Media Law, extending the definition of harm, for which publishers would be liable, to cover the "dignity and respect or any other right of the Republic of Croatia, bodies of state authorities or other legal entities". This would have amounted to a new catch-all offence for any criticism of the government and the President, regardless of its veracity. Following protests, Vladimir Šeks, the Deputy Premier and former State Prosecutor, abandoned the amendment and promised, instead, to bring an entirely new media law before parliament in the spring of 1994. Among his reasons for replacing the existing Law, Šeks cites its lack of a national security clause. Journalists are concerned that the government's intention in bringing in a new law may be to further limit the media rather than to address the many restrictions in the current Law.

In the field of general legislation affecting the media, while the situation is better than under Communism, some of the catch-all clauses inherited from the Yugoslav Federal Criminal Code, by which the authorities can punish critical comment, both spoken and written, remain

---

[23] Š Tanković, president of the SDA in Croatia, interviewed in *Ljiljan*, 25 Aug. 1993.

in force.[24] While Article 133 of the Criminal Code (which protected Yugoslavia's socialist system from criticism), was removed in February 1991, the retention of provisions such as Article 16 of the Law on Petty Offences Against Public Law and Order, means the government can still protect itself from criticism.

Article 16 prohibits "spreading false information" with intent to disturb the public. It was used in June 1993 to sentence the Croatian Serb politician Milovan Škorić to 60 days' imprisonment for alleging that detention camps for Serbs existed in Croatia. Škorić claimed his remarks were made at a private gathering, where a reporter secretly taped them for publication. Article 16 was again used in September 1993 to sentence Stjepan Kralj, a former security agent, to 15 days' imprisonment, for allegations of corruption against Deputy Premier Šeks. Amnesty International believes that the real reason for his prosecution may have been other allegations he had made, including that the Deputy Premier had protected the killers of a trade union leader.[25] Kralj likewise maintained that his comments were made privately; once charged, he went public by repeating his allegations in letters to the press.

Article 197 of the Croatian Criminal Code formerly carried a sentence of up to three years and, in exceptional circumstances, ten years, for persons found guilty of "spreading false information" with the intention of disturbing a large number of citizens or of obstructing the implementation of decisions or measures of the public authorities. In 1992 the article was first tightened and then, in response to public criticism, mitigated; it now carries a sentence of a fine, or up to six months' imprisonment. In 1993, the article was renumbered as 191.

Article 197 was invoked by the State Prosecutor several times in 1992, along with Article 75, covering slander of state officials. Three satirists from *Slobodna Dalmacija* were charged under these provisions, as were the editor-in-chief of the weekly political tabloid *Globus* and its best-known columnist, Tanja Torbarina. These cases never came to court. Journalist Jelena Lovrić was charged, under Article 75, with slandering Zdravko Mršić in his capacity as director of the government-run Agency for Restructuring and Development (ARD). The case had to be dropped

---

[24] For information on Yugoslav federal law, see Ch. 1.

[25] Amnesty International, *Concerns in Europe May-Oct. 1993* (London: Jan. 1994).

when Article 197 was amended to cover only four state officials; the President of the Republic, the Prime Minister, the President of the Constitutional Court, and the Speaker of the parliament. The State Prosecutor advised Mršić to bring a private case against Lovrić; he did so, and Lovrić received a six months' suspended sentence without right of appeal after a trial in which she was forbidden to speak in her own defence.

Article 197 was the basis for the prosecution of journalist Jasna Tkalec, convicted in 1993 for spreading false rumours. On 3 June 1991, only three weeks before Croatia's parliament voted on 'dissociation' from Yugoslavia, Tkalec published an article in the local Karlovac newspaper *Nokat*. The article would not have been published by any large-circulation paper (except perhaps the then independent newspaper, *Slobodna Dalmacija*) because it was highly critical of the Croatian leadership, especially its rehabilitation of *ustaša* ideology and the persecution of Croatian Serbs.[26]

"It is obvious that every hope in democracy is gone forever," Tkalec wrote, "like the hope for a peaceful solution [to the Yugoslav crisis], which doesn't yet mean that the *ustaša* and *neo-ustaša* will predominate among the Croatian people. Only the Croatian leadership wants to convince [us] and show it that way." She wrote that about 130 Serb-owned holiday homes around Zadar had been destroyed in two 'Kristalnachte', and monuments had been destroyed in Dalmatia. Tkalec also mentioned the "many thousands of Serbs removed from managerial positions, schools, hospitals, firms and institutions, the definitive 'cleansing' of the last Communists and Serbs".

Charged with spreading false information, Tkalec's trial took place on 29 June 1993 in a district court of Zagreb. In her defence, Tkalec pointed out that named government ministers had admitted both the growth of *ustaša* ideology in Croatia and that Serbs had been unjustly dismissed from work.[27] Judge Neven Svenda refused to admit these ministers as witnesses, and found Tkalec guilty under Article 197. He declared that she

---

[26] On *ustaša,* see Glossary.

[27] Minister of the Interior Josip Manolić had, she claimed, mentioned two tendencies in power, the partisan and *ustaša* lines; and Živko Juzbašić, a minister without portfolio, had mentioned a 'Kristalnacht' against Serbs in Zadar. She cited, too, Milan Djukić, leader of the SNS (Srpska Narodna Stranka, Serb People's Party), in Zagreb, who had also spoken of the sacking of Croatian Serbs.

had "the intention of ... stimulating animosity"; her "deliberate lies" and "warmongering propaganda" had been "disseminated to disturb citizens"; and it was not true that Croatia's leadership encourages *ustaša* ideology, or that so many houses were destroyed in Zadar. "Dangerous propaganda must be punished when it is an incentive to wreak violence against man and his community", Svenda adjudged, handing down a three-month prison sentence for approval by a higher court. He qualified this punishment as "adequate to the gravity of the offence and its consequences, and to achieve all purposes of special and general prevention".

The case is now under appeal. While the higher court may decide not to endorse the sentence, Svenda's cryptic final phrase spells his clear intention: to deter political criticism of the government, and encourage self-censorship, by making an example of the journalist.

Privatization of Media Companies

The privatization of media companies is governed by the Law on the Transformation of Socially-Owned Enterprises (April 1991). By this law, the Agency for Restructuring and Development (ARD), composed of government appointees, oversees the transition from Communist 'social ownership' (no titular owner) to private or state ownership. The ARD has also re-privatized companies which privatized themselves under federal legislation before Croatia passed its own law.

To facilitate the transition, the ARD can invest huge quantities of public money, via the Fund for Privatization; it can also impose a management board (*upravni odbor*) upon the company in question, with or without the company's consent. The board, usually five strong, may be nominated against the wishes of the company's own managers and it is empowered to decide the company's route to transformation: by sale to staff, to other investors, to the Fund, or a mixture of all three.

The process of transformation is highly complex and would be open to abuse even in stable circumstances; in the chaotic conditions of Yugoslavia's demise, it has been extremely corrupt. Contingencies such as state (that is, government) control of banks, the lack of money and stock markets, the government's extensive control over health, insurance and pension funds, the context of military emergency, and the frailty of the trade unions have laid the mechanism wide open to corruption. The discretionary power of the ARD and the management boards is immense, politically and economically. An unbroken chain of influence links the boards to the ruling party; staff changes can readily be foisted on a newspaper or a radio station by its management board in the name of economic necessity. The ARD sets the sale price of each company and can use this mechanism to retain state control by placing an excessively high value on the company. *Večernji list* was valued at 28 million Deutschmarks, for example, making it extremely difficult to find suitable private owners.[28] No watchdog body exists to intervene with the government on behalf of media which are abused by the process.

Catherine Lalumière, General Secretary of the Council of Europe, which has urged the government towards a more democratic media policy, told *Večernji list*:

> there are problems related to privatisation of the press [in Croatia], there is fake privatisation, friends of members of the government are buying media, which is dreadfully cunning.[29]

HINA News Agency

Hrvatska Izvještajna Novinska Agencija (HINA, the Croatian News Reporting Agency), was founded on 28 July 1990. Its headquarters are, fittingly, in the former Yugoslav Tanjug News Agency building in Zagreb, and there are bureaus in Rijeka, Split, Osijek, and Ljubljana (Slovenia). Its coverage is comprehensive: domestic and foreign politics, economics, culture and sport. It obtains international news through contracts with foreign agencies. With a staff of around 50 journalists and a wider network of about 100 correspondents, HINA issues daily bulletins in Croatian, English and German.

Officially HINA is 55 per cent state-financed, with the remainder raised by subscriptions. HINA has been well resourced, for, along with

---

[28] Council of Europe, supra note 22.

[29] *Večernji list*, 23 Oct. 1993.

television, it is one of the two load-bearing pillars in the government's media policy.

HINA's director is appointed by the government. The first director, Josip Šentija, said that a state news agency had been planned by HDZ since February 1990, before the first multiparty elections. In place of Tanjug, which he called "the state Yugo-agency", "Croatia had to build its own agency" as a tool of "the new state".[30] Thus HINA was intended from the outset as a political instrument for use as the authorities saw fit, in the tradition of eastern and central European news agencies.

Šentija's successor is Milovan Šibl, who used to head the now defunct Ministry of Information.[31] A senior member of the HDZ, like Šentija, and also a member of parliament, Šibl sits on the management boards of 10 news publications in Zagreb, including the Vjesnik group. He also edits the HDZ weekly organ, *Glasnik*, which has specialised in damning the party's media critics with extraordinary vindictiveness.

Referring to journalists at the independent news magazine *Novi Danas* before its forced closure in 1992, Šibl expressed his combative views very frankly:

> There are no real journalists in Croatia. Many of these journalists are of mixed origin, one Croat parent, one Serb. How can such people provide an objective picture of Croatia? ... They hate Croatia ... They hate President Tudjman and everything he stands for. The only place you can read the truth about President Tudjman is in HINA news.[32]

HINA easily dominates a news-media landscape that has withered under economic hardship and political authoritarianism. Few media have the resources to obtain their own information from abroad (including Bosnia) or to match the breadth of HINA's domestic coverage. As the state

---

[30] *Slobodna Dalmacija*, 8 June 1993. On Tanjug, see Ch. 2.

[31] When the Ministry of Information was terminated in 1993, as a relic of socialism, its functions were distributed among other government offices, notably the information department in the Ministry of Foreign Affairs.

[32] Quoted in L'Organisation Internationale des Journalistes, *Reporters and Media in Ex-Yugoslavia* (Paris: Les Cahiers de l'Organisation Internationale des Journalistes, Jan. 1993), 24.

news agency, it enjoys prestige as well as political power, and only editors who are wholly independent of state finance can choose to ignore it. In practice, only two printed news media shun HINA, except as a butt of satire or to illustrate its excesses: the independently owned weekly *Feral Tribune*, and *Arkzin*, the magazine of the Anti-War Campaign, Croatia's small peace movement.

It has been suggested that HINA reports are 40 per cent reliable.[33] But which 40 per cent can be trusted? Any given bulletin may be accurate, or a complete farrago, or anything in between. A minor example of HINA's routine manipulation of information was the bulletin carried by *Vjesnik* on 3 February 1993, reporting a Swedish delegation's reception in Zagreb. The Swedish Minister "conveyed a message from the Swedish government about the current situation in the south of Croatia". The content of this message, criticizing the use of armed force near Zadar on 22 January 1993, was simply omitted.[34]

HINA's reporting from Bosnia has been even more tendentious than its coverage of the war at home. On 8 August 1993, *Večernji list* ran a HINA bulletin which stated, "Croat witnesses who escaped from Zenica report that 35 Croats were hanged on the square in front of the Catholic church, for refusing to wear the uniform of the Muslim army." The report continued that Croats in the Zenica area were being forcibly issued with identity cards "with Turkish names and surnames" for which they had to pay 100-500 Deutschmarks. Any Serb or Croat who wanted to leave Zenica had to pay "the Muslim army" 900 Deutschmarks per head. The first part of the bulletin was repeated next day in *Vjesnik*. No other news or international source confirmed this report; and the United Nations Protection Force (UNPROFOR) found no evidence for the allegation following its investigation.

A second example illustrates one of HINA's standard damage limitation techniques when Croat forces are accused of aggression or worse. It concerns the massacre of 15 Muslim civilians, whose bodies were recovered by United Nations (UN) forces in the central Bosnian village of Stupni Do. The Muslims had been murdered on 23 October 1993 by HVO troops. According to the UNCHR Special Rapporteur: "They had either

---

[33] Id.

[34] CIFE Monthly Report, Feb. 1993. This report cites other examples of HINA's bowdlerizing.

been shot at close range or burned to death and included a group of women, found still clutching each other's arms. HVO representatives denied that a massacre had taken place, and for three days prevented international observers from visiting the village."[35]

HINA's reaction was simple. "Regarding the repeated news from Muslim media, and the reports of some foreign agencies about the alleged massacre of civilians in the village of Stupni Do", HINA offered the HVO's version: "following a Muslim attack on the village of Koplari, Muslim soldiers gathered in Stupni Do". Thus the report alleged that the village had been, against all evidence, a military base and hence a legitimate target. The bulletin is structured as a cool balance of views: on the one hand, the opinion of foreign news agencies, and on the other, the response of the alleged perpetrators of the alleged massacre — presented as if these sources were equally disinterested.[36]

Broadcasting

Croatian Radio-Television Law

Within two months of the 1990 elections, the Croatian Radio-Television Act had been rushed through parliament. The name Radio-Televizija Zagreb (RTZ) was changed to Hrvatska Radio-Televizija (HRT, Croatian Radio-Television), signifying its intended role as the media flagship of the nation-state. The Act established HRT as a public broadcasting organization, with certain obligations of public service. HRT broke with the federal broadcasting body, Jugoslovenska Radio-Televizija (JRT, Yugoslav Radio-Television), and with the Tanjug news agency.

The ownership status of the radio and television company did not change; it remained a public enterprise, hence 'state-owned'. The government intended to remould HRT from within, however, by replacing

---

[35] UNCHR, *Situation of Human Rights in the Territory of the Former Yugoslavia*, fifth periodic report submitted by Mr Tadeusz Mazowiecki, Special Rapporteur of the Commission on Human Rights, 17 Nov. 1993, 8.

[36] HINA bulletin in *Večernji list*, 27 Oct. 1993. For television coverage of the Stupni Do massacre, see section on 'Coverage of War in Bosnia' infra.

personnel from the top down. The new Law gave parliament the power to appoint and dismiss the director-general of HRT.[37] Directors of radio and of television would be appointed by the government, at the director-general's proposal.

The director-general was mandated to run the company with an Administrative Council of nine senior staff at HRT. One of the Council's functions is to issue rules and regulations "in accordance" with the government.[38]

The key public service organ provided by the Act was the Radio-Television Council, to be composed of 15 members of parliament (in proportion to the parties' standing in parliament), 10 HRT staff, and 10 delegates from cultural associations and churches. The Council would set guidelines for programming and evaluate output, reporting regularly to parliament. The Council would also choose the chief editors of radio and television, but would have no part in nominating the director-general or the heads of programming. The Council was not constituted for two years. Since it convened in 1992, it has not used even its limited powers to attempt to redress the imbalance of political coverage on HRT. The composition of the supervisory HRT bodies, the requirement that these bodies report to parliament or government, and the system of appointing senior staff, has facilitated government control of radio and television. The Council of Europe mission team's warning that these factors ran the undeniable risk that "programming will accommodate the leading political party" has been ignored.[39]

After the Act was passed, the incumbent director-general, Veljko Knežević, a Serb by nationality, was quickly replaced by a prominent member of HDZ, whose sole qualification was a year's experience writing television reviews for a weekly magazine.[40] Ines Saskor, editor-in-chief of news programmes, who had conceived the RTZ 'Elections '90' project, was also replaced. She says that senior officials at the television station

---

[37] This power had lain with an organ in RTZ called the workers' council; in reality, the central committee of the League of Communists of Croatia had decided the appointments.

[38] Council of Europe, supra note 22.

[39] Council of Europe, supra note 22 at 11. See section on 'Croatian Television' infra for an example of lack of access to opposition political parties.

[40] CIFE Annual Report, Feb. 1993.

were convened, told that an HDZ branch would be established at the station, and advised to resign (25 of them volunteered to do so at once).

Trade union investigations indicate that about 970 of HRT's 3,500 staff were removed over the next three years, hardly ever by dismissal. They were put on standby (paid most of their regular salary on condition that they not work for any other organization), or given early retirement.[41] Some lay-offs were justified through economic restructuring, but a disproportionate number of Serbs were removed.

The government repeatedly promised legislation to allow private media to operate and its failure to address private broadcasting was a major disappointment of the 1992 Law on Public Information. The long-awaited law on electronic media was presented by the Ministry of Maritime Affairs, Traffic and Communications for a first reading in parliament in November 1993. However, it contains a number of provisions which give serious cause for concern for the following reasons:

* failing to provide for an independent body to oversee the granting of frequencies to private bodies; instead the draft law grants the Minister wide-ranging discretionary powers over the allocation of frequencies, and over the content of private broadcasting;

* containing no overall plan for frequency allocation, and not even revealing the total number of available frequencies;

* stipulating that, unless private television stations produce their own news programmes, they would be obliged to carry HRT news;

* allowing for the banning of programmes which damage the security and constitutional order of Croatia;

* retaining government ownership of the transmitter network.[42]

---

[41] Id.

[42] Information from B Novak's paper to the Zagreb free media conference (see supra note 15), and from CIFE monthly bulletins, Nov. 1993-Jan.1994.

The bill was criticized by opposition politicians, journalists, and the Croatian Helsinki Committee, and it remains to be seen whether the government will accept any amendments before enactment.

Croatian Television

> In Croatia, which is terribly impoverished, there exists only one truly functioning means of information: HRT. ... [N]ewspapers have too small circulations to be able to influence Croatian public opinion. HRT presents and explains political life and its atmosphere. Everyone watches it, and many people are convinced that they need watch and listen to nothing else! There is still a fearful respect for television among our people, and its power is being exploited absolutely by one party![43]

The speaker is Vlado Gotovac, a political prisoner after the Croatian Spring, who remained on the media blacklist until the end of the 1980s. Now he is a member of parliament in the main opposition party, and president of Croatia's foremost cultural institution, the Matica Hrvatska.

The similarity between Gotovac's complaint and the remarks by Ivan Djurić, the Serbian opposition politician quoted in Chapter 3, is striking. For oppositionists in Zagreb, as in Belgrade, it is the 7.30 p.m. television news above all which symbolizes the ruling party's grip on the country's most important medium of information.

As in Serbia, access to opposition party views on state-controlled television has been strictly curtailed. Apart from a five-minute slot in a weekly programme for political parties, the main opposition party, the Croatian Social Liberal Party, (which won 17.7 per cent of the popular vote in the August 1992 elections) is virtually unrepresented on news programmes. When their issues are discussed, it is always as one of the last items on the news programme. As a gauge of their exclusion from prime time news and current affairs programmes, the party's leader,

---

[43] *Globus*, 15 Oct. 1993.

Dražen Budiša did not appear on the main current affairs programme, *Slikom na sliku*, until 5 November 1993.

HDZ's control of television is all the harder to accept because something better was not only possible: it actually happened. Gordana Grbić was one of the best-known editors of the main evening news in the late 1980s. Of the programme in 1989-1990, she says:

> I was proud of the job we did. We were really different from TV Belgrade [TVB]. We tried to give people the right information about what was happening. We used parts of TVB reports to show our different approach, for example to events in Kosovo, where we had our own reporter.
>
> We didn't oppose democratization. All parties were very satisfied with our coverage of the election campaign, including HDZ. But even during the campaign, we heard that 'six and a half [sic] Serb journalists' would be sacked from the news room. There were never more than three Serbs there anyway ... .

By September 1993, Grbić says, only two of the eight editors of the evening news team from 1990 still worked at HTV.

As a product, HTV news is superior to TVB's output. The format is less confusing and pretentious. Propaganda commentaries are less frequent and less obtrusive and the editor's delivery is more professional. In its content, however, it is a news service of the governing party and, at times, of one man, President Tudjman.

Two examples, from before and during the war illustrate this point:

*   On 24 January 1991, TVB broadcast a secretly made film (presumably prepared by the Yugoslav state security police or by JNA counter-intelligence) of Croatia's Minister of Defence, Martin Špegelj, negotiating to smuggle arms into Croatia in order to attack JNA personnel. TV Sarajevo had shown the film too, so parts of Croatia had seen it.

The film was an apparent attempt to intimidate the Croatian leadership, already under acute pressure from a Federal Presidency ultimatum to disarm the republic's defence units. The Federal Defence

Minister, General Kadijević, a Serb by nationality, had threatened that the JNA would use force to disarm the units if necessary. The ultimatum had expired at midnight on 21 January.[44]

As a result, the government feared that attack was imminent. Soldiers armed with bazookas were sent to guard the HTV centre from possible attack by the JNA. Light entertainment programmes were broadcast throughout the night, separated by news bulletins instructing people to stay calm and obey the authorities. At the same time, the authorities could not decide whether to show the film, or how to present it. They showed it the next day, followed by a two-hour rambling debate among a team of military experts and presidential advisers who clarified nothing. Was the film authentic? If it wasn't, was there any truth in the JNA allegation? How had the film been made? How worried should viewers be? These questions were raised but not answered.[45]

* In September 1991, television and other media carried reports about snipers in Zagreb and other Croatian cities, including Split and Šibenik. According to the weekly *Danas*, on at least one evening following the news, the television announcer offered a cash reward for information leading to the arrest of snipers.[46] Journalist Vesna Kesić noted that a wave of denunciations followed these announcements: "Citizens started to report every dubious phenomenon, [such as] neighbours with dubious [Serbian] surnames, and shop assistants refused to serve customers who had turned overnight into treacherous killers [because of their names]."

Then the alleged snipers vanished from the news. According to Kesić, the only solid information about the furore emerged during a phone-in programme on Zagreb's Radio 101. On 23 September, two guests were the commander of military special units in Zagreb and the commander of Zagreb's Territorial Defence (forerunner of the Croatian Army). They alleged that more than 600 snipers had been reported during one week at the height of the scare. Twenty-five people were taken in for questioning, of whom 23 were released immediately. The other two were released a while later. Media had been used to mobilize people by

---

[44] S P Ramet, *Nationalism and Federalism in Yugoslavia 1962-1991* (Bloomington: Indiana University Press, 1992, 2nd edition), 250.

[45] V Kesić, *Nedjeljna Dalmacija*, 3 Feb. 1991.

[46] I Z Čičak, *Danas*, 1 Oct. 1991.

whipping up panic and fear; and other media gave the game away with the phone-in programme.[47]

Profile of the Television Chiefs

With the fate of HRT in so few hands, it is impossible to portray the institution, its style, and its ethic, without describing the extrovert, authoritarian personality of Antun Vrdoljak, the director-general of HRT throughout the war, and Tomislav Marčinko, editor-in-chief of HTV news programmes.

Formerly an actor and reputable film director, Vrdoljak is an intimate of President Tudjman and a pillar of the ruling HDZ. He is a member of parliament and a member of the party executive.[48] He sits on the Council for National Defence and Security, a body appointed by the President and responsible for all aspects of policy.[49]

Independent polling agencies show that Vrdoljak appears on television more frequently than anyone except Franjo Tudjman.[50] Ranting garrulously against his critics, avowing his nationalism, praising HDZ's Croatia to the skies, crude and charming by turns, and dispensing trite folklore wisdom, Vrdoljak gives terrific value as an interviewee. Describing HTV as a "cathedral of the Croatian spirit", he swears (falsely) that "nobody was sacked from HRT who didn't flee from Croatia [because of] the war".[51] He despatches criticism thus: "They tell us, you [on HTV] didn't announce it at once when Vukovar fell. Let me frankly confess to you now: for me, Vukovar still hasn't fallen!"[52]

---

[47] V Kesić, "Arms for panic", *Svijet*, Nov. 1991.

[48] Article 16 of the Media Law (1992) stipulates that "any person with immunity from prosecution cannot be appointed an editor-in-chief" of a media organ. As an MP, Vrdoljak enjoys immunity (see section on 'Media and Law' supra).

[49] L'Organisation Internationale des Journalistes, supra note 32 at 27. He heads the management board at Croatia Airlines and is also president of the national Olympic Committee, and of the company which is building the new Split-Zagreb motorway.

[50] "The director and his boss are always seen together, sitting next to each other at conventions and festivals, the latter always whispering something into the President's ear." Kuzmanović, supra note 7.

[51] *Večernji list*, 15 Oct. 1993.

[52] Quoted in *Feral Tribune*, 16 Nov. 1993. See also section on 'Vukovar' infra.

"I understood my work [at HRT] as part of my duty to the homeland in its war for survival", Vrdoljak says, and adds that part of this duty was:

> to save the TV from foreign influences ... . [W]hen I ask myself if I have done anything for television, I think I can say: I have achieved my soldierly task. I never asked for rank, and when they gave it to me, I accepted uneasily, because I hadn't been at the front. Though working at the TV wasn't far away.[53]

Vrdoljak's right hand in the television centre is Tomislav Marčinko, editor-in-chief of news programmes. Marčinko, a Croat from the autonomous province of Vojvodina, was a high-ranking executive in the Vojvodina League of Communists until 1988, when he was ousted as part of the putsch engineered by Slobodan Milošević to gain control of the province. Less voluble than Vrdoljak, Marčinko also lacks the other's brass nerve, wavering under pressure. "HTV doesn't lie," he once said, adding "or just a little bit". And, "I can't say I am completely satisfied with our programmes, but we are at war ... ."[54] A diary piece written for *Danas* was forthright. On Vrdoljak, "Except for Dr Tudjman, I don't see anyone else in the HDZ who has done as much for his party and for Croatia." On HTV's coverage of Bosnia:

> At HTV we frankly supported the defence of Croat ethnic and historical space; from the first day we stood behind the ideas and practice of the Croat Community and later of the Croat Republic of Herceg-Bosna.[55]

Profile of Journalists

By the end of 1991, almost all independent-minded journalists had been removed from the screen. Among the news reporters who departed the station in 1991 were Aleksandar Milošević and Heni Erceg. Milošević

---

[53] *Slobodna Dalmacija*, 14 Aug. 1993.

[54] *Globus*, 8 Nov. 1991.

[55] *Danas*, 26 Oct. 1993.

began his career in 1987 on *Zagreb Panorama*, where many cub reporters learned the business in the late 1980s. He looks back at the period from 1988 (when he joined the TV Zagreb newsdesk) to 1990, when he made his name during the election campaign, as "the period of beautiful anarchy. The Communists were too weak to stop anything, and HDZ hadn't yet appeared".[56]

In 1990 and 1991, Milošević reported from the restless, then rebellious Serb areas in central Croatia. His work was considered informative and impartial. His coverage of the Croatian Serb rally on 25 July 1990 showed the radical Serb leader Jovan Rašković being loudly cheered for declaring "[t]his is an uprising of the Serb people!"; but the report stayed with Rašković as he continued "[b]ut it is an uprising without weapons", a conciliatory signal which drew only silence from the crowd.[57]

Milošević's reports from Plitvice on 31 March and 1 April 1991 were likewise impartial, though their reassuring calmness was the result of political manipulation. Milošević had clandestinely filmed a column of JNA tanks as they arrived by night in accordance, it emerged, with terms accepted by the Croatian authorities for the JNA to take control of Plitvice. After sending the film to Zagreb, he called Antun Vrdoljak, the new director-general of HRT, who only told him to stay put. "They never showed the film," Milošević says, "because people would have known that JNA tanks meant a Serbian border inside Croatia." Instead, his report on 1 April was followed by a studio interview with a minister who insisted that relations between the JNA and the Croatian Ministry of the Interior were "normal and correct"; the JNA had lent a helicopter to help evacuate the Croatian wounded. The news of the JNA's arrival was released a day later.[58]

While Milošević was reporting from Slovenia at the end of June 1991 he was pulled out, without explanation; thereafter he was sidelined. Other Serbs in the news department were being filtered out at the same

---

[56] A Milošević to author, 31 Aug. 1993.

[57] Contrast the Serbian press headlines in Ch. 3, section on 'Coverage of Serb Rebellion in Croatia' supra.

[58] For Serbian press coverage, see Ch. 3, section on 'Coverage of Plitvice' supra.

time.[59] Milošević wasn't only the wrong nationality; he had the wrong ideas. In 1990, he had complained in print of creeping censorship in television and a lack of professionalism among Croatian journalists.[60] On 30 September, he was banned from the HTV building along with other staff. On 14 October he received written notice, dated 8 October, that he had been dismissed on 30 September for being absent five days from work. Although his union forced HTV to reinstate Milošević, he knew he would not be allowed to work and was resigned to defeat. However, he did not go quietly, and his case became a minor scandal.

Asked to comment, editor-in-chief Marčinko said that Milošević was "certainly a very good journalist, but completely disoriented in the situation that Croatia was in. In my judgement he is Yugoslav-oriented in the toughest sense." Marčinko went on to remind readers that Milošević's father was a JNA officer.[61] Replying, Milošević identified the lies in Marčinko's version of events, and asked whether his criteria for removing journalists were national (making him a racist) or political (making him an unlawful censor). Marčinko's feeble riposte was that "all Miloševićes are psychiatric cases".[62]

Heni Erceg was an HTV correspondent based in Split. A generation older than Milošević, Erceg had made the transition from Communist to independent journalism. She reported from Slavonia in summer 1991. Information was received that the village of Laslovo, populated mainly by Hungarians, was being bombarded by Serb-JNA forces in a mainly Serb village called Palača. Against advice, Erceg went to Palača and found only "destroyed houses and a few terrified [Serb] residents". Erceg's corrective report went out that evening. "Next day, Branimir Glavaš [commander of Croatian forces in the Osijek region] called HTV and said I should be moved on, as journalists weren't allowed access to the Palača area. He was deciding where journalists could and couldn't go!" HTV called Erceg and ordered her out of the region. Erceg practically ceased reporting at the end of the year, because her editors stopped giving her work. She was suspended in summer 1992, and now works for the Split-based fortnightly, *Feral Tribune*, a rare refuge for independent journalists.

---

[59] A Milošević, *Danas*, 29 Oct. 1991.

[60] *Nedjeljna Dalmacija*, 26 Oct. 1990.

[61] *Globus*, 8 Nov. 1991.

[62] *Globus*, 22 Nov. 1991 and 29 Nov. 1991.

HTV's foreign correspondents too have been targeted. The Bonn correspondent was sidelined by the station in 1993 and wrote publicly that he had been "obstructed and prevented from performing the job of accredited correspondent" and that his reports had been censored.[63]

Proof that the line between independent and biased reporting on HTV is not fixed or impermeable is the late-night current affairs programme, *Slikom na sliku* (Picture on Picture). It runs for 45 minutes every night from around 11 p.m., after the second evening news (which gets fewer viewers than the main 7.30 p.m. news). *Slikom na sliku* is hosted by an editor who recapitulates the day's main stories aided by footage from HTV and foreign stations.[64] There are several editors, two of whom manage regularly to feature guests and show foreign networks' reports which expose disinformation in HTV's own reports.

However, the editors face harassment for their efforts. On 13 April 1993, Radovan Pavić, a political geographer, was a guest on *Slikom na sliku*, and offered a grimly realistic prognosis of Croatia's options for regaining the territory it had lost to Serb rebels. The programme editor, Dubravko Merlić, did not contradict his guest. The show was not repeated next day, as had been scheduled. That evening, the news editor read a criticism of Merlić for "disturbing the public" the previous night.

There is much speculation as to why the two editors are not purged altogether. However, the HTV directors can still oblige the editors to include propaganda material. In the aftermath of the Stupni Do massacre, for example, *Slikom na sliku* broadcast an HVO film which alleged that Stupni Do had been a military base and thus a legitimate target of attack.

Regulating Language and Tone

Language changed along with faces on the newsdesk before the war. Special readers were employed to ensure that editors and reporters used 'politically correct' terms. Even before 1990, nationalist ideologues had

---

[63] *Vjesnik*, 21 May 1993.

[64] Foreign satellite stations are available in Croatia, including CNN and Sky TV, but no figures are available for the number of households having satellite-receiving equipment.

been exhuming archaisms from Croatian dictionaries and 'cleansing' characteristically Serbian words and expressions.[65]

After the elections, these changes were accelerated and imposed as a matter of policy, but were not always systematically introduced. In mid-1991, the editors of the late evening news on Channel 2 were boldly calling Bosnia 'Herceg-Bosna', a name which implies Croat territorial claims, while editors on Channel 1 continued with the correct name.[66] People in the Serb-rebel centre of Knin were '*balvan* revolutionaries', while Knin's police chief Milan Martić, a rebel leader, was 'the sheriff'.[67]

These examples were cited by journalist Dejan Kršić, as evidence of HTV's "mistaken and counterproductive strategies of mythologization".[68] The spread of fighting in Croatia during August 1991, the month when the nature of the war began to clarify for many observers inside as well as outside the region, helped to entrench and normalize these strategies.

The basic repertory of linguistic techniques was the same as TVB's in Serbia. To take a single, crucial case: it became standard usage for television news to report that "Serb forces" or even "the Serbs" were shooting, burning houses, and so on in the occupied parts of Croatia.[69] The entire Serb nation was implicated in the attacks, so the entire nation became the enemy, which correlated precisely with TVB's simultaneous insistence that all Serbs must support the war effort, and those who did not were traitors. The same ploy was repeated during the war in Bosnia towards both other sides.

Serbian television never issued a code of correct titles and terms, presumably because it regulated these things more discreetly as well as more thoroughly. HTV, by contrast, faxed its regional studios with a 13-point 'decree' on the matter, on 28 August 1991. It was signed by

---

[65] Two guides to distinguishing Croatian from Serbian words are currently published in Croatia. "Words of foreign origin are excluded [from television news], old Croatian words are introduced ... . It is noticeable that new expressions are introduced the same day by journalists and presenters, as well as by correspondents from Rome, London, Mostar or Dubrovnik." (CIFE Monthly Report, May 1993.)

[66] Channel 2 news has since been discontinued.

[67] *Balvan* means log or tree-trunk. The first rebellion among Croatian Serbs had been the construction of log roadblocks around the central Croatian town of Knin.

[68] *Vjesnik*, 16 Aug. 1991.

[69] CIFE, supra note 34.

Tomislav Marčinko, news editor-in-chief, and Miroslav Lilić, editor-in-chief of programming, and deserves to be quoted in full:[70]

> 1. Reports must start with the latest information, and only then review the day's events.
>
> 2. Do not report future actions by MUP [Ministry of the Interior] and the [National] Guard.
>
> 3. Do not show people weeping and wailing.
>
> 4. Do not broadcast pictures of blown-up, badly wounded and shot Croatian soldiers (Guardsmen and police) or statements by wounded people.
>
> 5. Do not use the terms '*četniks*' and 'extremists' but only 'SERB TERRORISTS'.
>
> 6. Do not call the JNA anything except 'SERBO-COMMUNIST ARMY OF OCCUPATION'.
>
> 7. Do not use the term '*mupovci*' [members of the special police forces of the Ministry of the Interior] but instead 'police'.
>
> 8. Do not report the names of owners of blown-up houses.[71]
>
> 9. Casualty figures of Guardsmen and police must always be accompanied with "fell for Croatia's freedom", "gave their lives to defend the homeland", "heroes in defence of the homeland".
>
> 10. Expunge commentary from reports, give only facts.
>
> 11. Do not conceal defeats at the front, but stress the tremendous forces employed by the enemy and his unscrupulousness, and always finish such reports with optimistic declarations and avowals ("but we shall

---

[70] Adapted from the translation in M Malešić (ed.), *The Role of Mass Media in the Serbian-Croatian Conflict*, Psykologist Försvar Report 164 (Stockholm: 1993), 34-35.

[71] Owners of blown-up, or mined, houses (as distinct from shelled houses) were Croatian Serbs. Thousands of such properties were mined, before, during and especially after the war in Croatia. This injunction was intended to prevent Serbs from appearing as victims of the war.

bring back freedom to our Kijevo", for example).
Send reports of towns being successfully defended
for special programmes. Failure to adhere to the
above instructions will entail appropriate professional
and legal consequences.
12. We ask you to observe this decree with special
seriousness, bearing in mind that the Law on
Information in War Conditions has been enacted
TODAY.[72]
13. Footage must, in keeping with this Decree, be
previewed and approved by the editor before
transmission.

This decree was neither observed nor enforced to the letter, but it
illustrates the spirit of war coverage in the government-controlled media,
and it reveals the confusion ('only facts', plus 'optimistic declarations') in
the minds of those who wanted to manipulate the most powerful medium.

Regulating Images of War

HTV news presented a very confusing picture of the conflict. The
laser-like focus of TVB's message, Serb kinfolk threatened with genocide
by *ustaša*, was not achieved by HTV, which often veered in different
directions, as if it wanted to motivate viewers but was anxious not to
frighten them.

According to two analysts of the HTV evening news programme
between August 1991 and January 1992, until mid-August "the bulk of
information from the battlefronts was totally devoid of visual material".[73]
Only with the JNA attacks in western Slavonia, during August 1991, did
footage of soldiers and destruction start to feature regularly. Thereafter
Croatian casualties were sometimes shown to prove atrocities against
civilians. Much use was made of foreign news stations' footage.

---

[72] This refers to a a Presidential Decree, issued in accordance with Article 101
of the Constitution. See section on 'Media and Law' supra.

[73] Malešić, supra note 70 at 85-89. The two analysts of HTV were S Bašić and
V Cvrtila.

Overall, the analysts conclude, "instead of providing visual documentation, HTV became a very powerful propaganda apparatus, which created images of the war for the majority of the population". These images were very intense, emotive and generalized, depicting destruction, corpses, suffering, resistance, courage and so forth in an allegorical manner, often devoid of references to locate the story in a specific place.

Ivan Zvonimir Čičak, a well-known anti-HDZ patriot, who today heads the Croatian Helsinki Committee for Human Rights, had no doubt that HTV's coverage reflected a basic hesitancy in the political leadership about goals and means. He traced the later atrocious images on the news to the same source:

> Croatia compensates for losing on the battlefield by
> ... showing severed heads and massacred civilians ...
> to create a stronger feeling of hatred which could
> wipe away the feeling of aimlessness and bitter
> defeats.[74]

Čičak's argument leads outside the bounds of this report, into a full analysis of Croatian strategy during the war. But he is also arguing a clear point about the news media, a point supported by a former senior employee of HTV with many years' newsroom experience. According to this source, the question of propaganda was debated at the highest level in HTV early in the conflict. Should Croatia be presented as a victim: suffering and, implicitly, losing? Or as imminently victorious?

The debate was never resolved. An army officer was seconded to advise on coverage of military matters, but the arrangement was too informal to work. An 'information staff' was established to regulate national security information in the public media.[75] Its active role has not yet been revealed. The Minister of Information himself was very opaque when asked both about the staff and about the media involvement of the local political-military 'crisis staffs' around the republic.[76] Lack of central

---

[74] *Danas*, 10 Sept. 1991. Čičak may have had in mind the news on 5 Sept., which showed murdered villagers in Četekovci, Slavonia.

[75] J Šentija, *Slobodna Dalmacija*, 8 June 1993. As director of HINA, Šentija was a member of the staff. He says the staff was wound up in summer 1992.

[76] B Salaj, *Slobodna Dalmacija*, 31 Oct. 1991. "We don't have censorship by law, but we do have measures of readiness for the second degree."

regulation left matters of media access and liaison in local commanders' hands, who restricted coverage arbitrarily in the interests of military security. It also allowed characters like Branimir Glavaš, head of Osijek municipal council, and widely known as 'the sheriff of Osijek', to use their political and military clout as they pleased (see section on 'Profile of Journalists' supra.).

Reports of casualties continued to be censored in 1993. Following an HV action at the end of January 1993 to seize back territory held by Serb forces behind Zadar, in northern Dalmatia, Croatian casualties were not mentioned in the media for five days. Then the television news mentioned that 21 soldiers of the Croatian Army III brigade had been buried at Slavonski Brod, several hundred kilometres from the Zadar action. The report did not say where the soldiers had fallen. A month later, the brigade commander was asked on television if it was true that the press had suppressed information about casualties. "Not at all," he said, "*Glas Slavonije* [the regional daily paper for Slavonski Brod] published the obituary notices."[77]

Vukovar

The capture of Vukovar on 18 November 1991 was both the military climax of the war in Croatia and its nadir. It was Croatia's most savagely spectacular loss and the worst destruction in Europe since 1945. The handsome town on the banks of the Danube at the eastern edge of Croatia, with a population of 84,000 people, had been bombarded for 86 days by JNA artillery, river vessels, and aircraft, before it finally capitulated to the JNA and Serbian paramilitaries. Commentators, both within and outside Croatia, believed at the time that Vukovar was being sacrificed to the nationalist goal of winning international recognition for Croatia's independence. Whether this was so or not, Vukovar's destruction melted or tempered lifelong convictions.

During and after the siege, information about Vukovar was jealously controlled. Luka Mitrović, a popular HTV personality, has scarcely been able to obtain work since interviewing Mile Dedaković-Jastreb, commander of the town's defence during the siege, who criticized the government for not doing more to defend Vukovar. An issue of *Slobodni tijednik* (ST), the

---

[77] Ivančić, supra note 8.

extreme nationalist weekly, was banned for querying the official claim that everything possible had been done for Vukovar.[78]

Jastreb banned news cameras from the town to stop the besiegers gaining information about its defence. As a result, the town's image as a pure Croatian martyr was cultivated; only *Danas* mentioned the fact that some of its defending force were not Croats by nationality, as was logical, for Vukovar had been 43.7 per cent Croat, 37.4 per cent Serb, 7.3 per cent Yugoslav, 2.7 per cent Ruthenian: a Slavonian blend.[79]

According to Marjan Malešić's report:

> Vukovar became a symbol of the Croatian-Serbian war through narration ... television lost its visual function and became radio. The Croatian public heard daily reports of the destruction of Vukovar, but never saw it ... . [D]uring the final bitter battles for Vukovar (on 27 October 1991) reports consisted only of the disembodied voice of Sinisa Glavašević, a Radio Vukovar journalist, and a map of the area on which certain towns and villages were marked.[80]

Glavašević and his colleagues became national heroes during the siege. He disappeared after the fall and is widely believed to have been executed by his captors.

The evening before the fall, the voice of HTV's reporter spoke of "the dramatic situation of the people of Vukovar"; the screen showed a photograph of the town. A statement from the army general staff was read out: the army was defending the central part of the city and the hospital. Malešić noted: "News of the imminent fall of Vukovar had not yet been announced by the Croatian media; reports had been neutral, with no mention of fighting or defence, only the sound of shooting and detonations in the town. Enemy losses were reported, and mention was made for the first time of the need to save civilians."[81] Mention of enemy losses and the need to save civilians was meant to prepare viewers for the worst.

---

[78] For more on *ST*'s Vukovar crusade see section on 'The Weekly Press' infra.

[79] After 1961, the decennial Yugoslav census included 'Yugoslav' as an identity.

[80] Malešić, supra note 70.

[81] Id.

Malešić proposes that, when foreign news pictures of the devastation were transmitted around the world, after the town's capture, the previous dearth of images meant that "the propaganda effect on the Croatian public was exceptionally strong".[82] The effect, however, appears to have been an unintended benefit of Jastreb's military decision rather than a triumph of manipulation by television.

Coverage of War in Bosnia

Coverage of war in Bosnia has been designed to deliver simple messages: Croat forces in Bosnia are only defending themselves and their "centuries-old hearths"; all Croats must support this self-evidently just struggle; the other sides, the Serb forces and, since early 1993, the "Muslim forces" too (those loyal to the Bosnian government), are expansionist, aggressive and genocidal. The coverage of Stupni Do is a case in point.[83] Some 20 minutes into the evening news on 26 October, the newscaster announced that foreign media had that day reported a massacre at Stupni Do, and the HVO had prevented UN military observers from entering the area. There followed a report from Smiljko Šagolj, HTV's chief correspondent in Bosnia. "Muslim media and some foreign media are reporting this massacre", he alleged, before citing several HVO authorities, including a commander, denying any massacre or that access had been hindered.[84]

The following night, again 20 minutes into the programme, a report showed UN troops in the devastated village. UN information was given on the soundtrack: some 140 people were still unaccounted for, 15 corpses had been found, and half the houses had yet to be examined. No denial of HVO involvement was presented.

Later that night, on *Slikom na sliku*, Cable News Network (CNN) and Sky Television reports about Stupni Do were broadcast. CNN cited the UN claim that the Croat forces had tried to hide the massacre by refusing the UN access for three days. Sky reported that only now was the scale of the massacre becoming known, and added that the HVO only withdrew from the village when the UN threatened military action. The British UN

---

[82] Id.

[83] For background on Stupni Do, see section on 'HINA News Agency' supra.

[84] For more on Šagolj, see Ch. 5, section on 'Croat Media' infra.

commander's response was shown: "This is a disgusting war crime", committed not by soldiers but by "scum". Sky named Krešimir Božić as the responsible HVO commander.

On 29 October, the evening news report about Stupni Do spoke frankly of a massacre, without extenuation. *Slikom na sliku*, however, carried an interview with Slobodan Lovrenović, an official spokesman for the self-proclaimed 'Croat Republic of Herceg-Bosna'. We cannot speak of a massacre of civilians, Lovrenović said, until the HVO's own investigating commission has submitted its findings.

A ponderous HVO propaganda film was shown on *Slikom na Sliku*, on 23 November (one week after the release of the UNCHR report about Stupni Do), 'proving' that Stupni Do had been a military base, whence Muslim artillery had bombarded "Croatian Vares" (a fiercely-contested town which was 40.6 per cent Croat and 33.7 per cent Muslim before the war). The film presented no clear evidence to support this allegation, which contradicted the UNPROFOR's finding that there were no soldiers among the final tally of 25 corpses, and no weaponry in the ruins.

Such coverage has served Croatian strategic goals unremittingly and ruthlessly. Viktor Ivančić was reporting for *Slobodna Dalmacija* from the Kupres area in south western Bosnia in early April 1992. Reporter Silvana Mendušić was there for HTV. Ivančić reported when Kupres fell to Serb forces on 9 April. HTV did not. That evening viewers of Serbia's TVB news learned from a reporter, posing before a background of burning buildings, that, "After fifty years, Kupres is free!" For a further three days, Mendušić reported on HTV that "Kupres is securely in Croat hands". Consequently, *Slobodna Dalmacija* received angry phone calls, accusing it of defeatism. Refugees from the Kupres area later told Ivančić that they had believed the HTV reports and were almost caught in the Serb advance.[85]

---

[85] Information about TVB from L Bryant (confirmed by B Mihajlović, *Druga Srbija* (Belgrade: Plato-Beogradski krug-Borba, 1992). Information about Mendušić, from Ivančić, supra note 8. Heni Erceg remembers that Stipe Mesić, president of the lower chamber of parliament, was asked at a press conference to account for this disinformation. He explained that Bosnian Croats had to remain in their homes, because Tito's biggest mistake in 1941-1945 had been to displace the civilian population.

Regional and Local Television

Two local television stations opened in Croatia before the 1990 elections, under licences issued by the Federal Office for Radio and Telecommunications. Omladinska Televizija (OTV, Youth Television), began broadcasting to the greater Zagreb area in 1989. TV Rijeka started broadcasting in 1990, in both Croatian and Italian languages. Since the elections, stations have opened in Osijek (TV Slavonia), in Split (TV Marjan), in Djakovo, Zadar, Vrbovec, Opuzen, and Čakovec (TV Medjimurje). Others are planned in Sibenik, Kutina (TV Moslavina), and Istria.

The legal position of these stations is unclear, because no law yet exists to distribute frequencies. Hence the authorities have been able to permit and prevent private stations according to political criteria. TV Slavonia has had no difficulties, though it operates without a licence. It is owned by the National Stock Association (NSA), which also owns *Glas Slavonije*, the Osijek-based regional paper. The NSA, described by the CIFE as "the property of HDZ", was investigated by *Slobodna Dalmacija*, which was unable to trace even its telephone number. On 6 February 1993, the day before parliamentary elections, TV Slavonia broadcast *We Have Croatia*, HTV's two-hour eulogy of President Tudjman, first shown nationwide three weeks previously. This flouted the electoral commission's demand for a pre-election moratorium on media coverage of the candidates.[86]

OTV has had no trouble renewing its federal licence. Formerly owned by the Socialist Youth League (disbanded after the 1990 elections), the station is in the process of privatization. It has no economic or formal connections with government, but there is a strong tie in the person of Vinko Grubišić, the station's first editor-in-chief, who became Deputy Minister of Information in 1991, and is now on the staff of the HDZ central office. Grubišić continues to have a strong editorial input at OTV. While the station carries no news, its current affairs programmes feature personalities who would not be invited to appear on HTV — extreme nationalists, celebrities who have been labelled "Yugonostalgics", or, occasionally, opposition politicians in open debates with their HDZ counterparts. Its editorial perspective is, however, pro-HDZ, and it is rarely

---

[86] CIFE, supra note 34.

critical on key questions: the Serb minority in Croatia, and the government's policy in Bosnia.

TV Rijeka, by contrast, which obtained its original licence under the same conditions as OTV, is forbidden to broadcast because the government disapproves of its anti-nationalist outlook. TV Medjimurje has also been harshly treated. With the long-promised law to privatize frequencies repeatedly postponed, the station eventually started broadcasting without a licence in March 1993. It was closed down in April 1993 and, when it resumed in August for a short time, its content was a mix of movies from a Luxembourg-German satellite channel plus local news; this posed no significant threat to HTV's news monopoly. However, the management of the station is not controlled by HDZ and had resisted local HDZ pressure. Furthermore, the whole of Medjimurje is politically suspect because it voted against the HDZ in the 1993 elections to the upper chamber of parliament. The authorities, possibly fearing that the station might be deployed against them in the future, sealed the transmitter.

In Serb-controlled regions, local television stations were established, including at Knin and Beli Manastir, broadcasting local news and programmes from Serbia. The Serb local authorities also redirected HRT's transmitters in these regions to receive signals from Belgrade. The JNA-Serb forces twice attacked the Sljeme transmitter, which serves central Croatia, with rockets but failed to knock it out. For one brief period in 1991 only one powerful transmitter was operating in Croatia but HRT's engineers managed to keep HTV's Channel 1 on air throughout.

Radio

Croatian Radio

Under the 1990 Radio-Television Act, Radio Zagreb, which has three republic-wide frequencies, became Hrvatski Radio (HR, Croatian Radio), and passed under government control along with its network of some 50 local stations.

While there has been no independent monitoring of HR news during the war, as at HTV, there was more scope for balanced reporting before the January 1992 cease-fire in Croatia than after. It was symptomatic that HR banned or censored UNPROFOR newscasts at least eight times during the first year of UN deployment in Croatia. On 12 March 1993, for example, part of a report about Knin was cut, presumably because the information about UNPROFOR troops aiding Croats in the Serb-occupied territory spoiled an ongoing campaign by politicians and the government-controlled media to taint UNPROFOR as anti-Croatian.[87] The UNPROFOR head of civilian affairs has commented that it was the first case in his experience of a host country interfering with UN broadcasts.

Government pressure upon HR increased during 1993. The editor-in-chief resigned in August. Alleging interference, he said that his role had been reduced to that of assistant to the director. His replacement denies any political bias in the news, or that the government tries to influence the editorial policy.[88] Early in 1994, however, the following document was handed down to HR news staff, reportedly from the President's office.

> Editors of daily programmes, sub-editors, and journalists on news and current affairs broadcasts are kindly requested to observe the following:
>
> *   Commentaries on certain resolutions of the UN Security Council and other bodies about possible sanctions and pressures against Croatia (correspondents' reports, agency bulletins and so on) are to be broadcast 'discreetly', carefully, after special consultation, if necessary, with the news editor-in-chief, the editors of the particular programmes, the sub-editors, etc.
>
> *   Daily news broadcasts and reports, as also political party statements and so on, are to be transmitted without possible attacks on the overall policy of Croatia, the Leadership, the government and other bodies.

---

[87] CIFE Monthly Report, March 1993.

[88] I Lucev, *Danas*, 22 Feb. 1994.

*   Do not broadcast party quarrels,[89] unfounded attacks on persons in political life, on Agreements, Decisions and meetings which the highest representatives of Croatian power and state are negotiating, signing or arranging.

*   When "Party Forum" begins, reports of party meetings in daily [news] transmissions will cease.[90]

*   Live reporting from the Croatian parliament will continue, but journalists who work on daily transmissions should judge their reports in the light of their programme's tasks. The same applies with special summaries of parliamentary proceedings at 16.10 and 22.30.

*   Do not broadcast tendentious, scandalous stories such as "Argus", "Dalmacijacement" and so on, nor 'local' reports of municipal and county bodies, business affairs, unfounded complaints about the social situation ...[91]

*   Reports from Bosnia-Hercegovina are compiled as a rule from Z Vranješ[92] reports supplemented by agency reports (HINA, HABENA[93] and others) with

---

[89] A clear reference to a power struggle between radical and moderate streams within the HDZ.

[90] *Party Forum* was a daily radio programme open to politicians of all parties. The HTV board has plans to reintroduce it during 1994.

[91] Argus is a construction company in Valpovo which became the centre of a power struggle within eastern Croatia during 1993. Dalmacijacement was privatized in dubious circumstances, resulting in scandal which touched senior HDZ figures.

[92] Zlatko Vranješ, HR's correspondent in 'Herceg-Bosna', is widely regarded as a mouthpiece for government policy on Bosnia.

[93] HABENA is the Herceg-Bosna News Agency; see Ch. 5, section on 'Croat Media' infra.

spoken comments from Mrkonjić (Žepce), Šarić (Vitez), Katić (Usora) ..."[94]

Local Radio

Control of the local stations in the HR network has sometimes been fiercely contested, as will be seen from cases summarized below. There are also local private stations which received frequencies under the Federal Law on Telecommunications (1988), still the only such legislation in Croatia. This law allows municipalities to allocate frequencies by a process of selection which is dangerously vague. As many as 80 local stations may be operating in all.[95]

Among local stations in the HR network, only two, Sisak and Bjelovar, had been privatized by the end of 1993; economic incentives to invest could scarcely be weaker, and the privatization mechanism makes it simple to block politically unacceptable applications. The remaining stations are still responsible to the local companies and authorities which owned them during the Communist period. When these owners are not themselves controlled by HDZ, operating through its local branches, the radio staff cannot be changed at the convenience of HRT, the body that oversees both television and radio.

This has produced political struggles between stations and their parent bodies and the municipal politicians, as well as within stations. When this happens, the radio station is contested less as a news and information medium than as a local power base, an organ of civil society, which local authorities usually believe themselves entitled to control.

This was brutally clear in the treatment of Radio Valpovo during summer and autumn 1993, when Branimir Glavaš, the local military commander and head of Osijek municipal council, was manoeuvring to control Valpovo town council. The radio station was purged of supporters of the anti-Glavaš faction; these journalists' and technicians' professional record was utterly irrelevant.[96]

---

[94] Published in *Feral Tribune*, 15 Feb. 1994.

[95] CIFE Monthly Report, Oct. 1993.

[96] *Slobodna Dalmacija*, 7 Aug. 1993; *Večernji list*, 16 Oct. 1993 and 23 Oct. 1993.

The best-known local station is Radio 101 in Zagreb. It started, like OTV, under the auspices of the Socialist Youth League in the early 1980s, and has been able to renew its licence, but only at a price. The city council has kept the station under close scrutiny, by appointing a new director-general and an ARD management board which favours the HDZ. There is currently a stalemate; since the last election, the HDZ has had a reduced majority on the city council and is fighting to retain all its seats on the Radio 101 management committee.[97] According to one experienced independent observer, "the one alternative radio station dating from Communist times, Radio 101, has been turned into a harmless music emitter".[98]

Other stations, outside the capital, have fared worse. The editor-in-chief at Radio Daruvar, who belonged to no political party, was sacked on 21 January 1992 at the instigation of HDZ members in the town council. He was notified that "the present situation in our municipality" as well as Croatia's recent recognition as an independent state meant that Radio Daruvar needed an editor-in-chief with "refined political and patriotic sensibilities and a Croatian heart".[99] It should be recalled that, by 21 January, Daruvar was about to become the chief Croatian-controlled town in the UN-protected 'Sector West' area.

Radio Čakovec has likewise suffered apparent discrimination. Blaženka Novak, director and editor-in-chief, was suspended and then dismissed at the urging of HDZ members in the station and its HDZ-controlled management committee, which itself had been installed at the insistence of the local HDZ-dominated authorities. Her successor is an HDZ member. The Čakovec Court later overturned her dismissal and she now works as a cultural journalist at the station.[100] Čakovec is in the Medjimurje region, where HDZ was outvoted in the 1993 elections. In March 1994, five private radio stations were shut down in Medjimurje.

At Radio Karlovac, and at the local paper, the municipal authorities cited nationality as the ground for purging staff.

---

[97] CIFE, supra note 40, and R Baretić, *Nedjeljna Dalmacija*, 6 Oct. 1993.

[98] Kuzmanović, supra note 7.

[99] Z Krstulović, *Slobodna Dalmacija*, 10 Feb. 1993.

[100] Croatian Helsinki Committee report, report on freedom of media in Croatia, dated 7 July 1993; Z Krstulović, *Slobodna Dalmacija*, 11 Feb. 1993; and CIFE, supra note 40.

The existing editorial office was accused of being pro-Serbian because more than 20 of the 30 employees were purportedly of Serbian nationality. [In autumn 1991] a decision was reached by the local authorities, without any consultation with [editorial] personnel, about changes in the status of the company. It was stated that in a municipality where, at the outbreak of war, the population comprised 70 per cent Croats and 19 per cent Serbs, it was unacceptable that the majority of journalists should consist of Serbs. They [journalists] were also accused of 'sniping at the fledgling Croatian authorities from positions incompatible with HDZ supremacy in the municipal council'.[101]

At Radio Rijeka, the director and seven journalists were removed. No reasons were given. One of the journalists, Vedrana Rudan, believes she was demoted and later sacked for criticizing President Tudjman on air. However, six of the dismissed journalists were of Serb nationality; the seventh was Italian.[102] A year later, early in 1994, three private radio stations were abruptly closed in the Rijeka area, confirming the local authorities' determination to control the airwaves.

At Radio Osijek, in the domain of Branimir Glavaš, 17 staff were suspended without explanation on 16 October 1991. The list of their names had been faxed from HRT in Zagreb the previous day. One of these was Djordje Ivković, a sports journalist of Serb nationality. Following his suspension, Ivković volunteered for the HV (Hrvatska Vojska, the Croatian Army). He spent a year in uniform, was demobilized, and found menial work in Osijek market. While he was in the army, Tomislav Marčinko (editor-in-chief of HTV news) had offered him future work at HTV. In July 1993, Ivković was still waiting for this offer to be confirmed, when his dismissal notice arrived from Vrdoljak, citing "troublesome behaviour" and mistakes when reporting football matches as reasons for dismissing

---

[101] CIFE, supra note 40.

[102] Z Krstulović, *Slobodna Dalmacija*, 1 Feb. 1993, and CIFE, supra note 40.

him from Radio Osijek. The disciplinary commission at the station had no record of any criticism or mistakes.[103]

Other stations have benefited because of their HDZ connections. Radio Pazin was allowed to use the powerful transmitter at Učka, against regulations, presumably because Pazin is the HDZ's base in Istria, an economically important region which regularly votes against the HDZ.[104] Also in Istria, the frequency in Labin was granted to a company "close to HDZ ... [and] at Buje [also in Istria] the frequency was given to a firm owned by relatives of President Tudjman.

At Opatija [also in Istria], 11 applications were made, ten of them local, when the municipality called for tenders. However, the application from Zagreb was chosen for proposal to the municipal assembly. The company is run by three top HTV officials, including Ksenija Urličić, one of HTV's editors-in-chief and the sister of the vice-president of the Croatian Parliament."[105]

In war areas, local radio was perhaps more important for morale than information. In Gospić, where the local radio station was destroyed in the fighting, the journalists broadcast "from the back of a truck, from cellars, from kitchens".[106] However, regarding the war, the most influential radio station in Croatia was probably Radio Knin, nerve-centre of the Serb rebellion from its earliest days. It doubled as the 'Krajina Ministry of Information', where the 'minister' broadcast to scattered Serb communities who didn't trust any other news medium in Croatia. As part of its service, Radio Knin advertised war-booty stolen from local Croats, for sale and auction.

---

[103] Drago Hedl, *Arkzin*, Sept. 1993.

[104] Croatian Helsinki Committee, supra note 100.

[105] European Civic Forum, *Human Rights in Croatia* (Basle, Switzerland: 30 Jan. 1993).

[106] *Novi list*, 20 Sept. 1993.

The Press

Croatia's national news press consists of a daily paper, the republic's flagship *Vjesnik*; an evening paper, *Večernji list*; two weekly newspapers, *Globus* and *Feral Tribune*; and a weekly news magazine, *Danas*. All are based in Zagreb, and only the weeklies *Globus* and *Feral Tribune* are fully independent of government control. The others are more or less directly subject to the influence of HDZ.

There are three substantial regional daily papers which are distributed across the republic: *Glas Slavonije* in eastern Croatia, *Novi list* in the north-west, and *Slobodna Dalmacija* in the south-west. There are also a dozen or more local papers, and a few specialist magazines with news content, such as the privately-owned *Arkzin*, published monthly by the Anti-War Campaign and, at the opposite end of the spectrum, *Hrvatski vojnik*, a glossy review of military matters published by the Ministry of Defence.

The Vjesnik Group

Before it was dismantled in 1992, the Vjesnik group was Croatia's biggest newspaper publishing and distribution business, enjoying a virtual monopoly. It published 18 newspapers and magazines including two national dailies, *Vjesnik* and *Večernji list*, and owned some 80 per cent of all outlets for printed media in Croatia.[107]

The government moved slowly. As the Vjesnik group was a public enterprise under the control of the Socialist Alliance of Working People (SAWP) until 1990, the ARD was able to appoint a management board to oversee privatization, which then appointed a new director of the group and several new editors-in-chief.[108] In summer 1992 the new director removed 128 senior staff, replacing them with 35 preferred others. More were sacked or suspended at the end of the year.[109] Only three

---

[107] L'Organisation Internationale des Journalistes, supra note 32 at 30.

[108] On the SAWP, see Glossary.

[109] *Index on Censorship*, March 1993.

publications survived ARD's intervention: *Vjesnik, Večernji list* and the magazine *Arena*.[110] All other Vjesnik titles were closed down.

The printing and distribution businesses were hived off under new names, Hrvatska tiskara and Tisak respectively, but each maintains a virtual monopoly in their business.[111] Both are government controlled and awaiting privatization.

Vjesnik was placed, transitionally, in the ARD's hands, giving the government, which controls some 65 per cent of the newspaper's shares, indirect editorial control. The management board appointed a new editor-in-chief at *Večernji list*, Branko Tudjen, whose columns rage against the independent media. The board privatized the paper as a shareholding company, with 86.9 per cent of shares going to government-controlled bodies: INA, the state oil and gas company, and the ARD itself (with 58 per cent).[112]

When asked how *Vjesnik* and *Večernji list* had become state property without any state investment, Deputy Premier Vladimir Seks was evasive. "*Vjesnik* is part of the Croatian tradition, some kind of symbol of Croatia. As far as I know, the state subsidized it several times, helping to stabilize it, because of its significance. I know too that the intention is for *Vjesnik* to become the newspaper close to the government."[113] This proximity has allowed the paper to run up a printing bill of some 1.5 million Deutschmarks.[114]

Ten years ago *Vjesnik*'s circulation stood at 91,000; today, independent observers put the sales figure as low as 10,000, although the paper claimed a circulation of 40,000 in 1993. Since 1990, it has had a

---

[110] Kuzmanović, supra note 7. The ruling party's opinion of the solitary surviving magazine, *Arena*, is worth quoting. In November 1991, when the politically-neutral *Arena* was preparing for privatization, the HDZ organ *Glasnik* wrote that "its articles are shameful. At this time, when we are all united in defence of our country, *Arena* must choose between committing itself to the interests of the homeland or changing its name to *Duga*."(CIFE, supra note 40.) The fortnightly *Duga* was a leading nationalist publication in Serbia.

[111] See section on '*Danas*' infra for an account of how the virtual monopoly on printing and distribution was used to bankrupt this independent publication.

[112] Figures from A Gavranović, President of the Croatian Journalists' Association, presented at the Zagreb free media conference, 25-26 Nov. 1993, supra note 15.

[113] CIFE, supra note 95.

[114] *Globus*, 25 Feb. 1994.

flurry of editors-in-chief. Soon after the elections, the incumbent Stevo Maoduša (a Serb by nationality) was ousted by "a group around Hido Biščević", who then took over as editor.[115] Biščević later became Ambassador to Turkey; his successor was attacked by the HDZ organ, *Glasnik*, and accused of "Yugonostalgia", a dire offence. The third, Radovan Stipetić, stayed just long enough to purge the well-regarded cultural section of the paper. Then came Božidar Petrać, an HDZ member of parliament and former adviser to President Tudjman, who was replaced by Krešimir Fijačko in summer 1993.[116]

The paper has improved under Fijačko, presumably attempting to claw back readers, and is marginally less tendentious than *Večernji list* or *Slobodna Dalmacija*. The readers' letters pages, for example, appeared less rigidly controlled than previously.[117] Yet articles translated from the foreign press are still bowdlerized to remove criticism of Croatia and, above all, of President Tudjman. In October 1993, Mira Ljubić-Lorger, a member of parliament and the president of the small, regional Dalmatinska Akcija Party in Dalmatia, was evicted from her flat in Split by 16 men in Croatian military uniforms. *Vjesnik*'s Split correspondent Milan Mudronja filed the following report: "She moved out of her own free will and with no physical force. ... The citizens of Split mostly think that it is difficult to find any objection to this displacement, whether from a political, moral or even human point of view." Although the report was exposed as false by the Prime Minister's statement on the affair, on 27 October 1993, *Vjesnik* did not publish a correction.[118]

Večernji list claimed to be Yugoslavia's highest-selling paper for the first half of 1990, just pipping its Serbian rival, *Večernje novosti*.[119] Since then, sales have roughly halved, to about 170,000, but it is still the best-selling newspaper in Croatia. Under Branko Tudjen's editorship, *Večernji list* has become a byword for unconditional loyalty to the HDZ government.

---

[115] P Tašić, *Kako je ubijena druga Jugoslavija*, (Skopje: AI, 1994), 197.

[116] CIFE, supra note 34.

[117] CIFE, supra note 87.

[118] CIFE, supra note 95.

[119] *Večernji list*, 24 Oct. 1990.

Vjesnik and Večernji list

The *Vjesnik* press coverage of Croat-Serb relations in 1990 was thoroughly one-sided but rarely extreme in tone or demands. When the Serb-controlled 'Krajina' declared the autonomy of Croatian Serbs on 1 October 1990, *Večernji list* reacted with the headline "Autonomy proclaimed", and ran an extract from the declaration, almost without commentary. *Vjesnik*'s report, headlined "Kninska Krajina boiling", was factual, reporting the referendum results and the Serb leader's press conference without much comment. Another report, "Lies about specials", presented the Ministry of the Interior's demands for freedom of movement in the area.[120]

By the time of the Plitvice incident, the tone had changed (see also section on 'Profile of Journalists' above). On 1 April 1991, *Večernji list* announced "Terrorists' rebellion is strangled"; far from being thwarted, the rebels' capture of Plitvice had been sealed by the JNA's intervention. Next day, the reporter described the "Great Serb terrorists' rebellion". *Vjesnik*'s headline on 1 April was "Firm action by MUP against terrorists and rebels: Peace and order restored in Plitvice". The report used both Tanjug and HINA bulletins. On 2 April, *Verčernji list*'s main headline was (falsely), "Plitvice under control of police station", which was consistent with HTV's coverage.

Coverage of Borovo Selo was more outspoken but still markedly contained. "Police attacked in ambush" announced *Vjesnik* neutrally on 3 May, using MUP and police sources to describe how police had fought "terrorists", "*četnik* terrorists", and "Serb terrorists".[121] The following day's edition carried Tanjug reports headlined "12 Specials killed", "Warning in blood", and "Police massacred". On 5 May headlines included: "Bitterness and sadness over bloodshed", "Slavonia in mourning", "Appeal for pride, not tears" and "Serbs must shun terrorists".

---

[120] The special police force, known as 'Specials', is under the direct authority of the Ministry of the Interior (Ministarstvo Unutrasno Poslova (MUP)).

[121] It was after Borovo Selo, where self-described *četniks* really were active (see also Ch. 3, section on 'Reporting on Borovo Selo' supra), that the term *četnik* became widely used in Croatian media to describe any Serb paramilitary, with or without the actual *četnik* insignia.

Večernji list claimed, improbably, that its reporter had been in Borovo Selo with the police. His piece, "In the terrorist nest", confirmed the official version of events. Another headline vowed "Croatia is strong enough, *četnik* hordes won't get through".

The same day that the Specials were shot in Borovo Selo, the port town of Zadar on the other side of the country was shaken by demonstrations against the local Serbs (10.5 per cent of the population), provoked by the death of a local policeman at the hands of rebels in nearby Serb-controlled territory.

Vjesnik's report was headlined "Serb shops smashed" and claimed demonstrators had shouted "NDH, NDH!", and "To battle, to battle!"[122] *Večernji list* reported that people from the dead policeman's village wanted weapons. The Split daily, *Slobodna Dalmacija*, within whose regional orbit Zadar lies, headlined another crowd slogan "We are all the Croatian army", and reported 16,000 demonstrators, two cafés destroyed, and a number of *Borba*'s kiosks wrecked.

On 4 May, under the headline "Flags at half mast", *Večernji list* reported that some 20 Serb-owned cafés and bars and a similar number of other properties were destroyed in Zadar. Serb children had stayed away from school, and some JNA officers at the local base had moved their families into barracks.

This book's author, Mark Thompson, visited Zadar, arriving in the early evening of 2 May, as this demonstration was winding down. The atmosphere was electric. A gang of teenage boys filed purposefully through the town centre, carrying iron bars, and demolishing one Serb-owned property after another. Smiling policemen posed with members of the gang for a foreign news photographer. That night, road-blocks around the town were manned by groups of local men armed with hunting rifles and table legs. People spoke in slogans: "I have fought the [Communist] star with the cross all my life", "We've waited a thousand years for this, and the moment is now very close." Way after midnight, the author visited the local HDZ headquarters where he was told that the HDZ had organized the wrecking gang.

---

[122] These are nationalist slogans: "NDH" means Nezavisna Država Hrvatska, the *ustaša*-run Nazi puppet statelet of 1941-1945. "To battle, to battle for your people!" is an aria from a famous patriotic opera.

The Croatian press did not investigate the story. The estimated number of 'demonstrators' was hugely exaggerated, and the deliberate nature of the wrecking was not even mentioned; nor was the complicity of the police.

Serbian press coverage was identically misleading. "Zadar — devastated town" declared *Politika ekspres* on 3 May, reporting looting (which certainly happened, though unreported by the Croatian press). On 4 May *Borba* claimed "Destruction of Serb property", reporting 15,000 people on the rampage, only prevented by the militia from ransacking JNA officers' flats. The operation appeared controlled from start to finish; the notion that those men wanted to take on the JNA is altogether far-fetched.

The result was that both sets of newspapers collaborated to give the strong impression that thousands of Croats had arisen and acted as one. This nationalist fantasy of spontaneous, collective will suited only the élites and warmongers in both countries.

Coverage of War in Croatia

Along with other printed media, the Vjesnik papers helped to shape the official version of the conflict as pure aggression against Croatia. Analyzing these two dailies as well as the weeklies *Globus* and *Danas*, from August 1991 to January 1992, Marijan Malešić and his team found the basic definition of the war to be that "it is a 'defensive' war which Croatia is forced to fight to protect her territorial integrity. Therefore, Croatia is under attack and is defending herself, while Serbia is the aggressor, and is attacking."[123] This axiom has been perpetuated in coverage of the very different war in Bosnia. The words 'defence' and 'aggression' were the twin poles of media representation, as they were on the Serb side: having proclaimed their 'autonomous', soon-to-be 'independent' territories in Croatia and later in Bosnia, enemy actions could be defined as aggression against defenders who were protecting their homes. Linguistically, the two sides were identical in this respect.

Regarding actual combat, the analysts noted that attack and destruction were the key media concepts in Croatia. Destructiveness was alleged in three respects, of diminishing intensity: that Croatia itself was being destroyed; that 'symbols of national culture' were being destroyed

---

[123] Malešić, supra note 70 at 51.

(so emphasizing "the barbarity of the aggressor and his lack of culture [and] the history of destruction suffered by Croatian culture"); and that homes ('hearths') were being destroyed and plundered.[124]

Regarding the other side, the analysts found that terms like 'aggressors', 'extremists', 'occupying forces' and 'terrorists' vied in popularity with the term JNA and its derivatives: the Yugoslav Army, the army, the Yugo-army, and Yugo-soldiery. In third place came specifically nationalist terms: Serbs, Serbia, Serbian Communists, *četniki*, *Martićevci*, *Arkanovci*, and such like.[125] The intention was to seal forever the association in people's minds between Yugoslavia and aggression against Croatia. Consequently Yugoslavia as a still-existing state was hardly mentioned at all.

Since the war was frozen by international agreement in January 1992, the Vjesnik press has carried on with the same framework of interpretation. It is almost never reported that Serb-controlled areas are routinely bombarded and attacked by the Croatian Army.[126] On at least one occasion, in mid-September 1993, an Army statement claimed that "Serb extremists" had bombarded Knin themselves, to paint Croats as aggressors (a leaf taken straight from the Bosnian Serbs' propaganda manual).

To date, the HV has made two major incursions into Serb-occupied territory, the smaller of these being the raid south of Gospić, on 9 September 1993. Before withdrawing, Croatian forces killed inhabitants and destroyed livestock, dwellings and other property. UNPROFOR troops who moved into the area upon the Croatian withdrawal found 67 corpses. A further 25 people were missing. Most of the victims were civilians.[127]

Coverage of the massacre did not appear in *Vjesnik* until 13 September when the paper claimed that "Serb criminals" attack Croatian towns. On its back page, buried in a report about the Defence and National Security Council, was a single sentence: "In a limited action in the vicinity

---

[124] Id. at 53.

[125] Id. at 75. Milan Martić was the police chief in Knin. Arkan is the sobriquet of Željko Ražnatović, a Belgrade criminal who heads a paramilitary organization.

[126] The CIFE says that *Vjesnik* published, on 21 May 1993, the complete text of the UN Secretary-General's report to the Security Council about the future of the UN operation in Croatia. This report referred to the long-range bombardment of Benkovac, Obrovac and Kistanje in Serb-occupied territory.

[127] UNCHR, supra note 35 at 14.

of Gospić on 9 September, Croatian forces neutralized the infiltrating groups and liberated the areas south-east of Gospić from which the town was directly threatened." The atrocities of the 'liberators' were not mentioned.

On 1 October, the UNCHR Special Rapporteur advised the Croatian government that the HV attack had violated international law, and requested a full investigation. Replying on 9 October, Foreign Minister Granić said the government's own preliminary findings were that "persons killed in the action", including the elderly, "were all killed in combat".[128]

Coverage of War in Bosnia

The test of Croatian media objectivity in reporting Bosnia has been, above all, its presentation of the Croatian side, in both political and military aspects, since concerted fighting between the HVO (Croat forces in Bosnia) and the ABH (the Bosnian Army) began in mid-January 1993.[129]

Few texts containing criticism of the extreme nationalism of the 'Herceg-Bosna' leadership, of the HVO, or of Zagreb's support for both of these, have appeared in the Vjesnik papers.[130] The government's insistence that HV forces were not active in Bosnia, which has been exposed as a falsehood by foreign journalists, has gone unquestioned.

According to the CIFE monitors, the Croatian public did not learn officially that Croatian forces had also committed crimes in Bosnia until 3 May 1993, when President Tudjman unexpectedly half-conceded as much, during a press conference: "Crimes against Muslims were committed in Vitez, and by people who wore black uniforms and *ustaša* symbols from the Second World War, indicating that Croats were supposed to be blamed." This tortuously-coded admission drew no

---

[128] Id. at 16.

[129] Armija Bosne i Hercegovine (ABH, the Army of Bosnia-Hercegovina).

[130] Four such texts have come to ARTICLE 19's notice, two each in *Vjesnik* (4 April and 17 May 1993) and *Večernji list* (May 1993; the article is quoted in *67 Bosnia Briefing*, 26 May 1993; and 28 July 1993).

comment in the loyal media.[131] When the UNCHR Special Rapporteur's reports present evidence of Croat misdeeds, the press ignore them.[132]

Like HTV reports, press reports from Bosnia are typically confused and confusing, ignoring the difference between fact and suggestion, information and message, and turning everything into commentary. The press has dehumanized the Bosnian Muslims *in toto* more extensively than it ever did the Serbs. On 12 August 1993, *Večernji list* carried news of the killing of nine Muslims near Tomislavgrad, in Croat-controlled Hercegovina, on the night of 10/11 August. The positioning of the report was highly prejudicial: it was surrounded by other articles with the headlines "Muslims wound seven children" and "New Muslim forces to central Bosnia", and by a photograph of HVO soldiers praying over a comrade's grave.[133] Nevertheless, the news was printed.

The following day, however, the paper carried a piece by Slobodan Lovrenović, an adviser to the HVO leadership. It is very difficult to prevent such crimes as the Tomislavgrad killings, Lovrenović warned. "Cold analysis shows that the crime was really to be expected. The only question was where and when? ... The reasons for revenge are many, never mind how un-Christian it may be, one has to say that it is difficult to stop." He concluded that President Izetbegović's politics were responsible for the nine deaths, because Muslim victims are "a necessary part of the hellish plan for an Islamic Bosnia-Hercegovina".[134]

---

[131] CIFE, supra note 65. On 3 May 1993, perhaps more than on any other day, the Vance-Owen Plan for Bosnia (which President Tudjman and his proxies in 'Herceg-Bosna' wanted very much to be implemented) seemed about to be accepted by the Bosnian Serbs. The Bosnian Serb leader had signed the plan on 2 May; on 5 May, the Bosnia Serb 'assembly' would vote on it. The moment was right for Tudjman to appear conciliatory.

[132] V Ivančić, *2 Erasmus* (Zagreb: 1993). However, the CIFE report for May 1993 mentions that the Special Rapporteur's words about 'ethnic cleansing' of Muslim civilians by Croat as well as by Serb forces were twice reported in brief HINA bulletins during May 1993.

[133] Id.

[134] Id., and G Malić, *Feral Tribune*, 7 Sept. 1993.

The Regional Press

Slobodna Dalmacija

Slobodna Dalmacija is the biggest of Croatia's three regional daily papers. It has its own printing works and distribution network. While the national dailies were losing readers, *Slobodna Dalmacija* gained them, rising to 100,000 in 1990-1992. It was not aligned with any opposition party and, like the weekly *Danas*, it was targeted by the HDZ from the outset. It was the only paper to which President Tudjman did not vouchsafe an interview.[135] Its sister paper, the weekly *Nedjeljna Dalmacija,* had a more nationalist editorial concept, except for an adventurous cultural supplement called "Profil".[136]

Slobodna Dalmacija's coverage of deteriorating Croat-Serb relations was cautious and rather bemused, like the national papers. Its correspondent in Knin was a Serb who supplied solid, informative reports. When the massacre at Borovo Selo occurred, however, the paper lost its impartial tone. Headlines on 5 May 1991 included: "Beasts in human form", "Bearded animals on two legs", and "Bloodsuckers". Two days later it published photographs of the victims, and readers learned that "*Securitate* agents killed MUP police" (implying that Romanian assassins were involved, which seems unlikely).[137]

During the war in Croatia, *Slobodna Dalmacija* supported the government's war strategies but included sceptical queries about national goals and means. The war in Bosnia magnified the paper's editorial difference from other media. While it was certainly not always critical of Croatian policy in Bosnia the paper was not automatically uncritical, as other Croatian media. Nor did it usually intone the standard suspicions of the Bosnian government and abuse for its army.

Slobodna Dalmacija had transformed itself in 1990, under the federal legislation of 1989, into a shareholding company controlled by the employees who held 60 per cent of the shares. In October 1992, the ARD moved against the paper, claiming that the original transformation was an

---

[135] V Ivančić, "Un-Free Dalmatia", *Balkan War Report*, Feb./March 1993.

[136] The "Profil" supplement in *Nedjeljna Dalmacija* was stopped in Nov. 1993.

[137] Romanians have been freely slandered in both sides' propaganda.

illegal misappropriation of public property. A management board was appointed to protect public funds and property while facilitating the change of ownership. At its first meeting, on 2 October, the board promised not to change the editorial board, the staff, or the editorial policy. Nevertheless, during this meeting, the director of the paper was dismissed. The board instructed his replacement to amend the paper's contents ("please make sure that the next issue contains fair and honest reports. The truth as distorted by some individuals can't have space in our paper.").[138] The board also demanded that the paper's masthead be changed from (Communist) red to blue. The staff resisted these changes and international pressure was exerted on President Tudjman. There was an ill-tempered stalemate.

The ARD changed tack. The company's shares were revalued, lowering the staff-controlled portion to 24 per cent. In a highly irregular move, financial liabilities owed by the paper to Splitska Banka (The Bank of Split) were converted into a 42 per cent shareholding. Remaining capital was transferred to the Privatization Fund. Loans were arranged from state-controlled banks for approved members of staff and others to acquire extra shares.

By March 1993, 60-70 per cent of shares were held by state-controlled institutions. A strike was called, and received 80 per cent staff support. The new array of shareholders supported the management board, which replaced the editor-in-chief; the paper had been seized. The new proprietor is Miroslav Kutle, an entrepreneur from Hercegovina and an HDZ member who, *Globus* alleged, benefited from the extraordinary bank loans in order to buy Splitska Banka's 42 per cent of the share stock for 3.7 million Deutschmarks, a transaction which took place outside the stock market. With an additional 9 per cent which he bought on the stock market, Kutle then had a controlling interest.[139] Kutle's brother is a high-ranking HDZ member of parliament. Two members of the management board sit on Kutle's board of directors.

Throughout this struggle, HDZ officials and the government-controlled media were attacking and undermining *Slobodna Dalmacija*.

---

[138] "Chronological Overview of Developments Relating to the Privatization of '*Slobodna Dalmacija* — Novine D.D.'", a paper produced for the Information Department of the Croatian Ministry of Foreign Affairs. The instruction to the new director is quoted in 73 *CADDY Bulletin*, (New York: Nov. 1992).

[139] *Globus*, 15 Oct. 1993. No denial was issued.

HTV took the lead, trying to discredit the paper with reports about alleged scandals.[140]

One motive for acquiring *Slobodna Dalmacija* was economic: the paper's lucrative foreign sales made it a tempting target. Another motive was the paper's somewhat dissenting outlook on the war, of which examples have been given earlier in this chapter. Contributors who were most critical of Croatia's role in Bosnia, such as Jelena Lovrić and Ivan Zvonimir Čičak (themselves refugees from the seized weekly *Danas*), have not written for *Slobodna Dalmacija* since its takeover.

The differences between *Slobodna Dalmacija*'s view of the war and the consensus shaped by HRT, HINA and the two national dailies may appear slight as well as marginal, within the total volume of Croatian news output. However, it was targeted by the government because of its coverage. As evidence of the link between the paper's outlook and its fate at the government's hands, several incidents recorded by Helsinki Watch indicate that *Slobodna Dalmacija* was singled out for harassment by Croatian forces in Bosnia, months before the HDZ's first attempt to wrest control of the paper.

> On 28 April [1992], Zeljko Magajnić, a reporter for
> ... *Slobodna Dalmacija*, was beaten by three men in
> fatigues, presumably members of the HVO, in Livno
> in western Hercegovina [that is, inside
> 'Herceg-Bosna']. ... Between 22 and 28 April,
> Magajnić and Boris Dežulović, both reporters for
> *Slobodna Dalmacija*, were verbally harassed, were
> denied travel permits, and had their movements
> restricted by the military headquarters in Livno or by
> individual HVO soldiers in the area. Reporters for the
> Croatian government-controlled television station did
> not face such obstacles or harassment and were given
> ready access to the front lines.

---

[140] CIFE, supra note 40 and Ivančić, supra note 135.

The reason given for this harassment was that *Slobodna Dalmacija* had printed photographs which disclosed HVO military positions. The photographs contained no such information.[141]

Since the paper was re-privatized in March 1993, its coverage about Bosnia has included occasional criticism. Typical of its reportage and commentary, however, is this 5 August 1993 headline, "Yelling 'Allahu Akbar!' and 'Jihad!', the Muslim army is continuing its attack on centuries-old Croatian areas". One of its new regular contributors from Bosnia is Veso Vegar, a spokesman for the HVO and an author of its official statements.[142] Indeed, even by government-controlled media standards, its coverage has been exceptionally vicious toward the Bosnian Muslims. Before the March 1994 cease-fire, they and the ABH were identified en masse as "Muslim aggressors, criminals, hordes, extremists, *mujahedin*, Islamic fundamentalists, Ottomans ... ."[143]

Novi list

Novi list is a daily paper published in Rijeka for Croatia's northern littoral region. It has managed to sustain circulation and, during 1993, it was selling some 50,000 copies. This can be credited both to its rivals' decline in quality and to its own success in keeping the HDZ at bay, largely because of astute management and workers' solidarity.

In 1992 the management and staff applied to buy out the business, on the regular model of privatization. The government intervened in the usual way when it wants to control a medium where the HDZ does not dominate the local council. The ARD imposed a management board on *Novi list*, whose president was an assistant to the Minister of Internal Affairs.

The reaction was decisive. The staff protested loudly, appealing to public opinion and demanding a legal judgment on the ARD's "unlawful" action. Journalists who agreed to join the management board were suspended by the director of the company.

---

[141] Helsinki Watch, *War Crimes in Bosnia-Hercegovina*. A Helsinki Watch Report (New York: Human Rights Watch, Aug. 1992), 129-130.

[142] Cited by V Ivančić, *3 Erasmus*, (Zagreb).

[143] V Roller, formerly with *Slobodna Dalmacija*, writing in *Vreme*, 20 Sept. 1993.

In February 1993, the company was given the go-ahead to buy 97.6 per cent of stock. However, the ARD has the right to examine privatized companies periodically during the first three years. By the end of 1993, *Novi list* had already undergone five examinations, but the ARD could find no pretext to intervene again.[144] Assuming the ARD continues to scrutinize in vain, the paper's main problem is its antiquated machinery, such as its 70-year-old hot metal presses.

However, if the HDZ had really wanted control of *Novi list*, it would have succeeded. The reason it abandoned the attempt may have been the editors' canny restraint; they kept the paper regional, instead of seeking a national role as *Slobodna Dalmacija* had done. Within a regional brief, however, the editors and reporters have shown much quiet courage, an outstanding example of which was an article on 14 October 1992, by a young journalist called Dražen Herljević.

Under the headline "Veterans from Lika can't be traitors", Herljević reported a protest meeting in Rijeka, called by reserve soldiers and their families. These soldiers had been serving with the 111th HV brigade in eastern Croatia, when the brigade was asked to fight in Bosnia. Thirty-four reservists from the Rijeka region refused, on the ground that Bosnia was a separate state. These men were disarmed, threatened with deprivation of citizenship and with dismissal from their civilian jobs, and abandoned in a village. That night, the HV sent up more than 500 flares to show the village's position to the enemy. The men made their way back to Rijeka. Some went into hiding; others were sent back to the front. The HV claimed they were traitors.

In his article, Herljević takes the soldiers' side, covering himself by citing public demand for the truth about this "delicate matter". Herljević told ARTICLE 19 that an army officer had taken him aside at the protest meeting and told him that he must not write about this issue. He decided to write the piece anyway; there were no reactions to it, and no other medium picked up the story.

Not until January 1994 did the UN Security Council officially declare that the HV was in Bosnia. The Croatian government has still not admitted that HV forces fought in Bosnia. In a healthier media climate,

---

[144] CIFE, supra note 40; 19 *Balkan War Report*, April/May 1993; G Grbić to author, 3 Sept. 1993.

Novi list's story in October 1992 would have been enough to expose the official lies.

Glas Slavonije

The third major regional daily is *Glas Slavonije*, published in the eastern capital of Osijek with a circulation of 15,000 copies in 1993. Its editors were at odds with the municipal authorities, led by the HDZ and hardliner Branimir Glavaš.[145] As tensions rose in eastern Slavonia, throughout the spring of 1991, the authorities moved to take control of the paper. They ran a campaign of denunciation against *Glas Slavonije*, even forcing the editor-in-chief, Drago Hedl, to print an advertisement, paid for by the HDZ, calling on readers to boycott the paper.

Glavaš urged the ARD to impose a management board on the paper, which they did in June. Glavaš himself was appointed to head the board, and the director of the company was dismissed. The Workers' Council, a vestige from socialist times which formally managed the company, was suspended.

Hedl and the entire editorial board protested by handing in their resignations. Hedl later wrote, "a large part of the staff has been subjected to all manner of threats and pressures, including death threats". Hedl and the dismissed director were briefly drafted into the army. The intimidation culminated with an extraordinary show of force by Glavaš. On 26 July, he entered the newspaper's offices in full battle gear, escorted by ten armed soldiers. (He had arranged for the episode to be recorded by video camera.) All editorial staff were sacked. With the ARD's help, ownership of the paper duly passed to the National Stock Association.[146]

---

[145] On Glavaš, see also sections on 'Media, War and the Political Leaders' and 'Profile of Journalists' supra.

[146] CIFE, supra note 40, and CIFE, supra note 34. For more on the NSA, see section on 'Regional and Local Television' supra.

The Weekly Press

Slobodni tijednik and *Globus*

A feature of Croatian journalism since 1990 has been the role of two privately-owned political tabloid weeklies, *Slobodni tijednik* (known as *ST*) and *Globus*. As new media these papers could not be bridled from inside, by changing executives and editors or imposing management boards.

Their editorial recipe is familiar in Western Europe, and in Eastern Europe too since the fall of Communism: tongue-in-cheek banner headlines, political scandal, 'exclusive' exposés, gossipy profiles, photo-features, lightly-clad female models, demagogic editorials — flag-waving nationalism and noisy stabs at the ruling party, reactionary moralizing and gadfly cheek, servile and uppity at the same time.

ST and *Globus* boomed before and during the war. *ST* depended to a large extent on the charisma of its owner and editor-in-chief, Marinko Božić. Eventually, Božić's egotistical ways drove his better journalists to leave. Sales sank; Božić's health collapsed. The paper's old readership could not be won back; it tried turning serious, but no new readership was found. It eventually closed down in autumn 1993. *Globus*, however, has achieved some such shift.

Their success in 1990 and 1991 reflected conditions at the time. These papers were warmongering, issuing extreme demands, supporting Croatian expansionism in Bosnia, and whipping up hatred and fear in the name of patriotism. They exacerbated the media language of politics, by radicalizing every issue and scorning compromise. They actively encouraged vigilantism against individual citizens, mostly Serbs (sometimes identified with photographs, addresses, telephone numbers); they hounded people who questioned Croatia's purpose in the war; they ran fake photographs of real atrocities. When *ST* published the first story in Croatia about raped Muslim women in Bosnia, for instance, in July 1992, it illustrated the text with stills from a German violent pornographic film, without acknowledgement, implying they were images from Bosnia.

ST's extremist language was demonstrated in a rabid attack on a local journalist who had defected to Belgrade. Mila Štula was called "a great whore", "a sexually frustrated Serb woman", an "illiterate" who used her vaginal secretions for ink.[147]

ST listed the names of the editors of Serb nationality at *Glas Slavonije* newspaper, accusing them of being JNA counter-intelligence agents (a favourite and very dangerous smear).[148] *Globus* published an attack on five female writers and journalists who had criticized Croatian nationalism and the HDZ. "Croatia's feminists rape Croatia!" was the title of the anonymous piece, in the issue of 10 December 1992.[149] These writers were somewhat protected, at least, by their reputations and connections.

Both papers also attacked people with no such defence. On 29 June 1991, *ST* ran a piece called "KOS vampires are ready!" The strapline gave the gist, "Sisak: names of 14 apostles of evil". The article named 14 Serb inhabitants of the central Croatian town of Sisak, which had a 23 per cent Serb population before the war. The acronym KOS (Kontra Obavještajna Služba, the Yugoslav military counter-intelligence service) had long been used by Croats, Slovenes, Albanians and others as shorthand for Serb-dominated state terrorism.

The list of 14 alleged agents gave the men's names, employment (10 were retired policemen), with a few words of biography and, for some, their addresses and telephone numbers. In the weeks following the *ST* article's appearance, nine of the 14 Serbs were abducted by men wearing National Guard uniforms. Five of the nine were released; the corpses of three were recovered. The ninth, Dragan Rajšić, is still missing. All enquiries on behalf of the abducted and murdered men have come to nought and no charges have been brought against their abductors.

In *Globus*, Tanja Torbarina often uses her column to attack other, insufficiently 'patriotic' journalists. On 1 May 1992, she named Milan Jakšić, a Croatian Serb by nationality who had been suspended by *Vjesnik* and found employment as a correspondent for the Serbian daily, *Politika*. Torbarina insinuated, without providing any evidence, that Jakšić

---

[147] *ST*, 20 April 1991. Cited by V Kesić, *Danas*, 30 April 1991.

[148] *ST*, 28 June 1991. The timing indicates that *ST* was supporting an HDZ-led campaign to discredit the Slavonian paper. See section on *'Glas Slavonije'* supra.

[149] The campaign initiated by this instantly notorious attack generated remarkable quantities of rancid, misogynistic polemic. The five writers are suing *Globus*. One has been awarded damages of 19,000 Deutschmarks and the others' case is pending.

sympathized with Serb rebels in occupied Croatia. On 10 June, a bomb detonated in Jakšič's car outside his home.

Marinko Božić, *ST*'s owner, was given to such avowals, in his editorials, as "I am ready to be crucified for Croatia like Jesus on the Cross."[150] In summer and autumn 1991, *ST*'s recipe of "raw Croatian populist radicalism and 'neo-bolshevism', particularly intolerant towards anyone with different political views" had made it the most popular and influential paper in the country.[151]

Then Božić overreached: he took up the cause of Vukovar, attempting to exploit the gap between the government's careful screening of news from the besieged town and the public's hunger to know what was really happening. On 7 November, less than a fortnight before the town fell, he asked a dangerous question: "In whose interest mostly is it to hide the truth that weapons aren't reaching Vukovar any longer? At noon today they assured me at the Ministry of Defence that weapons are being sent from Zagreb ... ." A few weeks later, on 8 January 1992, *ST* printed a telephone conversation between President Tudjman and Mile Dedaković-Jastreb, the military commander at Vukovar. According to *ST*'s transcription, the President promised Jastreb that weapons would be delivered; *ST* implied that the deliveries were never made.[152]

The government banned this issue of *ST* under the old Federal Law on Public Information (1985) which gave the Minister of Information the right to ban media for revealing military secrets. Minister Salaj claimed that the Tudjman-Jastreb transcript was a military secret. He also prevented *ST* from appealing against the ban by citing a Presidential decree enacted in 1991 which, he claimed, authorized the banning of media in wartime without a right of appeal. *ST*'s lawyers filed a petition challenging the legality of the denial of a right of appeal but the Public Prosecutor did not respond. The banning of the weekly appears to have been a reprisal for its support for Jastreb, rather than for any genuine national security concerns since the information was already in the public domain. *ST* had published the transcript in a previous issue, as had another paper, *Nedjeljna Dalmacija*, without attracting any prosecution. The manner in which the

---

[150] *ST*, 8 June 1991.

[151] D Hudelist, *Novinari pod šljemom: O nekim tendencijama u hrvatskom novinarstvu za obambrene rata 1991/92*, (Zagreb: Globus Books, 1992).

[152] See Helsinki Watch, supra note 141 at 347.

newspaper was confiscated also indicated that the banning had been well organized. The issue was seized from news kiosks across the country within two hours of *ST* receiving the prosecution document from the Ministry of Information. According to *ST*'s lawyer, the speed was suspicious because "post-publication bans used to take two days to implement in former Yugoslavia."

Globus is a more complex phenomenon. It has a running feud with certain leaders in the HDZ, especially those who control the media. Antun Vrdoljak, director-general of HRT, is a favourite butt. It has also investigated top-level corruption scandals involving HDZ leaders. During 1993 it changed its attitude to Bosnia, covering stories which the state media ignored. For instance, *Globus* published the UNCHR report of 21 May (with its information about the massacre of Muslims by HVO at Ahmići) and the Croatian Primate's criticism of Croatian policy in Bosnia. It has been able to maintain its circulation at around 170,000 weekly.[153] At the end of 1993, it caused a sensation by publishing a leaked Ministry of the Interior document about the alleged criminal activity in 1991 of forces led by Tomislav Merčep, a prominent HDZ personality and advisor to the Minister of Defence. Merčep's lawyer has sued for defamation, demanding huge damages of 800,000 Deutschmarks.

Danas

The weekly *Danas* was one of those publications, like *Vreme* in Serbia or *Oslobodjenje* in besieged Sarajevo, which became symbols of independence in dark times. During the 1980s, *Danas* was far bolder in its criticism of Serbian nationalism than other Croatian media. While it was more cautious about democratization, *Danas* alone, according to Danko Plevnik, "did much more for the transformation [from communism to pluralism in Croatia] than those meaningless, endless meetings of Croatian Communists from the party cells right up to the central committee".[154]

The HDZ had targeted *Danas* from the start. In their view, it was "Croatia's foremost guilty publication";[155] guilty, that is, of being anti-Croatian, 'Yugo-unitarist', 'Yugonostalgic', for being a newspaper

---

[153] According to CIFE, supra note 65.

[154] D Plevnik, *Slobodna Dalmacija*, 8 Jan. 1993.

[155] I Z Čičak's phrase, *Danas*, 23 July 1991.

which stood on the sidelines and comments, rather than being politically 'engaged' in the war.

Nothing proved more clearly than the persecution of *Danas* that Franjo Tudjman and his party had no intention of allowing and defending freedom of expression in post-Communist Croatia. For it was *Danas* that "opposed especially, from the beginning to the very end, the authoritarianism of Slobodan Milošević".[156] As far back as 1989, the League of Communists of Croatia denounced the paper for an attack on Milošević.[157]

By June 1991 the ARD had used the magazine's financial difficulties as a pretext to impose a management board at *Danas*. In August the government tried to stop publication on the ground that the company was bankrupt. The courts rejected this. The HDZ stepped up its attacks through its party organ, *Glasnik*. The management board stalled the process of privatization for some six months, violating the legal term within which it was obliged to declare itself on the concept of transformation.

Meanwhile the war was cutting circulation in its own way. Then HTV refused to take *Danas*'s advertising, and the Vjesnik group refused to print or distribute it. "Of the 3,000 newspaper kiosks in Zagreb, only seven would handle the paper. There were mountains of unsold copies. In Istria and Dalmatia circulation dropped by as much as 60-70 per cent."[158] By mid-1992, the magazine was bankrupt. A private entrepreneur bought it and launched it as *Novi Danas* (the name was changed for legal reasons) with the same staff and the same editorial views.

Vjesnik's near monopoly of distribution was used again, to convince the new proprietor that *Novi Danas* was not viable. The Vjesnik group simply banned the magazine from its kiosks (a patently political decision, given that "the first two issues had sold very well").[159] "In the two months of *Novi Danas* we changed office three times", recalls journalist Maja Razović. "They would cut off our electricity and our phone. But the only thing we couldn't deal with was Vjesnik telling us they wouldn't

---

[156] Plevnik, supra note 154.

[157] G Grbić to author, 3 Sept. 1993.

[158] CIFE, supra note 40.

[159] A Lisinski, *Novi Danas*, 31 Aug. 1992.

distribute us."[160] The entrepreneur admitted defeat after half a dozen issues.

The title was sold to a pro-HDZ entrepreneur, Boris Ivan Peko. In December 1992, he relaunched the title, with the same design, as a nationalist publication. Not much need be said about the third *Danas*. Being so close to power, it has been able to attract large quantities of advertising and to disdain printer's bills: "It is an open secret that *Danas* has not paid a single dinar of its printing costs" to Hrvatska tiskara.[161] By February 1994, these costs ran to more than 1 million Deutschmarks.[162] Sales reputedly are under 10,000 copies. (In the late 1980s, *Danas* sold 100,000 weekly.) On Bosnia, the litmus test, the "basic editorial attitude" criticizes the Bosnian government and supports Croatia's backing for the HVO and Herceg-Bosna.[163]

More interesting for this report is how the war in Croatia undermined the old *Danas'* approach to the conflict. This approach, pursuing objectivity against the torrent of competing mutual accusations, grew out of an analysis reaching back several years, which identified responsibility for Yugoslavia's crisis on both sides, and supported Yugoslavia's evolution into a confederal state and Ante Marković's economic reforms. In August 1991, *Danas* was still taking

> an 'objective' stand in its war reports, quoting losses and violations of human rights on both sides in the conflict. However, following massacres carried out by the JNA and Serbian reservists in a number of Croatian villages, *Danas* distanced itself from its previous approach. ... It can be said that ... after the fall of Vukovar ... one can no longer speak of the existence of any 'opposition opinion' [in Croatian media] to the war.[164]

The 'Vukovar Effect', again.

---

[160] M Razović to author, 31 Oct. 1993.

[161] M Marković, *Slobodna Dalmacija*, 28 June 1993.

[162] *Globus*, 25 Feb. 1994.

[163] CIFE's analysis of the first 15 issues of the new *Danas*, supra note 65.

[164] Malešić, supra note 70 at 443.

Feral Tribune

Until March 1993, "Feral Tribune" was a weekly satirical feature in *Slobodna Dalmacija*. Its three authors selected some political event from the previous week and satirized it with photomontages, huge headlines, and wordplay. The HDZ's blunders and President Tudjman's pomposity made ideal targets for "Feral Tribune". The three satirists were charged, in February 1992, by the public prosecutor with insulting the President of the Republic; the case never came to court.

When the government gained control of *Slobodna Dalmacija* in March 1993, the three satirists (who are also news journalists) took their title and registered it as a separate publication. On 1 June *Feral Tribune* appeared in a format new to former Yugoslavia: a fortnightly newspaper of two parts, one satirical as before, the other with news items, cultural reports, columns and interviews. This, the serious section, carries news which cannot be found in other media, and views which are otherwise unpublishable. In 1994, *Feral Tribune* became a weekly.

The new management of *Slobodna Dalmacija* tried and failed to stop the three founders from using the title. It also refused to sell the new fortnightly in its kiosks. The Tisak kiosks carry it, however, and it manages to sell 40,000 copies. The Ministry of Culture and Education refused to exempt the new newspaper from heavy taxes, for example on imported newsprint, which are not levied on the rest of the press except the pornographic weekly *Erotika*.

A serious case of harassment against *Feral Tribune* occurred on 5 January 1994, when editor-in-chief Viktor Ivančić was taken by police to the military barracks in Split, and charged with failing to respect a draft notice served on 31 December 1993. The notice, which was unsigned and served only three days after Ivančić had received Croatian citizenship, clearly was politically motivated. Ivančić had repeatedly criticized Croatian policy toward Bosnia and recent issues of *Feral Tribune* had publicized military misdeeds in Split. Throughout the second half of December, Croats from Bosnia were being drafted to fight with the beleaguered HVO in central Bosnia (Ivančić was born in Sarajevo). It is the first case of the use of a draft notice against a serving editor-in-chief in Croatia, although the tactic was employed previously in summer 1991 when Drago Hedl was briefly drafted into the army after his forced resignation as editor-in-chief of *Glas Slavonije*.

Conclusions

*   In 1991 Croatia's government was driven by its ambition for independence from Yugoslavia to risk everything. The government declared Croatia's "dissociation" from Yugoslavia without means to defend the country and its people. Finding itself engaged in war and hugely outgunned, it was resolved to press forward, trying to hold its own on the battlefield while suing the European Community for support (in the form of recognition). The government wanted to inspire the people to resist, but without demoralizing them by showing them how badly Croatia was faring. (By early September 1991, even the government admitted that a third of the republic was in Serb-JNA hands.) For their part, the media were still partly bewildered by events. Hence the vacillation in media coverage of war, which gave the privately-owned weeklies a lucrative monopoly on shock-horror photo-stories of devastation, especially in July and August.

*   The government's authoritarian hostility to independent media predates the overt military threat to Croatia. (The latter became clear only in January 1991.) This hostility was shown by its treatment of the radio-television network, of Tanjug, and of the Vjesnik group, and other abuses of the mechanism of privatization. It is this abuse, exploiting government-controlled funds to create a façade of private companies, which represents the closest continuity with the methods of Yugoslav 'self-management socialism' (preserving one-party power by dissembling it into an assortment of supposedly independent institutions).

*   War enabled the government to tighten its grip on news and media. It produced emotionally heightened situations in which it was easier to advance propaganda, disinformation and lies, and more difficult for its audience to distinguish lies from truth, commentary from fact. It gave a pretext for the enactment of Presidential decrees and the use of old federal legal provisions against the media, in the name of national security. (These decrees could be abused, and were: the famous case of *ST*, which was banned for printing the Tudjman-Jastreb conversation a month-and-a-half after the fall of Vukovar.) The war added to the insidious pressure upon journalists to censor themselves, 'for the sake of the people', though the beneficiary was the government, not the people.

* It was the HDZ policy toward Bosnia (a policy of ambiguous support for the government, later turned into aggression) which triggered the most repressive and manipulative treatment of media in Croatia. This is logical. The support for the Bosnian government was insincere, so the government did not want the truth to be told about it; then the land-grab in central Bosnia and concomitant 'ethnic cleansing' of non-Croats, in 1993, were unprovoked and barbarous, so again the government did not want the truth to be told. It was not a coincidence that the policy toward Bosnia has been championed by the same groupings ('the Hercegovina lobby') and individuals (Tudjman and the radical tendency in HDZ) which have been most hostile to media independence.

This grip on media continued to tighten after the January 1992 cease-fire in Croatia. While this fact may be taken as confirming the nature of the HDZ government, it should be seen in the light of the ongoing campaign of persecution against Croatian Serbs. According to Ivan Zvonimir Čičak, president of the Croatian Helsinki Committee for Human Rights, some 10,000 dwellings belonging to Croatian Serbs in government-controlled territory were damaged or destroyed during the 15 months *after* the cease-fire.[165] This persecution, apparently tolerated by the government, went practically unreported in the Croatian media, which were still concentrating their energies on depicting Serbs as mortal enemies of Croatia.

* It was more than chance, therefore, that the March 1994 cease-fire and accord between the HVO (backed by Zagreb) and the Bosnian government coincided with a flurry of new publications in Croatia: a news fortnightly *Start Nove Generacije*, a literary paper, *Vijenac*, a political review, *Hrvatska ljevica*, and others. Nor was it chance that several leading members of HDZ split with the party soon after, in mid-April, citing the Croat-run concentration camps in Hercegovina as a prime reason.[166] It

---

[165] More than 5,000 persons have been illegally evicted from their homes during 1992 and 1993 according to the International Helsinki Federation for Human Rights in *Forced Out: Illegal Evictions Continue With Impunity in Croatia* (March 1994).

[166] The breakaway faction was led to Josip Manolić, whose uneasy response to a question about the camps was quoted in the section on 'Media, War and the Political Leaders', supra. Manolić returned to the subject with new boldness, in the 1 April 1994 issue of *Globus*:

> Who took the political decision to start concentration camps in Herceg-Bosna? Further, who took the political decision to keep east Mostar

was as if the cease-fire broke a psychological 'spell' on would-be critics of the government, allowing political normality to resume.

*   Yet, the government's actions have had a disastrous effect on the media environment. Croatia is a small country: if 50 or even 25 independent journalists are bullied into giving up the professional struggle, the effect on the next generation of journalists will be profound. "Croatian war reporting is Croatian war lying", Viktor Ivančić has written; and "it will take decades for the profession to recover from producing so many lies".[167]

*   A final note of bleak optimism: the government will not be able to ride roughshod over media professionalism for ever, if only because fewer and fewer journalists will tolerate the results.[168] The editor-in-chief of Croatian Radio resigned in August 1993, complaining that the new reorganization of the station meant that his editorial role had been reduced to that of assistant to the director: "I can't honestly perform my work."[169] In the same spirit, the Bonn correspondent of HTV wrote to *Vjesnik* explaining his absence from the screen, on the ground that he had been "obstructed and prevented from performing the job of accredited correspondent". He mentioned "censorship of reports".[170] These men have been forced to swell the ranks of 'journalist-dissidents', and the chorus of frustrated professionals. If the chorus makes enough noise, it will be difficult to ignore.

---

under siege for several months? Who took or permitted the decision to destroy the Old Bridge [in Mostar, in November 1993]? The final consequence of all these questions is: who decided that Croats would wage war against Muslims? This is a question to which the Croatian public must sooner or later have an answer. So, who started the war against Muslims? Whoever started that war must be held responsible.

[167] Ivančić, supra note 8.

[168] The government is also vulnerable to international pressure regarding media independence as evidenced by its relations with the Council of Europe — even if that pressure has not yet yielded much.

[169] M Pajalić, *Slobodna Dalmacija*, 28 Aug. 1993.

[170] *Vjesnik*, 21 May 1993.

Chapter 5

BOSNIA-HERCEGOVINA LEFT BEHIND

Introduction

As the only Yugoslav republic without a titular nation, Bosnia-Hercegovina (hereinafter Bosnia) was the only republic that could not be a nation-state. In its balance and blend of peoples of different faiths and national cultures, Bosnia was the epitome of Yugoslavia. None of its three nationalities, Muslim, Serb and Croat, had an absolute majority; according to the 1991 census, Muslims were 44 per cent of the 4.35 million population, Serbs were 31 per cent, and Croats 17 per cent.[1]

Tito's Partisan leaders drafted a charter for the future republic in 1943 which laid down that it would be "neither Serbian nor Croatian nor Muslim but rather Serbian and Croatian and Muslim". Bosnia was multinational in conception and in practice. Muslims, Serbs and Croats were all 'constituent peoples' in Tito's Socialist Republic of Bosnia-Hercegovina; none was a constitutional minority. National quotas were broadly observed in government institutions and organizations, including the executive ranks at the republic's radio-television station, Radio-Televizija Sarajevo (RTVSA, Radio-Television Sarajevo).[2]

---

[1] The collective political status of Muslims in the Socialistika Federativna Republika Jugoslavia (SFRY, Socialist Federative Republic of Yugoslavia) was a controversial matter. Until 1971, the decennial census offered Yugoslavia's Muslims the option of identifying themselves with Serb or Croat nationality. In 1971, the census recognized Muslims as a constitutive nation, equal with Croats, Macedonians, Montenegrins, Serbs and Slovenes. This promotion, capping a decade of effort by Bosnian Muslim leaders, and representing a defeat for Serb (and Croat) nationalists, was perhaps the boldest stroke of Titoist policy on the national question (a policy characterized by the principle of 'divide and rule').

[2] RTVSA was renamed Radio Television Bosnia-Hercegovina (RTVBH) in May 1992. Below, TVSA or TVBH refers to the television station, RSA or RBH refers to the radio station, and RTVSA, RTVBH, or just RTV in quotations, refers to the radio and television service.

Communist rule in Bosnia was generally harsher and more pervasive than in other republics, because of the national question.[3] Control over media was correspondingly tight. When the League of Communists of Bosnia began to lose authority, the resulting instability was even more complex than elsewhere.

Multiparty elections were held in Bosnia in November 1990. The results reflected national demography. Most seats were won by the main Muslim party, the Stranka Demokratske Akcije (SDA, Party of Democratic Action). Second was the Serb party led by Radovan Karadžić, the Srpska Demokratska Stranka (SDS, Serb Democratic Party, the same name as the radical party of Serbs in Croatia). In third place came the Hrvatska Demokratska Zajednica (HDZ, the Croatian Democratic Community) an offshoot of the party which had won the elections in Croatia earlier that year.

Alija Izetbegović, leader of the SDA, used the collective Presidency of the republic to construct a coalition government of the three national parties. The collective Presidency had seven members: three from the SDA and two each from the SDS and the HDZ. First among equals was the President of the Presidency, a position which was to be rotated among the three parties every two years. This role possessed none of the unimpeded executive power enjoyed by the Serbian and Croatian Presidents under their republics' new constitutions. The first President of the Presidency was Alija Izetbegović, the President of the parliament was Momčilo Krajišnik of the SDS, and the Prime Minister was Jure Pelivan of the HDZ. Cabinet positions were shared among the three parties; the Minister of the Interior was SDA, the Minister of Defence was HDZ, and the Minister of Information was SDS.

The arrangement appeared to function, but co-operation was superficial. Serb members of the Presidency and the parliament repeatedly blackmailed the SDA and the HDZ by threatening to walk out. Even before the elections, the SDS had created a 'Serb National Council' in the northern stronghold of Banja Luka as a legislative body independent of the legal government in Sarajevo.[4] The SDS and the HDZ were following

---

[3] As late as 1983 a show trial of 'nationalist' Muslim intellectuals, including Alija Izetbegović, was held in Sarajevo resulting in harsh sentences for four of the accused.

[4] L Bryant, *The Betrayal of Bosnia* (London: University of Westminster, 1993), 32.

national agendas set by developments outside the republic, while the SDA was a movement of religious dissidents (like Izetbegović), former apparatchiks, Communist entrepreneurs and intellectuals who all, however, agreed that Bosnia must be indivisible.

Neither the SDS nor the HDZ had campaigned on a demand for partition of the republic, but the SDS rapidly turned its stronghold areas in the north, west, and south-east of the republic into a party fiefdom, ungovernable by Sarajevo.

As open conflict loomed in Croatia, the SDS raised the stakes. By May 1991 the SDS was demanding outright that large tracts of northern and western Bosnia should secede to form 'Bosnian Krajina', plainly, to become a partner to the Serb-held 'Krajina', with its headquarters at Knin, just across the border in Croatia.[5] Later that summer, the SDS began to act as a paramilitary organization, working secretly with the Jugoslovenska Narodna Armija (JNA, Yugoslav People's Army) and the Serbian Ministry of the Interior to deliver weapons to Bosnian Serbs. The JNA base in the northern Bosnian town of Banja Luka, an SDS stronghold, became a centre of operations against Croatia.[6]

With Croatia and Slovenia seeking recognition by the European Community (EC), the aim of the SDS was to pre-empt moves by the other governing parties in Bosnia toward independence. Pre-emption had a political aspect: the SDS could, and did, block consensus on any key issue facing Bosnia (SDS members of parliament blocked legislation to declare the republic's neutrality between Serbia and Croatia). It also had a military aspect: by preparing the Bosnian Serbs for war, both psychologically and practically, the SDS was demonstrating that a move towards independence would precipitate a terrible conflict.

In September 1991, the SDS leadership declared the desired tracts of Bosnia to be 'Serb Autonomous Regions'. On 15 October the parliament in Sarajevo declared the republic to be sovereign (entitling the republican legislature to overrule Yugoslav law and JNA commands) and neutral between Serbia and Croatia. During the debate before the vote, Radovan Karadzić had warned the parliament that if Bosnia became independent, it would "go to hell" and the Muslims would not be able to defend themselves in the event of war. When his intimidation failed to

---

[5] N Malcolm, *Bosnia: A Short History* (London: Macmillan, 1994), 224.

[6] On the situation in Banja Luka, see section on 'Serb Media' infra.

deter the other parties, he led his members out of the parliament and later denounced neutrality as an "anti-Serb act". The SDS set up a separate 'Serb National Assembly' a few days later in Banja Luka. The 'Serb Republic of Bosnia-Hercegovina' was proclaimed on 21 December 1991.[7] The Bosnian Serb parallel state, or state-in-waiting, was in place, and the Sarajevo government could do nothing about it.

The HDZ leader in Bosnia, Stjepan Kljuić, was a moderate who believed in the integrity of the republic, unlike the hard-liners in his party.[8] However, Kljuić agreed with nationalists that President Tudjman was the leader of all Croats, not only those in Croatia. This ambiguity would soon be exploited by a hard-line faction backed by the parent party in Zagreb.

The HDZ set up two autonomous regions in majority-Croat districts in November 1991, one in the north and the other in the south-west. The second and stronger of these, the 'Croat Community of Herceg-Bosna', was declared on 18 November. 'Herceg-Bosna' was not hostile to the Sarajevo government, as the 'Serb Autonomous Regions' were, and its claim to be a defensive arrangement was justified by the recent unprovoked Serb-JNA attack against the majority-Croat village of Ravno, near the SDS stronghold of Trebinje in Hercegovina. Also, 'Herceg-Bosna' did not proclaim its independence until 2 July 1992. The portent, however, was clear. The HDZ was already establishing its own armed forces in Croat communities, with the help of the Hrvatska Vojska (HV, the Croatian Army). These forces were called the Hrvatsko Vijeće Obrane (HVO, the Croat Defence Council).

Until December 1991, the HDZ voted with the SDA against any partition of the republic. On 2 February 1992, control of the HDZ was won by the hard-line faction, which drew its support from the predominantly Croat areas of western Hercegovina, a traditional breeding-ground of nationalism.[9] (Two-thirds of Croats in the republic, however, lived elsewhere, mingled with Muslims and Serbs in central and northern Bosnia.) While Kljuić handled the hard-line Hercegovina

---

[7] The name was abridged to 'Serb Republic' on 12 August 1992.

[8] "We are for a sovereign and indivisible Bosnia-Hercegovina", Kljuić told the magazine *Bosanski pogledi* (8 Aug. 1991). Quoted by P Garde, *Vie et mort de la Yougoslavie* (Paris: 1992), 371.

[9] Bryant, supra note 4 at 35.

challenge ineptly, it is safe to assume that Zagreb was instrumental in engineering the change of leadership. The new leaders, headed by Mate Boban, brought the party into line with the partitionist thinking of Croatia's President Tudjman.

As an historian and then as a politician, Franjo Tudjman had not tried to conceal his conviction that Bosnia should be divided between Croatia and Serbia. He knew exactly which portions of the neighbouring republic he wanted, and he is widely believed to have sought opportunities to settle the matter with President Milošević (including at the Karadjordjevo talks in March 1991), over the head of the Sarajevo government. Given Franjo Tudjman's fixation and his client Boban's highly conditional support for the Sarajevo government, the Serbian government and its proxies in the SDS had reason to believe that, were war to be launched upon Bosnia, the HDZ would, in the absence of international intervention, turn against its allies and carve out its own national territory.

This was the situation early in 1992, as Croatia and Slovenia gained international recognition of their independence, the United Nations (UN) prepared to send 14,000 peacekeepers to Croatia, the JNA withdrew personnel, tanks and artillery from Croatia into Bosnia, and the EC vacillated over granting recognition to Bosnia.[10] Eventually, the EC prescribed a referendum as the way forward: an untimely move given the increasing belligerence of the SDS and the JNA.

The referendum took place on 29 February and 1 March 1992. Some 64 per cent of the electorate took part, of whom 99.5 per cent voted for "a sovereign and independent Bosnia-Hercegovina, a state of equal citizens and nations of Muslims, Serbs and Croats and others who live in it".[11] The SDS forbade Serbs to vote in the referendum, then provoked a crisis by setting up roadblocks in Sarajevo. A great show of solidarity against the violence by the citizens of Sarajevo helped to defuse the crisis. Elsewhere, the Serb onslaught was about to begin. In late March, a tripartite force launched attacks against non-Serbs in northern and eastern Bosnia. The force was made up of the JNA (95,000-strong in Bosnia by this time), irregular formations of Bosnian Serbs armed by the Yugoslav

---

[10] The JNA's transfer to Bosnia was intended to forestall Bosnia's moves towards independence.

[11] Malcolm, supra note 5 at 231.

Army, and paramilitary and volunteer bands from Serbia, with names like White Eagles and Tigers and fronted by high-profile allies and agents of the Serb leadership, such as the SRS leader Vojislav Šešelj[12] and the racketeer and gang-leader Željko Ražnatović-Arkan.

By 19 May 1992, the United Nations High Commissioner for Refugees (UNHCR) reported that 1.2 million Bosnians had been displaced by the onslaught, which was clearly intended to smash the republic beyond repair. In mid-August, a US Senate Foreign Relations Committee report put the death toll at 35,000, of whom 20,000 had been killed in the course of 'ethnic cleansing'.

Media Before the Onslaught

By March 1992, many multinational organs and institutions in Bosnia had already been subverted by the SDS, with the HDZ sometimes following suit. Two which had resisted, however, were the main broadcasting service, RTVSA, and the main daily paper, *Oslobodjenje*. When subversion proved impossible, these media were discredited by propaganda and then pounded by artillery. Meanwhile, the national parties set up parallel media (television and radio stations, magazines, news agencies and press centres) alongside their parallel 'autonomous' territories, governments, and ministries, including ministers of information, all inside the borders of Bosnia.

Whereas news media in Serbia and Croatia were centralized and consolidated, in Bosnia they were split and reconstructed in triplicate. News media, or rather propaganda media, multiplied with the casualty statistics, and, with every new medium, the sum of political pluralism diminished.[13] These new media were spawned as accessories to the

---

[12] On the SRS and Šešelj, see Ch. 3, section on 'Supporting the Drive for Volunteers' *supra*.

[13] The most bizarre propaganda medium in this war was surely the 'Camp Press' in the Serb-run detention camp at Manjača, in northern Bosnia; it testifies to a mania among the Bosnian Serb leaders to disseminate propaganda. A survivor writes: "Our daily news was provided by the Camp Press, a non-existent news agency. In the morning the news was bad, in the afternoon so-so, and in the evening it was good, to wish us sweet dreams. I suspect that this news was actually spread by the camp authorities via the grasses, or camp informers." (O Bosnević [a pseudonym], in R Ali

military force wielded by hostile political factions. As the Serb military juggernaut rolled through northern and eastern Bosnia, and Croat forces resisted in the south east, it was the duly elected government of the internationally recognized republic (whose laws RTVSA and *Oslobodjenje* respected) which as yet had no army.[14]

The Transmitter War

The media war which foreshadowed open conflict between Serbia and Croatia was waged through words and images. In Bosnia, the media war was also waged in terms of physical force. From autumn 1991 through to April 1992, the republic dwindled swathe by swathe, medium by medium.

TVSA's signal was broadcast throughout the republic by 11 main transmitters and some 186 relay stations. By the end of March 1992, no fewer than five of the transmitters had been seized by the JNA-Serb side. The first to go, on 1 August 1991, was Kozara covering north-central and north-western Bosnia, including the towns of Banja Luka, Prijedor, and Sanski Most (which would be 'cleansed' with utmost brutality the following spring and summer). On 28 October, Plješevica was seized and adjusted to receive the Serbian television frequency; this transmitter stands inside Croatia, but it was used by TVSA to cover north-western Bosnia. On 3 February 1992, the transmitter at Doboj, in north-central Bosnia, was taken. (The SDS later admitted responsibility.) On 13 February, Majevica in north-eastern Bosnia was taken and redirected. On 23 March, Trovhr was destroyed, depriving south-eastern Bosnia of the TVSA signal.

By the time Bosnia was recognized as an independent state on 6 April 1992, up to half its territory was covered by the Radio-Televizija Srbija (RTS, Serbian Radio-Television) signal. When the onslaught began, three more transmitters were seized. Velez, near Mostar, covering

---

& L Lifschutz (eds.), *Why Bosnia? Writings on the Balkan War* [Connecticut: 1993], 112.)

[14] The Armije Bosne i Hercegovine (ABH, Army of Bosnia-Hercegovina) was formed during summer 1992 from a volunteer militia, the Patriotic League; the official Territorial Defence; Green Berets, an SDA militia; and the tiny republican anti-terrorist police force.

Hercegovina, was redirected at the end of April with the result that Hercegovina could not see Channel 2 of TVSA after 8 p.m.[15] TV Belgrade was broadcast instead, and TVSA's Channel 1 was transmitted on the Channel 2 frequency which had a weaker signal. TVSA's Mostar studio lost its electronic link to Sarajevo on 29 April. Two days later, the Vlašić transmitter in central Bosnia was taken; an engineer was killed in the operation, and the rest of the technical crew were taken prisoner. In June, in eastern Hercegovina, the Leotar transmitter was redirected.

Of the three remaining transmitters, Tusnica in western Hercegovina was redirected by the HVO, and Bjelašnica on the southern rim of Sarajevo was destroyed in August 1993. The JNA had tried to disable Hum, just north of the capital, before evacuating Sarajevo at the start of May 1992; tanks shelled the transmitter from inside the city barracks but Hum was never knocked out, even when a JNA jet attacked it with rockets. Even so, Serbian television covered some 70 per cent of Bosnia.[16]

RTVBH's remarkable engineers, who improvized and maintained a network of portable transmitters to carry the Hum signal to other government-held territory, managed to restore TVBH to 20-25 per cent of the republic. TVBH could be seen in parts of north-eastern Bosnia, central Bosnia, Zenica, Tuzla, and sometimes in Mostar. According to the Ministry of Information, most of the 30 employees of RTVBH killed during the war were engineers.[17]

The station's connections to other republics, and the world beyond, were lost along with the outlying transmitters. In television as in everything else, Bosnia was thoroughly enmeshed in Yugoslavia. TVSA's usual access to international exchange networks (such as Eurovision) lay through Zagreb and Belgrade. Only satellite links remained.

The Serb side exploited its stolen access to develop the traffic between Bosnian Serb television and RTS; the Bosnian Serb station in

---

[15] *Oslobodjenje*, 29 April 1992.

[16] L'Organisation Internationale des Journalistes, *Reporters and Media in Ex-Yugoslavia* (Paris: Les Cahiers de L'Organisation Internationale des Journalistes, Jan. 1993), 96.

[17] Information from: Ministry of Information, *Information on the Current Situation in the Radio-Broadcasting Network of the Republic of Bosnia-Hercegovina*, prepared for UNESCO, 10 Sept. 1993; interview with M Memija, *Dani*, 10 March 1993; and interviews with RTVBH engineers in Sarajevo, Nov. 1993.

Pale, near Sarajevo, uses the optical microwave link installed between Zagreb and Belgrade (for the 1984 Winter Olympic Games held in Sarajevo) in order to exchange broadcasts with TV Belgrade.[18] According to one source, information was exchanged by satellite too, using the transmitter at Kozara. (For examples of the traffic between Belgrade and Serb-held areas in Bosnia see section on 'Serb Media', below.)

The significance of this media interpenetration would be difficult to exaggerate. For more than six months before the Serb attack began in March 1992, the Serbs of northern Bosnia were saturated with propaganda about the Bosnian government (and the Serbian version of the war in Croatia) which the government was impotent to challenge.

The Communications Breakdown

The loss of television transmitters, post and telecommunications, and road and rail links rendered much communications technology redundant.[19] The flow of information across the country now depended on runners, ham radios, field telephones, television studios operating like urban radio stations, and satellite links. Sarajevo, Tuzla and Zenica, all controlled by the government, have been isolated like late Roman colonies amid a sea of barbarians; but these colonies have satellite phones and fax machines, satellite dishes, a few private power generators, crews of foreign journalists, and detachments of UN peace-keeping troops.

The fragmentation is limitless; in Sarajevo, outposts of resistance can see but not touch each other. Sarajevans could speak by satellite to an audience of 72,000 at a London rock concert in August 1993, but they could not find out what was happening 20 kilometres away. Television

---

[18] P Jenkins, "Propaganda unlimited", *The Guardian*, 3 May 1993.

[19] Serb fifth-columnists destroyed the Sarajevo telephone exchange in May, and Serb forces cut off the power supply to the main PTT telecommunications tower on Mount Trebević, at the edge of the capital, in June 1992. Lines around the republic and to Serbia were briefly restored in July, then cut. International lines could have been rerouted via Croatia, but the Zagreb government has refused to comply, apparently as a lever against the Bosnian government. (*Oslobodjenje*, 22 Sept. 1992 and 30 *Bosnia Briefing*, 25 March 1993.)

conveyed precious information across battle lines within Sarajevo, like carrier pigeons:

> It is horrible to hear the artillery and the machine guns firing from the hill nearby, and to know that they are killing innocent people in the city, who can't even fire back. The statistics on TV every evening, when we've got electricity [to watch it], are terrifying. So are the pictures, but we can't stop watching, because of all our people on 'the other side'.[20]

An American reporter told of a man in a cellar, in the besieged Sarajevo enclave of Dobrinja, who wired his television set to a bicycle dynamo every evening, and pedalled furiously for half an hour in order to watch the news.[21]

Zlatko Dizdarević, the *Oslobodjenje* columnist, tells another story of regression in Dobrinja. People there, he says, "are producing handwritten leaflets, and somehow manage to duplicate them. They even have a working fax on which, page by page, they get *Oslobodjenje* and clippings from the foreign press. Then all this information moves under cover of darkness, from window to window, balcony to balcony."[22]

Media are not merely victims of this breakdown, this medievalization (which the outside world can watch nightly via satellite); for they matter in new ways. Public appetite for information is very keen, making people on all three sides in Bosnia easy prey for propagandists.

---

[20] R Rehnicer, *Sarajevo Journal (May-Dec. 1992)*, excerpted in *Liber. Revue européenne des livres*, 14 June 1993: a supplement to No. 98 of *Actes de la recherche en sciences sociales*. Rehnicer is a Croatian-born Jew living in Sarajevo; however, the words 'our people' refer to neighbours from the author's apartment block who had fled from this Serb-controlled zone to other parts of the city.

[21] *New York Times* reporter J Burns in W Tribe's as yet unpublished account of the war, *Sarajevo: A Return*, written in 1993.

[22] Z Dizdarević, *Sarajevo: A War Journal*, (Fromm: 1994), entry for 27 June 1992.

Media in the War

Media life in Sarajevo has been lively despite nearly two years of continual shelling.[23] Two newspapers are published, the daily *Oslobodjenje* and the lesser known *Večernje novine* which appears twice-weekly, depending on the availability of newsprint. There is also a remarkable, independent news magazine, *Dani*. There has been a little boom of tabloid weeklies, especially in the first months of 1994 prior to the March truce: *Bosanski Avaz, Oglasi, Narodne novine, Sarp, Bosna* (launched by Senad Avdić, former editor-in-chief of *Slobodna Bosna*), *Sarajevo Times*, and *Behar* (which claims to be "the first paper in the Bosnian language"). There are also oddities like the beautifully-produced *Tenis*, the first tennis magazine ever in Bosnia according to its editor; and *Leo News*, a satirical news sheet posted daily on a city-centre wall. As well as the radio and television service, RTVBH, there are some eight independent FM radio stations, including Radio Vrhbosna, launched in spring 1993 by Napredak, the Croat cultural society.[24]

Other media were forced to close before or shortly after Bosnia was attacked. The case of Yutel has been described in Chapter 2. TV Dobre Vibracije, a private TV channel broadcasting for Sarajevo, was commandeered by SDA hard-liners; the station had to close in June 1992 because of its proximity to the front line. Several news magazines also shut down: the satirical monthly *Vox*, which ran out of money; the fortnightly *Naši dani*; the fortnightly *Walter*, and the weekly *Bosanski pogledi*. Meanwhile more than 200 new publications and radio stations have registered at the Ministry of Information since April 1992, awaiting better days to start up.[25]

---

[23] The siege of Sarajevo began in April 1992.

[24] Napredak dates back to 1907. During the war, Napredak did not align itself with the nationalists of 'Herceg-Bosna'. The fact that Radio Vrhbosna could function, and even include many Hrvatski Radio programmes in its nine hours of daily transmission, despite the belligerence of 'Herceg-Bosna', indicates the full duality of Croat political attitudes inside Bosnia.

[25] It isn't only media entrepreneurs who are looking ahead: a state airline, 'Air BH', was legally registered in Sarajevo in December 1992. (*Oslobodjenje*, 19 Dec. 1992.) However, one motive for this proliferation of registered media titles was the desire to evade conscription into the Army by procuring an official journalist's accreditation. Best of all was UNPROFOR accreditation, which gave access to UN

The media picture outside Sarajevo is chaotic and desperate, but not entirely bleak. The two Sarajevo newspapers have regional editions: *Večernje novine* in Tuzla and *Oslobodjenje* in Zenica, which also has a would-be daily of its own, *Islamski glas,* and another paper, *Štit. Slobodna Bosna*, which moved from Sarajevo to Zenica at the end of 1992, appeared sporadically during 1993. North-eastern Bosnia has *Bosnoljubljen* and *Čelić. Trn* newspaper appears in Tešanj. A news magazine, *Vrelo*, is planned in Tuzla, which also has *Zmaj od Bosne* and a local television station, FS3 (Front Sloboda 3).[26]

Local television became a Bosnian phenomenon during the war; some 15 or 20 local stations started broadcasting in government-held territory outside Sarajevo. There were five in the Tuzla area alone broadcasting for several hours a day. Zenica had 'Zetel' (Zenička televizija), and central Bosnia had studios in Visoko, Kakanj and Vitez. They broadcast a schedule of local news, 'notice-board' programmes to connect separated families, interviews with visiting personalities (UNPROFOR[27] commanders, SDA or other politicians, and popular singers), and pirated videos of feature films.

Local radio stations and printing presses have been rigged up to convey local news and personal messages. When the HVO overran western Mostar on 9 May 1993, the Mostar 'war studio' of Radio BH moved across the River Neretva to the eastern part of the city, and "manage[d] to transmit eight hours a day" while a printing press next door ran off newsletters.[28]

The media situation in the north-western pocket of government-controlled territory, known as Cazinska Krajina, was fragmented in an unusual way in September 1993. For here, both sides were Muslim; indeed, the leaders on both sides belonged to the same party, the SDA. Cazinska Krajina, surrounded on all sides by Serb-held territory in Bosnia and Croatia, was, until the autumn of 1993, under the political control of

---

flights out of Sarajevo.

[26] Mention should also be made of Bosnian media outside the country. Apart from the weekly international editions of *Oslobodjenje, Večernje novine* and *Ljiljan* (printed in Slovenia), *Bosna Press* is produced in Frankfurt and *Asyl Times* in Sweden. There are also Bosnian radio stations or special programmes in Berlin, Denmark and Australia, as well as refugee bulletins in a number of other countries.

[27] United Nations Protection Force.

[28] *The Independent*, 8 Feb. 1994.

Fikret Abdić, a Communist entrepreneur turned SDA entrepreneur. Unfettered by nationalist beliefs, Abdić steered a clever course between Croat and Serb forces. He was a member of the collective Presidency, closely involved in the rounds of doomed negotiations to save the republic. President Izetbegović and the Sarajevo clique of SDA leaders were reputedly suspicious of him, because of his background and his great popularity in Cazinska Krajina. During the Geneva peace negotiations when Izetbegović was being pressurized to accept 'partition' of the republic, Abdić declared part of Cazinska Krajina to be the 'Autonomous Province of Western Bosnia', fully independent of the government in Sarajevo.[29]

Abdić did what all partitionists in Bosnia do: he established his own media. Zapadnobosanska Informativna Agencija (ZBIA, the Western Bosnian News Agency) issues bulletins bearing the letterhead of Agrokomerc, the agricultural combine in the region which is Abdić's original power base. After Abdić had signed peace agreements with the Croats and Serbs in October, TV crews from Zagreb and Belgrade were welcomed to the pocket-sized 'province', whence they sent identically positive reports; for they could both support Abdić against the common enemy, the Sarajevo government.

But Abdić had not carried the local brigade of the ABH with him. On 30 September, forces loyal to the Sarajevo government took control of Radio Cazin. Early on 3 October, the same forces stormed Radio Velika Kladuša, in Abdić's home town. Before withdrawing a few hours later, they destroyed the station's equipment.[30] As well as Cazin, the ABH hold Radio Bihać, which also has a television studio in its cellar, one of the regional studios of RTVBH. Cazin and Bihać produce anti-Abdić news while a few kilometres down the road in 'Western Bosnia', the radio station at Velika Kladuša produces pro-Abdić news, as does a weekly newspaper, *Zapadna Bosna*, privately registered in Zagreb by a Bosnian businessman. Its issue of 18 March 1994 was presented as "the first European number!". Above photographs of four Muslim leaders in Sarajevo, the headline promised to "expose all the lies and tricks of the warlords!".

---

[29] The 'Autonomous Province' was declared on 26 Sept. 1993.

[30] *VIP Daily News Report*, 4 Oct. 1993.

Meanwhile, media loyal to the Bosnian government demonized Abdić as a national enemy. The newspaper *Ljiljan* even rushed a book into print: *Abdić's Road to Treachery*, which appeared early in 1994.

Media and Censorship

No media legislation has been enacted in Bosnia since the 1990 elections.[31] The government failed to pass a bill to bring the radio-television service under its control early in 1990, largely because it was too deeply riven by different agendas and goals.[32] This situation continued until spring 1992 but, with the outbreak of war, the government, through the collective Presidency, took formal control of the radio and television service by appointing senior executives. These appointments did not lead to a marked tightening of control at RTVBH until the end of 1992, when the government appointed SDA members as directors of both radio and television. (See section on 'Television' below.)

In 1990, new federal laws on media privatization were incorporated into republican statutes. The pre-1990 republican criminal code is still intact, with its catch-all articles against 'hostile propaganda' and 'hostile association'. Since the war began, there have been no preconditions for new private media in Sarajevo to register with the Minister of Information. Private radio stations require a licence from the Ministry of Traffic and Telecommunications to obtain a frequency.

The government effectively controls the supply of newsprint. The OKO printing company, part of the Oslobodjenje group until 1991, has a monopoly in Sarajevo. In 1991, it was converted into a joint stock company with the state as the main stockholder. The managing director, Petar Škert, claimed in response to a *Dani* interviewer that the company has "no relations" with the government. This statement was belied the next month when OKO delayed the printing of an issue of *Dani* for six weeks

---

[31] A Constitutional Commission began work on a new constitution in March 1994 to replace the pre-election 1990 Constitution; until the principles of a post-war Bosnian state are known, assuming the state survives in some form, the Commission remains a hostage to military and diplomatic developments.

[32] See section on 'Television' infra for discussion of the bill.

because it contained a controversial article (see below). While printing costs are relatively low, paper cannot be obtained without connections in high places (government circles, the UNPROFOR, the local black marketeers or international charities which support media) or without large sums of Deutschmarks (the local currency, known as 'coupons', was good for little except to buy bread and a daily newspaper). *Oslobodjenje* had the cooperation of UNPROFOR in securing paper supplies from international donors; no other medium had this benefit and some spent months waiting for essential donations to be transported from the Croatian ports or farther afield, pending clearance by the UN or the besieging Serb forces.

The government's control of other media also tightened in 1993, as the following cases show:

* On 17 July 1993, the independent station, Radio 99, in Sarajevo was closed down after announcing that it would carry an interview with Fikret Abdić later that evening.[33] An engineer arrived from government-controlled RTVBH and shut down the station, which was not allowed to resume broadcasting until 15 September.

* In the same period, the magazine *Dani* republished an interview with Fikret Abdić from the Croatian weekly *Danas*. The state-controlled OKO printing company used its monopoly to delay the issue's publication for six weeks.[34] *Dani*'s editor-in-chief, Senad Pečanin, has no doubt that the Abdić feature was the reason. In 1994, OKO again delayed an issue of *Dani* for two months because it contained an article criticizing the SDA.[35]

* Journalists who expressed views opposed to the government have been liable to individual harassment and intimidation. A radio journalist at RBH alleges that he was beaten up by one of President Izetbegović's bodyguards, inside the Presidency building in June 1992, because of an article he had published in *Oslobodjenje*. The journalist does not suspect a conspiracy but rather that the bodyguard was "acting on his own". In January 1994, Senad Pečanin was detained by police for parking his car illegally, an absurd charge in besieged Sarajevo. The policeman then

---

[33] On Abdić, see section on 'Media in the War' supra.

[34] It was eventually published on 30 July 1993.

[35] *Globus*, 1 April 1994.

criticized Pečanin for not including President Izetbegović among *Dani*'s list of leading personalities of 1993.

*   Journalists of Serb nationality (automatically under suspicion) were particularly vulnerable. One victim was TV journalist Ljubomir Ljubojević. After criticizing the government, he was mobilized to join the Bosnian Army. He tried to escape from Sarajevo and was caught by Serb troops who took him to Pale "and forced him, publicly over Kanal S, to spit on himself for serving 'Muslim television'."[36] Mobilization has been used as a means to discipline unruly journalists since the end of 1992, according to one RTVBH editor: "The list of exempt journalists was reduced and reduced."

*   Rade Jevtić, business manager at independent Radio Zid, said that the Ministry of Information had called several times to suggest that the station was not filtering information in the expected way, although these calls involved no actual threats.[37] The Ministry denies that any calls were made.[38]

While the independent media did not run the risk of legal prosecution, they had no legal protection either. The aim was to encourage self-censorship, so that journalists would not express critical views of the government's and the President's performances before and during the war; of the Army's role; of atrocities perpetrated by the Army; and of hard-line Muslim elements in and around the governing party and among the international volunteer forces fighting with the Army. TVBH avoids these sensitive issues; since mid-1993 so does RBH.

Ironically, the foremost beneficiary of censorship by intimidation in Sarajevo during 1993 was the rogue commander of a Bosnian Army brigade in Sarajevo: Mušan Topalević, known as Caco. For months Caco's men plagued the city with impunity, dragging civilians off the streets to dig trenches on the front line, among other crimes.

A privately-owned, popular music radio station, Radio M, was partly destroyed by Caco's men because they disliked the manager's

---

[36] M Ćamo, 18 *Balkan War Report*, Feb-March 1993.

[37] R Jevtić to author, 10 Nov. 1993.

[38] S Kreso, assistant to the Minister of Information, to author, 11 Nov. 1993.

choice of music (he played some Serbian songs). The manager, a Muslim by nationality, said that seven foreign news networks reported the attack, but inside Sarajevo, only *Večernje novine* and one minor opposition political party published anything about it.

Gordana Knežević, deputy editor of *Oslobodjenje*, made no excuse for not writing about Caco, even when his men detained three of her staff. "The day after we ran an investigation of Caco, his people would have come and taken us all away. My rule is to do nothing which could prevent us from publishing."[39] Except for a 30 July propitiatory interview in *Dani*, Caco was hardly mentioned in the Sarajevo media until he was killed in October. The biggest story in the city could not be told in its media.

Terminology in the Media

The question of terminology was uniquely tortuous in Bosnia. During the war in Croatia, the main Bosnian media generally avoided prejudicial terms for the JNA and the Serb and Croat forces. Even when the intention and scale of the attack on Bosnia became clear, in April 1992, this abstinence continued, reflecting two primary facts. First, the Bosnian government and its forces were composed of all three Bosnian nationalities; second, the main theme of Serb (as, later, of Croat) propaganda against Bosnia was the alleged Islamic sectarian ambitions of the leading Muslim politicians, and the 'treachery' of those Serbs (or Croats) who supported the government's defence of Bosnian sovereignty and integrity. Therefore, media which shared this position had to be doubly wary of language which implicated, or might seem to implicate, all Serbs (or, later, all Croats) in the aggression against Bosnia.

Later, these media adopted the convention, used informally by many Bosnians, of calling the Serb forces '*četniki*' in order to protect the Bosnians of Serb nationality who supported the government. Thus there were Serbs in Sarajevo or Tuzla, but the people shelling those cities were *četniki*. Always a fragile distinction, by the end of 1993, it seemed to have broken down in the main Sarajevo media adding to the anxiety of Serbs

---

[39] G Knežević to author, 12 Nov. 1993.

and Croats in government-controlled territory. In the eyes of Muslim hard-liners, calling the principal enemy '*četniki*' was side-stepping the issue: "Nowhere in the world are the people who are once again committing genocide against Bošniaks [Bosnian Muslims] known as *cetniki*, but rather as Serbs. They call themselves Serbs too."[40]

In autumn 1993, the Chief of Staff of the ABH, General Rasim Delić issued an order to the Sarajevo media to call the HVO by that title (not "*ustaša* forces"), and to call the Serb forces "paramilitary units of Bosnian Serbs" or "Yugoslav Army" (not "*četniki*"). The order did not work for long, even in RTVBH, and least of all in the Army Press Centre, which continued to use such terms as "*ustaša* hordes".

News Agencies

BH Press

BH Press is the news agency of the Republic of Bosnia-Hercegovina. It was founded by the government in April 1992, when the republic gained international recognition, and has operated only under war conditions. Its few staff occupy small offices in the Presidency building in central Sarajevo. Some 30 young reporters scattered around the government-controlled parts of the republic send information by telephone. The agency stopped operating in Croat-controlled areas early in 1993; even before that, its reporters were not notified of press events in 'Herceg-Bosna'. The agency has no contacts in Serb-controlled territory.

The function of BH Press, according to its director, Zlatan Husarić, is "to report the activities of the Presidency, the government, and the Ministry of the Interior, and to publish their statements". It also disseminates statements by the Bosnian Army Press Centre.

BH Press has disseminated a number of propaganda pieces. In 1992, it issued an untrue report of the funeral of Serbian paramilitary leader Željko Ražnatović-Arkan, adding that the militant SDS leader

---

[40] E Duraković, *Ljiljan*, 16 March 1994.

Biljana Plavšić had wept for her close friend. Other ill-advised fictions were the 'news' that the son of SDS leader Radovan Karadžić had joined the Bosnian Army, and that Karadžić himself was in a state of nervous collapse.

Husarić admits that BH Press has not regained the credibility lost by these adventures in disinformation. In addition, the agency has a reputation for low professional standards. A journalist at RTVBH told ARTICLE 19 that BH Press used to summarize the contents of the satellite television station reports which were relayed on TVBH's own news broadcast. The summaries were then circulated to Sarajevo's media as BH Press bulletins.

Unlike government press agencies in Serbia and Croatia, the BH Press Centre is practically irrelevant in Sarajevo. Members of the government do not channel their statements or appearances through it, and the foreign press do not need to use it because Sarajevo's very accessibility is to the government's advantage (on the ground that the more coverage of actual conditions in the city there is, the more chance of international support for their cause). Husarić believes that the government does not try to raise the agency's profile, because it does not consider the agency's work to be a priority. This mirrors the complaints of many journalists in Sarajevo that the government underestimates the importance of information. The government holds the view that, unlike its counterparts in Serbia and Croatia, it is not pursuing goals which need to be dissembled or legitimated by strong propaganda and disinformation, preferring instead to rely on its victim status.

The Bosnian Army Press Centre

The BH Army Press Centre was established in autumn 1992. After a false start (the first team at the Centre began a statistical content analysis of reports about the war: not what was required), the Centre has become the Army's propaganda wing. Before the Centre began to function, the ABH had targeted journalists. In September 1992, *Oslobodjenje* published an anonymous bulletin from the "Information Office of the Staff of the Supreme Command of the Armed Forces of the Republic of Bosnia-Hercegovina" warning that "journalist-agents" were active in the city, and asked how unnamed "journalists and editors at RTVBH" were still working in Sarajevo.

Nerzuk Čurak, the director, believes that the government does not sufficiently control the media: "We haven't yet grasped the importance of information in a state of war, and we have more democracy here than we should have."[41]

The Centre uses the standard prejudicial terms for the HVO and Serb irregulars (*ustaša* hordes, *četniki*, and so forth). Its propaganda efforts have been analyzed by the *Dani* columnist Ivan Lovrenović, who gives the following two examples. One, which drew mockery from the columnist, was a claim in the Centre's bulletins that "a great quality of the [BH] Army [was] its 'simulation of weakness'". However, the Centre's propaganda was also more insidious; another bulletin referred to "the fundamental people in Bosnia-Hercegovina". The whole context left no room to doubt, Lovrenović noted, that the people in question were the Muslims. "If one people is fundamental," he asked with irony, "what must the others be? Non-fundamental? Unfounded? Foundationless?"[42]

Television

Introduction

The fate of Bosnia was foreshadowed by the fate of its radio-television network. The will of the SDS and the readiness of the HDZ to destroy the republic was first clearly revealed in their hostility to the institution of Radio-Television Sarajevo (RTVSA).

The republican Union of Journalists had won a remarkable measure of legal autonomy for RTVSA in the late 1980s by exploiting the League of Communists' loss of authority. In June 1989, at the initiative of the Union, the Bosnian parliament enacted a law allowing RTVSA staff to elect their executives by secret ballot, subject to the parliament's approval. It was the first such law in the history of Yugoslav media; its enactment was a measure of the anxiety which was driving the League to muster some reformist credibility.

---

[41] N Čurak to author, 15 Nov. 1993.

[42] I Lovrenović, *Ex tenebris: sarajevski dnevnik* (Zagreb: AGM, 1994), 98.

RTVSA executives had previously been nominated by the Socialist Alliance of Working People (SAWP). In each republic, the SAWP took its tone from the League of Communists and, in Bosnia, it took a hard line against democratization almost until it disintegrated in 1990. The 1989 law did not alter the ownership status of the station; it remained a 'public enterprise' in the socialist definition, without a titular owner.

When the parliament approved the staff's choice, RTVSA became safe from co-option by any single party during the rocky transition to democracy, which began formally in April 1990 when multiparty elections were scheduled for the end of the year. Competition among the three leading national parties to influence RTVSA, especially TV Sarajevo (TVSA), got seriously under way. According to Nenad Pejić, the staff-appointed editor-in-chief of TVSA at the time, party 'spies' were infiltrated into the news department.[43] These were party journalists who kept their respective parties abreast of editorial discussions and plans. The news department came under the most pressure, because political information was the most prized and contested resource in RTVSA. Since the elections, no fewer than 28 editors have presented the evening news; a massive turnover, which began well before the war.

The station's election coverage in 1990 was regulated by a voluntary code, drawn up by Pejić in accordance with the station's statutory public-service responsibilities, and agreed by the major political parties. All parties declared themselves satisfied with the result. After the election, however, the SDA-SDS-HDZ coalition government in Sarajevo, like the new governments in Zagreb and Belgrade, sought to bring the broadcasting service, as well as the Oslobodjene publishing group, under its control. A broadcasting law was drafted which would have led to RTVSA splitting into three national services, which was the ambition (not yet explicit) of the SDS and of radicals in the HDZ.[44] The SDA's motives were simpler: its leaders sought the same servility from 'their' broadcasting service that Communist leadership had enjoyed for so long.

---

[43] N Pejić, "The Role of Television in a Period of Ethnic Tensions", a lecture printed in 51-52 *The South Slav Journal*. This section of the report draws on Pejić's paper, as well as on his interview in 6 *Index on Censorship* (London: 1992), and on interviews with him and other past and present editors and journalists in the television and radio newsrooms.

[44] The draft law would also have given the government the right to appoint the director and editor-in-chief of RTVSA.

Not until the middle of 1991, rather late, did the SDA recognize that partitioning RTVSA would greatly facilitate the partitioning of the republic.

RTVSA took its case against the draft law to the Federal Constitutional Court, arguing that the law would contravene recent federal legislation on the control of public companies and on employees' rights, which took precedence over republican law.

A campaign was put together with the help of the daily *Oslobodjenje*, which organized a protest rally in front of the parliament. It was March 1991, and 5,000 Sarajevans joined in the first non-national rally in post-Communist Bosnia. The paper also mustered international pressure, for example by asking the British and American Embassies in Belgrade to express concern about the case to the federal government led by Ante Marković. The court duly upheld RTVSA's objection by a majority of 8-1.[45]

Meanwhile, the three governing parties were variously intimidating, cajoling, and bribing journalists. The SDS was organized inside RTVSA, reflecting a numerical advantage where it mattered; there were 18 Serb journalists in the newsroom (as compared with seven Muslims), and five Serb senior editors in the television station as a whole, as compared with one Croat and one Muslim.[46] The SDS leadership held weekly meetings with Serb journalists. Among senior Croat and Muslim journalists only a few were believed to be involved with political parties.[47]

Pejić describes the pressure as systematic: "All the ethnic parties tried to win their way into the team [of news editors], with offers of jobs, money, and threats of removal." The governing parties could not cut the station's budget because it did not receive state funding. Instead, early in

---

[45] Information from G Knežević, deputy editor of *Oslobodjenje*, to author, 12 Nov. 1993, and from N Pejić to author, 25 Feb. 1994.

[46] While the national quota system was not maintained rigidly, except at the very top, the over-representation of Serbs is partly explained by the fact that avowed 'Yugoslavs' were a separate group in the quota, and most 'Yugoslavs' were of Serb nationality. In the 1991 census, Yugoslavs were 5.5 per cent of the population in Bosnia.

[47] It is worth remarking that Stjepan Kljuić, the relatively moderate leader of the HDZ until he was replaced in Feb. 1992, was a radical himself when it came to branding Croat journalists who refused to be recruited to the HDZ as enemies of the Croat people.

1991, the parties called on their supporters to boycott the licence fee, in protest at TV Sarajevo's 'anti-Serbian', 'anti-Croatian' and 'anti-Muslim' coverage. One third of fee payers heeded the call, depriving the station of a huge amount of its income. Pejić adds: "Until the end of 1989 only 9 per cent of [RTVSA's] income had come from advertising, while the remaining 91 per cent came from the licence fee. By the end of 1991 only 74 per cent came out of the fee."

By this time the SDA had reconsidered its hostility to the station; otherwise its income would have fallen even further. Even so, by March 1992 the station was bankrupt. Strike action was planned, to strengthen demands for state support but was called off because of growing Serbian aggression following the referendum. The station has continued in a state of financial crisis, with journalists working for little or no pay (the local currency is practically worthless) and, like most Sarajevans, relying on humanitarian aid for survival.

Attempts to Split Up the Service

In November 1991, the SDS called outright for TVSA to be split into national channels. TVSA had three channels: Channel 1 covered 91 per cent of the population, while Channels 2 and 3 reached 78 per cent.[48] The SDS proposed that the three national parties rotate control of the channels. The recently self-proclaimed 'Assembly of the Serb People of Bosnia-Hercegovina' would appoint the Serb editor, explained Radovan Karadžić.

"It was absolutely crazy," Pejić says, "and if not a technical impossibility, a logistical one." Feasibility was not the point: the intention was to destroy programming, above all news programming, which sought objectivity and multinational audiences.

The SDS claimed that division was necessary because television coverage was unfair to Serbs. The real reason was that the only acceptable alternative, editorial control of the whole station, was impossible, given the balance of party power in the parliament and the commitment of RTVSA to multinational principles (which included the national quota for executive positions). The SDS demand was repeated up to the very brink of war: one

---

[48] Figures from Ministry of Information, supra note 17.

223

of the SDS's two key conditions for removing the barricades which its armed supporters erected around the capital on 2 March 1992, after the referendum on independence, was a Serb television channel. Instead, President Izetbegović offered only access to Serbian television.[49]

In January 1992 the HDZ followed the SDS example and echoed its demand, rather as Croat forces would later follow the Serb example in the strategy of 'ethnic cleansing'. The SDA did not want a separate channel; as usual with any large strategic issue, the SDA didn't altogether know what it did want. It was caught between playing the Serb-Croat radicals at their own game (partly from well-founded fear, partly from its own radical members' ambitions) and stoutly defending the unity of the broadcasting network.

TVSA had already polled its viewers to see how many wanted three national services. The result vindicated its resistance. Only 35,000 supported the idea of breaking up the single service, while 330,000 were against. The SDS response, according to Pejić, was to say that TVSA "had no right to ask people for their views. 'We know what they want'." Under pressure, Pejić compromised by increasing the amount of programming from Serbian and Croatian television. Channel 2 of TVSA broadcast 11 hours of Serbian and Croatian television on alternate days, right into April 1992. Channel 2 also broadcast the pan-Yugoslav Yutel television news every evening.

War in Croatia

TVSA's coverage of the war in Croatia was uncommitted. Broadcasts presented a range of different perspectives, depending on the editors' and reporters' outlook. The American writer Brian Hall watched the news in the middle of 1991, as Croatia slid into war:

> Many of those grey Communist journalists had colourized into Serb, Croat and Muslim journalists. All of them went their own way, and none could be disciplined by the studio bosses without provoking the wrath of their co-religionists in the government or

---

[49] *The Guardian*, 4 March 1992.

in the streets. You could usually predict the slant of a piece by the name of the reporter at the bottom of the screen. This had the interesting effect of making Sarajevo TV coverage simultaneously narrow-minded and broad-based.

A sample of one evening's news:

A car full of kalashnikovs had been discovered heading for Hercegovina; Serbs were suspected (Muslim reporter).

Explosions and shootings continued throughout Slavonia. Serb peasants led the camera through trashed houses, putting fingers through bullet holes in windows; Serb mothers cried about rampaging animals (Serb reporter).

Shells fired by 'the so-called Yugoslav People's Army' destroyed several homes in a Croat village (Croat reporter).

Milan Martić, leader of the illegal Serb militia of the so-called 'Autonomous Region of Krajina' [in Croatia], marched with a column of his militant adventurists to the town of Titov Drvar, in Bosnia, and held manoeuvres, and announced the end of the border between the Croatian Krajina and the Bosnian Krajina. He was welcomed by Serb town officials, who called the Bosnian Krajina 'Serbian territory' (emphatically not a Serb reporter).

... Yugoslav affairs had taken an hour. The announcer said, 'Not much of interest happened in the rest of the world today. And now for the weather ... .'[50]

This random partiality endangered roving TV crews. TVSA news editors compiled a list of 48 attacks or threats against reporters during

---

[50] B Hall, *The Impossible Country: A Journey Through the Last Days of Yugoslavia* (London: 1994), 220-221.

1991 and early 1992.[51] This list (which omits "'ordinary' examples like threatening letters, telephone calls, or threats to parents and children") illustrates the extraordinary difficulty, and danger, of refusing to take sides. The vicissitudes of one crew, comprising a Serb, a Croat and a Muslim, are particularly vivid.

The TVSA crew of Aleksandar Kojović, reporter, Tomo Marić, cameraman, and Semsudin Čengić, technician, managed to get into Dubrovnik, together with some other reporters. "The Dubrovnik authorities accommodated them in the Hotel Argentina as their guests. Five minutes before curfew, armed soldiers of the HV dashed into the room ordering the TVSA crew to leave Dubrovnik within 30 minutes. After an hour of persuasion, the crew was allowed to stay til morning."[52] Next day, the HV supervised the crew's movements and filming, before ordering them to leave on pain of being thrown into the city catacombs. On their way to Dubrovnik, through JNA lines, the trio had been warned not to return or they would be arrested.

Shortly afterwards, Kojović, Marić and Čengić were declared *personae non grata* in Trebinje, the SDS headquarters in Hercegovina, because of their report "from the village of Ravno, destroyed by the JNA on the pretext that members of the Croatian Army were there. A campaign started, with the local radio station and press [in Trebinje] constantly agitating against TVSA. The crew could not buy petrol at a Trebinje petrol station, and the guard outside the town Assembly pulled back the bolt on his rifle and threatened them: 'You damn traitors, the whole lot of you should be killed!'."[53] That same month, a fourth TVSA journalist, cameraman Zoran Gudelj, was beaten in Trebinje for reporting from Ravno.

The same pressures were applied to the headquarters. Nenad Pejić gives the following example:

> In October 1991, Serbian TV broadcast a story about
> an Orthodox priest who was beaten up by Croatian

---

[51] RTVSA, "Examples of Obstruction of Work and Harrassment of TV Sarajevo Journalists", signed by N Pejić and prepared by TVSA news editors for the UN Human Rights Committee, March 1992.

[52] Id.

[53] Id.

forces. The same day Croatian TV broadcast a story about a Catholic priest who was beaten by Serbian forces. The point is that both stories were true, but Serbian TV did not broadcast the story about the Catholic priest and Croatian TV did not broadcast the story about the Orthodox priest. Sarajevo TV broadcast both stories. During the first minutes of the broadcast story about the Orthodox priest ... Croat viewers ... protested, calling us 'ethnic TV'! A few minutes later, when Sarajevo TV broadcast the story about the Catholic priest, Serb viewers called us and protested 'you are *ustaša* TV'![54]

TV Journalists and the Question of Impartiality

As the future of Bosnia hung by a thread, TVSA was attracting a huge audience for the most comprehensive television news service in former Yugoslavia. It was also the last major public institution, along with the newspaper *Oslobodjenje*, to withstand national fragmentation.[55]

None of this means, however, that the station's own news coverage presented the crisis in the republic clearly. The editor-in-chief of *Slobodna Bosna*, then the most perspicacious news medium in the republic, expressed his disdain for TVSA's evasive coverage of the 2 and 3 March 1992 crisis in the city (when the SDS mounted roadblocks and sniper nests near the parliament) and advised its journalists to divide into national channels if they so wished because they were useless united. "On Sunday evening [3 March] one could not [even] learn from your programme that Sarajevo was sealed off."[56]

---

[54] Pejić, supra note 43 at 26.

[55] N Pejić claims that TVSA's own research suggested that 1.7 million viewers watched the news on both channels. Pejić told the author that the station "became a substitute state, with people calling for advice about their anxieties and their practical problems, like what to do about an electricity cut, and was it true that the water supply in such-and-such a place had been poisoned".

[56] S Avdić, *Slobodna Bosna*, 5 March 1992. By contrast, Avdić praised Yutel's coverage of the crisis and claimed that Yutel's director, Goran Milić, had averted war in the capital merely by reporting events in a professional way.

With the start of open aggression a month later, pressure on TVSA massively increased. The editorial watchword was still impartiality but editorial decisions were becoming quasi-military decisions, putting lives directly at risk. Pejić recounts that in mid-April, some Muslim soldiers occupied the dam above Višegrad and threatened to blow it up. The newsroom had two calls in quick succession. The first was from the SDA: "Mr Pejić, if you do not broadcast our live telephone conversation with the soldiers on the Višegrad dam, they are going to destroy it." The second was from the SDS: "Mr Pejić, if you broadcast live the telephone conversation with the Muslim terrorists on the Višegrad dam, we will shell your transmitters." Pejić decided to broadcast the conversation with the Muslim paramilitaries on the dam, "and just a few minutes later a Serbian paramilitary group started to shell TVSA's transmitter".

RTVSA's use of sources and terms in reporting the war appeared to reflect a view that impartiality required the presentation of all parties to the conflict as more or less equal, and equally responsible for the descent into violence, without regard to the context or content of each side's position. RTVBH's director-general, Mufid Memija, reflected this view of impartiality when he was challenged about the frequent criticism that television had not prepared citizens for this war. He evaded the question but noted that impartiality "means you are affirming criminality as a real alternative to a normal civilized project".[57] Memija's meaning of impartiality implies that it buttressed the Serb side by equating it and its self-justifying arguments with the Bosnian government side and its arguments in favour of an indivisible, democratic republic.

A former news editor says that Tanjug reports were used, uncredited, as the source of most TVBH news items "until we saw that their reports about Sarajevo were false".[58] As for vocabulary, it remained mystifyingly vague long after the nature of the assault was visible around the world. Zlatko Dizdarević remarked tartly as late as 2 June 1992 in his *Oslobodjenje* diary that "journalists at the International Press Centre want to know, 'When will Bosnia-Hercegovina's television start to use a terminology about this war that describes what is actually taking place?'

---

[57] M Memija, *Dani*, 10 March 1993.

[58] For Tanjug, see Ch. 2 supra.

(In the interest of moderation, Bosnian TV journalists have avoided naming the aggressor or any of the parties involved in the conflict.)."[59]

RTVBH radio journalist, Rade Trbojević, a Serb by nationality, has suggested two reasons why "everyone was afraid to say publicly that the JNA was attacking Sarajevo". First, some Serb journalists were still not committed to staying in Sarajevo, and wanted to keep the option of leaving open by not damning the SDS and its forces. The haemorrhage of Serbs from the television station and other media through the early weeks of violence may corroborate this claim, though journalists of other nationalities left too. The second reason was fear. When Trbojević did publicly identify the Serbs as aggressors (he claims to have been the first), he was branded a "*jihad* journalist" by Srpska Republika Novinska Agencija (SRNA, the Serb Republic News Agency). Threats then ensued from Serbs in Sarajevo, to the point that Trbojević moved his family to a different address.[60]

However, this is not enough to explain why RTVBH strove to misrepresent the evidence of everybody's eyes, even after the JNA had finally evacuated the city and the republic, in the last week of May 1992. Another consideration is the notion of impartiality in its Bosnian context. Yutel's director, Goran Milić, (who should know something about the pitfalls of impartiality in the midst of war)[61] says that RTVBH's general approach in the late 1980s, as Serbian storm clouds thickened over Kosovo, Slovenia and Croatia, was one of: "don't get into that mess, don't report those bloody events. Report about the economy instead."[62] As a result, RTVBH's effect on its audience was precisely opposite to that of TV Belgrade and TV Zagreb on theirs; it disarmed them psychologically.

In this respect, many journalists and editors were deluded by the same sort of thinking that SDA and some HDZ leaders persisted in until April 1992. Several factors contributed to this delusion:

---

[59] Z Dizdarević, supra note 22.

[60] Rade Trbojević, *Dani* magazine, 30 July 1993. Trbojević suspects that his father, who died in an unexplained fall, was killed by Serb neighbours in revenge for the son's outspokenness.

[61] See Ch. 2, section on 'Yutel' supra.

[62] G Milić to author, 27 Aug. 1993.

*   The political factor. The SDA leadership calculated that its best chance of preserving the republic lay through constant negotiations, trying to defuse the mine to prevent it from exploding, as one of the SDA leaders put it.[63] In September 1991, President Izetbegović tried to persuade the EC to support the provision of salaries and pensions for JNA officers in Bosnia. At the end of December, JNA chiefs of staff visited Sarajevo and assured President Izetbegović that the JNA would not impose solutions on Bosnia by force. Early in 1992, President Izetbegović allowed the JNA to disarm the Bosnian Territorial Defence Units.[64] Thus, continual negotiation was the policy, whatever its merits, and journalists duly fell into line.

*   The psychological factor. The belief that the JNA could never turn against Bosnia, regardless of what it might have done in Croatia, and that the outside world ('Europe') would never let a general war happen, was widespread in Bosnia, including among journalists.

Senior journalists with good connections in the political establishment, including those at RTVSA, *Oslobodjenje*, and Yutel, appear to have been more, rather than less, deluded; and less willing than others to identify the onset of aggression as such.

Two Serbian writers of the non-aligned opposition are among those who have touched on the heart of this matter. Ivan Čolović quotes a sentence by David Rousset: "'Normal people do not know that everything is possible.' This apparently banal but truly terrible constatation seems to me to summarize our present situation very precisely", says Čolović. In a similar vein, Miloš Vasić of *Vreme* has written that "the possibility of a war in Bosnia-Hercegovina was so appalling to everyone that it bordered on the unthinkable, like a global thermonuclear war, from the Yugoslav standpoint".[65]

*   The professional factor. Taking RTVSA part-way out of the system in 1989 was easier than taking the system out of the station. RTVSA was

---

[63] E Ganić quoted in E Vulliamy, *Seasons in Hell: Understanding Bosnia's War* (London: Simon & Schuster, 1994), 74-75.

[64] The Territorial Defence Units were the forerunner of what became the ABH.

[65] I Čolović, "Ceux qui petent le feu", *Les Temps modernes*, February 1993. M Vasić, *Balkan War Report*, Jan. 1993.

peopled with ideological journalists who were habituated to working for, and within, a totalitarian system. Only some of the youngest staff were open to the influence of the younger group of free-thinking print-journalists who were active in Sarajevo at the end of the 1980s, such as those at the weekly *Slobodna Bosna*. (This factor was to have consequences, as the SDS, the HDZ, and their backers outside the republic, exacerbated tension in Bosnia. Many journalists yielded sooner or later to the siren call of nationality.)

Secondly, many journalists did not know how to cover the threat to their republic. Their framework of interpretation was ideologically pro-Yugoslav and pro-JNA; they could identify the perennial demon of 'nationalism' as the enemy, but they could not or would not identify the scale of danger represented by the SDS, even when it was obviously subverting the republic from inside its government, arming paramilitary bands, seizing transmitters, and openly colluding with the JNA.

* The cultural factor. Bosnia and Bosnians were traditionally the butt of patronizing humour and disdain, or worse, for Serb and Croat nationalists. A portion of this hauteur was internalized by generations of Bosnians themselves during the 70-plus years of Yugoslavia, and particularly by Muslims, whose national identity (not fully recognized until 1971) was often an enigma to themselves as much as to others. One consequence was a Bosnian tendency to give the benefit of the doubt to the self-confident champions of Serb (and Croat) 'national rights'.

War Conditions

The RTV centre stands at the western edge of Sarajevo, not far from the *Oslobodjenje* building. Both were built in time for the 1984 Winter Olympics, which Sarajevo hosted. In May 1992, the *Oslobodjenje* journalist Zlatko Dizdarević watched the RTV centre "gradually being transformed into a gigantic sieve".[66] The centre never became unusable, however; it was built to withstand bombardment and it has successfully done so.

---

[66] Dizdarević, supra note 22.

By early May 1992, the sieve had already leaked many personnel. Sarajevo was a dangerous place and journalists were particular targets of Serb threats; Nenad Pejić, editor-in-chief of TVSA, left suddenly, as did Besim Cerić, director of TVSA. Director-general Nedo Miljanović also departed, and settled in Montenegro. About 20 Serb editors and reporters left to work in the 'Serb Republic'; about 10 Croats went to 'Herceg-Bosna'. Others went to Belgrade and Zagreb, or farther afield to rebuild a normal life beyond reach of snipers and artillery. Others stayed in Sarajevo but did not go to work, from fear of the shelling and sniping or from concern that their work at the station would place them in even more danger.

The result was chaos in the newsroom. Much equipment was stolen, and many journalists in Sarajevo believe that it ended up at the television studio of the 'Serb Republic' in Pale. Other equipment was destroyed in the shelling of the city.[67] During April and May, nobody knew who would turn up for work on any given day. One editor of Serb nationality, Dragan Božanić, took the opportunity during April to insert pro-Serb reports from international stations into the news; he later left for Pale. The Serb leadership sent an 'open letter' to RTVSA on 9 April, stating that the station had become an SDA organ, under the physical control of that party.[68] Clearly this was untrue, but with half the republic already deprived of the TVSA signal, people in Serb-controlled areas could not judge this propaganda for themselves. The letter was undoubtedly also intended to intimidate staff at the station.

RTVSA employed 2,300 staff before the war. By early 1993, according to one journalist, some 1,800 had left, "including all the senior staff". A skeleton crew of around 140 journalists and technicians kept the services going.[69] Twenty-seven staff had been killed (engineers and technicians mostly) and many more wounded. Finding experienced replacements proved impossible. Cub reporters were promoted to war correspondents, resulting in poor quality of reporting.

---

[67] On 3 May [1993], UNESCO reported that TVBH's only remaining professional camera had been destroyed in the fighting in Sarajevo, preventing future live reports by the station (*Index on Censorship*, July-Aug. 1993).

[68] *Borba*, 10 April 1992.

[69] M Saki-Hatibović, quoted in 48 *UNESCO Sources*, June 1993, 114.

By early 1993 the evening news, and a half-hour round-up of international satellite stations' coverage of the war, were TVBH's only daily productions. The rest of the 12-hour schedule was filled with archive material (old serials, documentaries, movies), folk music and rock video clips, satellite football matches and movies, plus an occasional current-affairs or cultural programme. The production team was picked up each morning in the city centre and driven to the RTVBH centre, accelerating along the most exposed route, known as 'sniper alley'. Snipers routinely targeted the RTVBH bus.

The technical and visual poverty of TVBH news is due to circumstances which are beyond the station's control: the war waged against the republic by one and then another army. This rapidly brought the station to chaos. From April 1992 its reporters could not work in the two-thirds of Bosnia which the Serb side conquered; in 1993 they could not work in the Croat-controlled portion either. Contact between Sarajevo and the rest of government-controlled land in central and northern Bosnia is extremely difficult.

These conditions encouraged the newsroom to focus exclusively on Sarajevo, which could at least be filmed, while relying otherwise on a handful of their foreign correspondents whose pieces were received on the station's sole satellite telephone in the editor-in-chief's office. This left other communities in Bosnia feeling abandoned and distrustful, however, which suited the Serb and Croat sides very well. An official from Konjic and Jablanica, only 80 kilometres from the capital, complained: "we have been completely cut off from all important information, TV and Radio BH were engrossed in the problems of Sarajevo, they've treated all other parts of the state marginally".[70]

The poor quality of content cannot be explained in the same way. One local critic has described TVBH's war reportage as "very noisy and incomprehensible" and illustrated with "maps from geography schoolbooks". He continued:

Maybe we can forgive this because of war shortages, but we cannot approve the shamefully small quantity of facts and information offered to the most patient listeners and viewers. Instead of precise and clear

---

[70] S Ćibo, quoted by S Avdić, *Ljiljan*, 1 Sept. 1993.

facts about the situation in the war areas, we have to listen to a repertoire of political pamphleteering by a ham radio operator. Instead of casualty figures in a town, we hear how the people and soldiers are ready to fight the aggressors, to struggle for a united, sovereign, free ... etcetera.[71]

Television News Under Government Control

Formal control of RTVBH passed to the government during spring 1992. The hierarchy of authority in RTVSA disintegrated under the impact of the attack on Sarajevo: the trio of top executives had left, and the procedure for electing successors lapsed. The government initially appointed an executive committee to run RTV. Its nine members, led by Mehmed Agović, were all journalists at the station and comprised all three nationalities. At the end of April, the committee banned Serb leaders and SRNA information from the airwaves. The committee imposed no other direct orders upon journalists.[72] The republican Constitution directed that an enlarged Presidency should assume executive and legislative power if war prevented the parliament from meeting. This was done on 1 July 1992 (a 'state of war' having been declared on 20 June), and the Presidency took charge of executive appointments at the RTVBH.

Several journalists said that a pro-Muslim, or rather a pro-SDA, perspective began to be imposed towards the end of 1992. It was at this time that the ABH started to publicly criticize journalists; and SDA members were appointed as director-general of RTV and as director of the radio. (The previous director-general, Mehmed Agović, was a Muslim by nationality but not by political conviction, and was not a party member.)

Mufid Memija, the new director-general, was a classic example of the 'journalist-convert'.[73] Before the advent of democracy, Memija was

---

[71] D Hrasnica, *Dani*, 27 Oct. 1993.

[72] The taboos on criticism of the SDA and of the HVO (until February 1993) were applied informally, and only occasionally broken on the radio news.

[73] On 'journalist-converts', see Ch. 4, section on 'Journalists and War' *supra*. Memija was replaced in early 1994.

"a highly agile exponent of self-management socialism and the politics of non-alignment".[74] At the end of the 1970s and in the first half of the 1980s, Memija was one of the three best known TV journalists in Sarajevo.[75]

With Memija at the helm, standards at TVSA declined. A news journalist described to ARTICLE 19 how an international satellite report — about the HVO's threat to shell a Muslim settlement in central Bosnia — was inserted in the news one evening in February 1993, without the editor's knowledge. Any questioning of the HVO's increasingly hostile role had been taboo at RTVBH, so this insertion signalled a major shift in editorial policy. It also exposed the news editor to the danger of reprisal by Croat soldiers in Sarajevo (the HVO had its own unit in the city until it was dissolved in October 1993), for, as everywhere in former Yugoslavia, the editor (who also presents the programme) is responsible for the content of the information he or she broadcasts.

A former TV news editor says that Mufid Memija "is Izetbegović's man but you can't say that he conducts Izetbegović's policy because Izetbegović has no policy. I was the first here to ask for clear guidelines about censorship in war. But no guidelines were given, nothing! So we do the best we can."

Another former television news editor recalls Memija trying to insert items in the evening news, soon after his appointment. The editor dissuaded him but his disenchantment grew and a few months later he left Sarajevo. The editor estimates that altogether about 60 staff, mostly Croats and Serbs, left RTVBH in the first four or five months of 1993, largely from distaste for the creeping manipulation. (Only two of these, to the editor's knowledge, went 'national': a Serb crossed the lines to Kanal S, in Pale, and a Croat made his way to TV Široki Brijeg, in 'Herceg-Bosna'.)

While ARTICLE 19 heard of no suspensions or dismissals of non-Muslims at TVBH on national grounds, non-Muslims felt marginalized in 1993. With increasing reason, they began to feel they were a token

---

[74] The description by his interviewers from *Dani* magazine (issue of 10 March 1993).

[75] The others were Ilija Guzina, who defected to become the chief news editor at Kanal S television in the 'Serb Republic', and Smiljko Šagolj who reports for HTV Široki Brijeg in Croat 'Herceg-Bosna', both of whom have gained notoriety for their role in spreading propaganda. See section on 'Croat Media' infra.

presence: that their loyalty to the idea of a multinational, multi-confessional Bosnia was being abused. This feeling was strongly bolstered on 20 September 1993, when some 25 of the better-known Muslim journalists from RTVBH were asked to a meeting in the name of President Izetbegović. No non-Muslims were invited. There they were told that the Bosnian government would soon sign the Geneva plan for a so-called Union of Bosnian Republics. The journalists' task was to prepare the public for the shock of this about-turn. The meeting dispersed and the journalists awaited orders, which never came, because the President didn't sign.

Shortly after this episode, a change was introduced in the TVBH schedule. A Bosnian folk-song was played before the evening news (and also after the main evening radio news). The song is associated with the SDA party, and is sung by a famous Muslim choir, from the Gazi Huzrev-beg mosque. This was understood by staff and audience alike as a further signal of Muslim political predominance, or even of Islamization.

In 1993 TVBH repeatedly delayed the release of negative information from the public. The station delayed releasing the news of the 8 January assassination of Deputy-Premier Hakija Turajlić for several hours. Director-general Memija's account of why the information had been withheld was neither coherent nor convincing, except for the defensive admission that Hrvatska Televijia (HTV, Croatian Television) had been free to broadcast the foreign station's report "because the information wasn't so relevant for its public".[76] When the Sarajevo suburb of Otes fell in a bloody assault in January, the extent of casualties was not revealed. A journalist from *Dani* magazine wondered why viewers did not learn that Mount Igman (at the very edge of the city) had fallen to the Serbs on 31 July-1 August 1993 until TVBH's Geneva correspondent mentioned in a report that President Izetbegović was demanding their withdrawal.[77]

Usually, however, according to a TVBH editor who is not a Muslim and who criticizes the station freely, TVBH's gaffes and omissions owe more to incompetence and disorganization than to intention:

> The news doesn't give a proper, comprehensible
> picture of events. There are no editorial guidelines

---

[76] M Memija, *Dani*, 10 March 1993.

[77] D Hrasnica, *Dani* magazine, 27 Oct. 1993.

for what to do in certain situations, so everything is up to personal initiative. Memija appears at seven o'clock with a commentary to be inserted in the programme, which goes out at 7.30! Politicians exploit opportunities like the destruction of the Mostar bridge to barge in with ideological commentaries. Editors decide the agenda of items for themselves. They all make mistakes, but they aren't attacked for it because no one bothers that much. Our confused TV news reflects the government's confused politics.

Radio

The conditions at RBH (formerly Radio Sarajevo) during the war have very closely resembled that of the television station. The two services are part of the same company, and war has forced them to pool their resources, to the extent that the television news is transmitted on RBH at 8.00 p.m.

However, there have been differences. The radio lost fewer of its staff through defection and emigration, and it was not hit so hard by loss of transmitters. RBH's main transmitter, at Visoko, some 30 kilometres north-west of Sarajevo, was disabled by Serb shelling in the autumn of 1992. For some three weeks, the station was reduced to broadcasting on FM, and was audible only in the capital. RTVBH engineers managed to repair Visoko, which now transmits in medium- and short-wave.

For the first month of the Serb attack, the radio kept a very open editorial stance. Arguments from all sides (government, Serb, Croat, JNA) were presented with minimal comment by the news editors. Todor Dutina, the director of SRNA, faxed his daily bulletins to RTV from his base at Pale and even rang up the radio station, which transmitted his call. On one occasion, in the first half of April, Dutina called the station with an ultimatum: "Unless you immediately release frequencies of Radio Sarajevo for the needs of 'Serb Radio', the RTV centre will be bombarded!" Shells began to hit the centre soon afterwards.[78]

The editorial openness did not last. At the end of April 1992, the second radio channel was shut down, in order to concentrate resources on the principal programmes, and the RTVBH executives banned Serb leaders and SRNA information from the airwaves. According to a member of the news editorial team, no other directives have been handed down. However, as on television, the coverage of relations between the HVO and the Bosnian Army was tightly controlled; the HVO could not be criticized until February or March 1993, and the taboo on criticism of the government and the ABH continues.

Until the end of May, correspondents in Tuzla, Bihać, Zenica and other government-held towns could telephone reports to the RTVBH centre. Then the Serb forces cut telephone links, and the only regular news from around the republic came via amateur radio operators (see below). The network of local stations has been broken up, and many of the stations have been taken over by Serb and Croat forces.

Staff at the station say that no journalists were suspended from the radio for political reasons. One editor was demoted in October 1992 after inquiring, on air, whether Alija Izetbegović was acting, during a visit to Hercegovina, as President of the Republic or of the SDA.

Early in 1993, Nadja Pašić was forced to resign as director of the radio station. She was replaced by Šaćir Filandra, a member of the SDA, and with no relevant qualifications. RTVBH staff say that the radio retained some slight distance from the government until the summer.

Private Radio

In Sarajevo there are two radio stations offering a broader diet of news than RBH supplies. Nezavisni Student Radio 99 (known as Radio 99) was set up in February 1992 by Altermedia, a private company formed by a group of young intellectuals and journalists under the auspices of the Socialdemokratska Partija (SDP, Socialist Democratic Party, the former League of Communists). The station is situated in the basement of the former Central Committee building.

---

[78] K Kurspahić, *Oslobodjenje*, 18 May 1992.

Radio 99's news bulletins aim to present "pure information with just linking comments", according to editor-in-chief Adil Kulenović, formerly an information officer with the Socialist Democratic Party. Bulletins last no longer than 15 minutes, and draw on CNN, Sky News, Radio France Internationale, Voice of America and Deutsche Welle, as well as Hrvatski Radio. Radio 99 also carries interviews and phone-in programmes. The station can be received in Pale, says Kulenović, and "SRNA often quotes us, especially when we attack the government. SRNA calls us the only independent medium in Sarajevo. Which is dangerous."

By travelling abroad during the war, Kulenović says, he became aware of the danger of distortion in Sarajevo media. Putting together brief reports about Bosnia culled from a dozen foreign sources, "you give the impression that the wide world is deeply concerned about Bosnia, and that something must therefore be done about it soon". This fostered citizens' vain hope — encouraged already by state radio and television — of foreign military intervention to end their suffering. Not that the station disregards the need for hope: "We don't say 'this is the nineteenth month of war' but 'this is one day closer to the war's end'. It is almost a crime to insist on proving to people how much they suffer, how difficult life is. Nobody broadcasts the suicide statistics for Sarajevo, and sometimes a single word can change a person's mind when he or she is on the edge."[79]

Radio Sarajevo Zid is the city's favourite FM music station, anchored by disc-jockeys and journalists in their twenties, and owned by a well-known personality in Sarajevo, Zdravko Grebo.[80] The station started broadcasting in March 1993. "As an independent radio station, Radio Sarajevo Zid shall have a defined autonomous political attitude. It will not come from any ideology, dogma, party codex", wrote Grebo in his ringing 'International Manifesto' for Zid.

Zid's news bulletins are conceived as part of the station's cultural mission to educate listeners against nationalism and intolerance. "People don't expect us to have comprehensive news", Grebo says. "My own view is that it is equally important to have news from outside former Yugoslavia as about Sarajevo. Even if our news about Bosnia and former Yugoslavia

---

[79] A Kulenović to author, 9 Nov. 1993.

[80] *Zid* means wall, and it puns on Grebo's name: Zdravko i društvo, Zdravko and company.

is all true, without information from abroad the picture can only be half true."[81] The station has no news reporters of its own; its bulletins use information ad hoc from international networks and from foreign newspapers when it can get them.

Outside Sarajevo, the environment could hardly be more hostile to "autonomous political attitudes", as the fate of Radio CD proved very clearly.

Radio CD was a private station in the central Bosnian town of Zenica, whose population is predominantly Muslim. It was started in autumn 1991 by a young journalist, Zoran Mišetić (a Croat who supports the integrity of Bosnia), who wrung some start-up capital from the town authorities. He broadcast a mixture of music and current affairs; any politician could speak on Radio CD, on condition of taking listeners' questions. Mišetić freely criticized the town's SDA-dominated authorities for favouring Muslim managers; and when an SDA leader told a press conference that Bosnia had no room for independent media, Mišetić accused him of fascism. Municipal and republican SDA politicians attacked him, but the station gained a following; when Radio CD organized an anti-war rally, thousands attended.

On 19 April 1993, a gang of armed and masked men tried to kidnap Mišetić. They went to his family's flat, where they threatened his family with death unless they revealed his whereabouts. (The gang, who described themselves as *mujahedin*, took two television sets and other valuables.) The gang took Mišetić's mother to the radio station. According to the hotel manager who leased premises to Mišetić, the gang disarmed the police guarding the hotel, and forced their way into the radio station. Mišetić wasn't there. He was at the hospital, giving blood for the people wounded in the mortar attack on central Zenica a couple of hours earlier. The gang left, kidnapping two of the radio's journalists, one a Croat by nationality and the other a Serb. Essential equipment was also stolen.

The pretext given by the *mujahedin* gang for wanting Zoran Mišetić was that his reports for Voice of America were helping the Serbs by revealing which targets in Zenica had been hit. In reality they wanted hostages to exchange for "our *mujahedin* brothers arrested at HVO checkpoints on different dates since December 1992". These words come from a handwritten document from the gang, dated 19 April and addressed

---

[81] Z Grebo to author, 15 Nov. 1993.

"To the UN Büro Zenica". The document lists 15 men with Arabic names, with the dates and locations of their arrest by the HVO. The unnamed authors added: "we inform you that another HVO-cooperators [sic] from Radio CD were taken and added to the list of HVO-hostages on our hand". When members of the EC Monitoring Mission tried to investigate, they found the studio locked by persons unknown. The Zenica authorities appear to have done nothing to protect the station or, later, to find the criminals. When ARTICLE 19 questioned the Minister of Information in Sarajevo about the Radio CD case, he said that he had never heard of the station.

Zoran Mišetić escaped to Croatia with the help of members of international and Bosnian church organizations, and foreign journalists. The two kidnapped journalists were later exchanged as hostages by their captors. Radio CD has not broadcast since 19 April. Mišetić has since been commended by a Flemish peace organization for his work in "opposing intellectual cleansing".[82]

Amateur Radio

More than a thousand radio hams were registered in Bosnia when the war started, organized in some 250 radio clubs covering the whole republic. About 160 of these clubs reacted to the attack in March and April 1992 by co-ordinating a message service.

Radio hams would work regular hours at their machines, communicating with each other and with a few friendly clubs in Serbia (15 out of 120) and in Croatia. Even before telephone connections were broken in summer 1992, their network was a substitute telephone service operating across battle lines.[83] While ham radio news reports were of variable professional and technical quality, they were indispensable for RTVBH news, especially for getting information from the Serb-besieged and bombarded enclaves in eastern Bosnia. "Radio amateurs are doing a heroic

---

[82] Z Mišetić to author, 30 Oct. 1993.

[83] Information in this paragraph comes from a paper by M S Mandrino from Pančevo, Vojvodina, entitled "Humanitarian Aid on the Air: the Role of Radio Amateurs in the Bosnian War", made available by the Institute for War and Peace Reporting, London.

job, achieving the impossible", wrote *Oslobodjenje*'s Zlatko Dizdarević.[84]
Ed Vulliamy of *The Guardian* vindicates that tribute in his description of
the radio ham network:

> A voice that had become familiar to those huddling
> around radio sets in Sarajevo was that of Ismet
> Mustafić, a radio ham in Cerska. On the first day of
> March [1993] ... that voice sounded unusually
> nervous. 'The Serbs are about to enter Cerska', he
> reported. 'They have moved to the edge of town and
> have been shelling all night. Thousands are preparing
> to flee.' The following day, the radio sets reported
> that Cerska had fallen. The torment of Cerska and
> Srebrenica was a drama that unfolded down crackly
> radio receivers belonging to hams like Izet Karaman
> in Tuzla, who had rigged up his kit and tape
> recorders in the garage of his block of flats, the walls
> covered with signal numbers and names of people he
> had never met who were now speaking to the world
> via his equipment.[85]

It was a radio ham who broke the story of starvation in Žepa. It
was also ham radio which informed the world when General Morillon, UN
commander in Bosnia, resolved to remain in besieged Srebrenica until aid
arrived.

However, the network was not only serving the media: it was often
the only method of political and military communication between Sarajevo
and the government-controlled enclaves. It was also the only means to
make personal contact across the battle lines. The mosque and the
synagogue in Zagreb, for example, both maintained radio links with
Sarajevo.[86]

Salko Hukelić, of the Bosnian League of Amateur Radio, told
Oslobodjenje that solidarity "was not lacking" among the republic's radio

---

[84] Dizdarević, supra note 22, diary entry for 7 Aug. 1992.

[85] Vulliamy, supra note 63 at 273.

[86] *The Independent*, 30 July 1993.

hams.[87] This modest claim was true, but radio hams participated in, as well as resisted, the conflict. Velibor Čolić, a writer from Posavina who served with government forces in 1992, has told grim stories of radio treachery during the war: the Muslim radio ham in Modriča who helped the Serbs to direct their artillery, and the Croat radio ham who similarly helped the Serbs in Donji Kladari. The latter was captured and executed: he allegedly told his executioners that he had done it for money and because his daughter was married to a JNA officer.[88]

The Press

Oslobodjenje

One surprising effect of the war has been the rise to global fame of an obscure Bosnian daily newspaper. Before the war, *Oslobodjenje* was selling some 80,000 copies in Bosnia and up to 10,000 in other republics. By 16 September 1993, the day when 72 newspapers (on four continents and with a total circulation of 22 million in 40 languages) published a facsimile page or longer insert from *Oslobodjenje*, in recognition of its 50th birthday, it had surely become the best-known and most praised newspaper in the history of south-eastern Europe.

The newspaper's building, which has been destroyed by shells and fire, is near the RTVBH centre at the edge of the city, only a few score metres from the front line. Yet the paper has barely missed a day since the war began. Staff work in shifts, sleeping in the building which has no electricity, water or heating. The editors work from a nuclear fall-out shelter in the cellar, often by candlelight. The paper is printed there, and staff take turns to transport copies by truck to vendors around the city.

"The publication of *Oslobodjenje* is a daily miracle", declared the International Federation of Newspaper Publishers (FIEJ) early in 1993. "FIEJ also praises the determination of the newspaper's editors to remain

---

[87] *Oslobodjenje*, 25 May 1992.

[88] V Čolić, *Les Bosniques* (Paris: Editions Galilee/Carrefour des litteratures, 1993), 22-23 and 67-68.

above the ethnic conflicts which have torn their country apart, in keeping its multi-ethnic staff and in respecting professional standards of objectivity in its reporting."[89]

Croatian journalist Danko Plevnik has written that *Oslobodjenje*'s tenacious survival has turned the paper into "a symbol of the struggle of the people of Bosnia for their freedom and independence".[90] The paper's editor-in-chief concurs: "Despite the material and human losses we have suffered (five journalists killed, more than 12 missing without trace, and about 30 wounded) the free spirit of our paper is stronger than ever. The staff of *Oslobodjenje* are the exact image, not only ethnically, but ethically, of Bosnia-Hercegovina."[91]

The Oslobodjenje group was Bosnia's equivalent of the Vjesnik and Politika groups in Croatia and Serbia. By 1990, it was publishing two dailies (the other is *Večernje novine*), 15 weeklies and four journals. It had its own distribution network, with 800 kiosks and 200 delivery vehicles.

Oslobodjenje was one of many Yugoslav newspapers which began life as a Partisan news-sheet during the Second World War and then passed into the ownership of the SAWP. In Bosnia, both the League of Communists and the SAWP were highly orthodox and conservative: qualities which *Oslobodjenje* fully reflected. Unlike *Politika* in Serbia and *Vjesnik* in Croatia, *Oslobodjenje* had never been the flagship of a reform movement, because Bosnia never had a reform movement.

In the run-up to the 1990 elections, the SAWP renounced its ownership privileges and allied itself with the League of Communists. This left the paper in ownerless limbo. After the elections, the coalition government wanted to reorganize *Oslobodjenje* along national lines, just as it wanted to divide RTVSA into three national services. A law was drafted to constitute a parliamentary group which would implement a national policy at the paper and at RTVSA.

Editor-in-chief, Kemal Kurspahić led the resistance which has been described in the section on 'Television' above. All 2,000 staff at *Oslobodjenje* supported Kurspahić, although they were 51 per cent Serb

---

[89] Resolution of FIEJ, published in *IFEX Bulletin*, 8 Feb. 1993.

[90] Plevnik, *Hrvatski obrat* (Zagreb: Durieux, 1993), 57.

[91] K Kurspahić, in the 50th anniversary special edition.

by nationality.[92] Deputy editor, Gordana Knežević explains how "a bit of gossip" helped to forge this solidarity. Rumour had it that the SDS had earmarked a Serb television journalist to manage the nationalized *Oslobodjenje*,[93] and that his task would be to bankrupt the newspaper in order to justify the introduction of three national dailies.[94] Faced with this prospect, the staff stuck together and defeated the planned reforms. The paper began the process of transforming itself into a joint-stock company, a process which was completed in March 1992, on the eve of war.

The ownership limbo was matched by an editorial impasse. The modern history and the mixed national make-up of Bosnia meant that its main daily paper could not switch from being a republican to a national organ. In any case, its essence, as with RTVSA, was anti-nationalist. Tactical support for one national party against others was out of the question.

This, along with the paper's strident dogmatism, explains why it could never entrench itself in readers' affections or capture their deeper loyalties in the way that *Politika*, to take the obvious example, could do with Serbs. A 1989 survey of public opinion about the press indicated that a smaller proportion of citizens in Bosnia relied on their republican press for information than in any other republic; the figure for Bosnia was 26 per cent, as against 79 per cent for Croatia (the highest proportion) and 42 per cent for Serbia (including Vojvodina). When Bosnians were asked which publication they respected most (the leading Serbian and Croatian dailies were also sold in Bosnia), *Oslobodjenje* won less than half the survey's sample of votes gained by *Politika*, and only the same number that Croatian dailies gained.[95]

Just as the republic itself was prevented by nationalist factions from developing a post-Communist, democratic identity, so too *Oslobodjenje* could not reconstruct itself after 1990. Being extremely pro-Yugoslav and pro-JNA, it could neither penetrate the Yugoslavist mask

---

[92] According to L'Organisation Internationale des Journalistes, supra note 16, by September 1992 the proportion had fallen to 31 per cent.

[93] Ilija Guzina, now the main news editor at Kanal S, in Pale.

[94] G Knežević to author, 12 Nov. 1993.

[95] Survey results printed in *Borba*, 2 Oct. 1989; cited in S P Ramet, "The Role of the Press in Yugoslavia", in J B Allcock, J B Horton and M Milivojevic (eds.), *Yugoslavia in Transition: Choices and Constraints. Essays in Honour of Fred Singleton* (New York & Oxford: 1993), 414-441.

of Serbian nationalism nor detect how the JNA was aligning itself with that nationalism. It often just blankly condemned developments. Its report of Slovenia's move to independence, for example, revealed sheer incomprehension. "Slovenia no longer part of Europe" was the headline over a disapproving piece.[96]

Editor-in-chief Kemal Kurspahić has said: "I was one of those who simply could not believe that war could ever come to this city. 'Impossible!' I said to the many foreign visitors, journalists, diplomats, friends, who came to visit *Oslobodjenje*."[97] When war did come to the city, it created conditions which revived *Oslobodjenje*. The bombardment vindicated the paper's anti-national dogmatism.

The paper was no better placed to report the aggression against Bosnia than any other Sarajevo medium; with two-thirds of the republic shut off, and only sporadic contact with the remaining third, it became a city paper.

While the news coverage is thin, the paper's commentators do not lack trenchancy. They have criticized the President's interference with military operations, the Foreign Minister's aloofness, and the nepotism in diplomatic circles.[98] However, such criticism is occasional and 'balanced' with adjacent pro-government articles; not because the government controls the paper (it doesn't) but because the editorial team shares the government's view of its priorities. The team holds that, when the public is suffering so much already, it is pointless to demoralize it further by attacking the authorities for faults which everyone knows about anyway. The result of this policy is that the news coverage has on occasion distorted information. The fall of the central Bosnian town of Jajce, on the evening of 29 October 1992 is a good example. RTVBH announced the fall, but on 31 October *Oslobodjenje*'s front page ran: "BH Army counter offensive". "The *četniki* have not severed the life of the 600-year-old Bosnian town of Jajce", said the report, then added that "more than 90 per cent" of Jajce's population were in flight.

---

[96] *Oslobodjenje*, 26 June 1991.

[97] K Kurspahić, in Ali & Lifschutz supra note 13.

[98] "The local daily *Oslobodjenje* has charged President Izetbegović with impeding offensives whenever it seemed they might have a chance of breaking the siege. All of these accusations have been met by a notable silence by the government." (M Ćamo, 17 *Balkan War Report*, Jan. 1993.)

Such distortion can be rationalized politically, in terms of the effect on morale in Sarajevo. However, in the case of *Oslobodjenje*, the upbeat rhetoric of the Jajce reports also reflects something else: the paper's chosen role as the living symbol of Bosnian resistance to the madness of 'ethnic' politics. Pride in this role is perceptible in the war diary of the columnist, Zlatko Dizdarević, who wrote on 2 June 1992: "What moved me were the requests from many people all over Bosnia-Hercegovina who have a fax machine and who want to receive any information they can get from us, without doubting for a moment its veracity or reliability. I am moved to tears by the fact that day after day, in so many Bosnian towns, people queue in front of the windows that display a single telefaxed copy of this newspaper."[99] Thus it was that *Oslobodjenje* won a place at last in Bosnian hearts.

The Serb-JNA forces were aware of the paper's importance, and they targeted *Oslobodjenje* accordingly. The Sarajevo building was systematically shelled, regional correspondents were killed,[100] and premises in Serbia were seized.[101]

Slobodna Bosna and Ljiljan

Slobodna Bosna, a weekly tabloid newspaper, was launched in the autumn of 1991 by Altermedia.[102] The editor-in-chief, Senad Avdić, gathered a team of young writers hungry for political scoops. The newspaper's style was fearless and sensational.

Its fourth issue made it famous. "Sarajevo in the *četniks'* sights — SECRET PLAN TO ATTACK SARAJEVO" screamed the cover headlines on 21 November. This "super-exclusive" story by the paper's investigative

---

[99] Dizdarević, supra note 22, entry for 2 June 1992.

[100] The *Zvornik* correspondent, Kjasif Smailović, was killed on 8 April 1992 on the doorstep of his office, by the Serb 'liberators' of the town. He had seen them approach as he filed a piece which included the words, "This will probably be my last report." In May, the Doboj correspondent Ferid Ćehić was killed in his office.

[101] The Belgrade offices shared by RTVBH and *Oslobodjenje* were taken over on 16 May 1992 on the authority of the SDS. On 24 June, the Novi Sad bureau was broken into and the locks were changed. "Members of the Serbian Radical Party were reported to have moved in." (*Index on Censorship*, Sept. and Oct. 1992).

[102] On Altermedia, see section on 'Private Radio' supra.

team explained how the SDS was preparing a strategy to blockade Sarajevo on three sides, using paramilitary units armed and trained by the JNA. Some details in the prognosis were wrong (for example, the team claimed that the SDS would try to evacuate most of the 150,000 Serbs in Sarajevo before attacking) but many were proved correct four and a half months later.[103] Almost as striking as the article's accuracy, however, is its adequacy to the moment.

The paper published interviews with political leaders who also contributed articles. Events in Croatia were reported without euphemisms. Whatever the topic, one question hovered over all: will there be war in Bosnia? The yellowing pages of *Slobodna Bosna* still crackle with the tension of those months before war broke out.

When war came, the team dispersed. Muslim journalists remained at the paper and, over time, endorsed Bosnian Muslim (political) nationalism. One former member of the *Slobodna Bosna* team, Nerzuk Čurak, now heads the Army Press Centre. At the end of 1992, *Slobodna Bosna* escaped the static quarantine of Sarajevo to Zenica, the second largest city in Bosnia, to cover the war at closer quarters. The paper appeared in Zenica every month or two, when paper was available.

Several of *Slobodna Bosna*'s key writers, including Senad Avdić and Medina Delalić, also contribute to *Ljiljan*, a Bosnian Muslim nationalist weekly published first from Zagreb and later from Ljubljana. A Bosnian edition is printed in Visoko, and the newspaper also has a bureau in Zenica. *Ljiljan* was launched in late 1992, with support from Saudi Arabia. During 1993, the paper shed its non-Muslim contributors, and concentrated on smoking out 'fifth columnists' and 'traitors', in cheer-leading for the BH Army, and in trying to develop Bosnian Muslim national identity, including an Islamic dimension.

A typical sample of *Ljiljan*'s rhetoric is this 17 November 1993 report: "In the very neighbourhood of Ahmići, the village where those fascists [the HVO] massacred around a hundred [Muslim] civilians, fighters of the Army of Bosnia-Hercegovina liquidated 120 of Boban's fighters."

---

[103] According to one journalist who worked at *Slobodna Bosna* at the time, the information was leaked from the JNA leadership.

Dani

Dani is a privately-owned news magazine, similar in format to the independent Belgrade weekly *Vreme* and the former Zagreb independent weekly *Danas*. It owes much to the vibrant Sarajevo youth culture of the late 1980s. With short news pieces, lengthy features, a satirical supplement, city gossip, interviews and wide-ranging cultural back-pages, *Dani* is a rich product. Its tone is lucid and rather hard-bitten, avoiding the pleading and dogmatic victim-rhetoric which often marked the Sarajevo media. It was launched in autumn 1992 as *BH Dani*, which became *BH Ratni Dani* before all prefixes were dropped.

The name was chosen to associate the paper in the public mind with *Naši Dani*, the organ of the official Youth League of Bosnia (one of the components of the SAWP). In the late 1980s, bold criticism of the government made *Naši Dani* the leading political paper in the republic, selling up to 100,000 issues fortnightly. The Youth League elected to break with the SAWP in spring 1990, so it could campaign freely for the end-of-year elections as a separate party. Political independence brought *Naši Dani* financial ruin: state support for the SAWP expired at the end of 1990, leaving the Youth League (which, as the Democratic League, had crashed in the elections) high and dry. *Naši Dani* closed early in 1991.

Dani is owned by a private company belonging to Senad Pečanin, its editor-in-chief. Capital was supplied by Alija Delimustafic, a Communist entrepreneur who became a leading member of the SDA. He was Minster of the Interior until autumn 1992, when he left Sarajevo after a quarrel with the party leadership. From his new base in Austria, Delimustafic has continued to invest in the magazine.

Dani is widely regarded as the most independent-minded medium anywhere in Bosnia — not necessarily a recommendation, in a good many eyes. Supporters see the magazine as a beacon of professionalism; critics believe that the paper's owner set up *Dani* in a spirit of revenge against the government which sacked him, and that Pečanin and his team's reputation for editorial independence has been built at the expense of demoralizing the public.

Dani is equipped with a satellite telephone, a precious asset which has enabled the magazine to "break the information blockade of Sarajevo," Pečanin says, "so we could publish the opinions of Bosnians outside Bosnia, and also of commentators throughout former Yugoslavia". It has also been able to obtain reports from the besieged enclaves in eastern Bosnia.

Dani's regular team includes writers of all nationalities. It has covered stories which other media do not touch, including, for example, war-time prostitution in Sarajevo. It has criticized Bosnian Army commanders for the loss of their soldiers' lives, and attacked corruption in high places. According to Pečanin, when the government convened a group of editors in May 1993 and requested them to criticize burgeoning Muslim radicalism in the city, only *Dani* dared to do so.

Serb Media

Banja Luka in northern Bosnia was the bridgehead of Serb media expansionism in Bosnia. With a Serb population of 51 per cent, Banja Luka was the first stronghold of the SDS. As early as 1 August 1991, the SDS redirected the transmitter on Mount Kozara to receive Serbian television instead of TVSA. Later that month, Federal Premier Ante Marković released a taped conversation between Milošević and Karadžić, in which the SDS leader learned that his next delivery of weapons would come from the JNA Commander of the Banja Luka garrison, General Nicola Uzelac.[104]

Rasid Durić, a teacher of Yugoslav literature at Banja Luka University (until sacked by the Serb authorities in June 1992 for being 'nationally unsuitable': his nationality is Muslim), dates the beginning of war in the region to the seizure of the Kozara transmitter. "The seeds of propaganda hatred toward Banja Luka's Muslims grew from month to month: a little ball of disorientation ... swelled into an unbearable burden of personal and collective fear."[105] Petar Luković of *Vreme* takes much the same view of Serbian television's strategy: "They needed just six months. Serbian TV during that period [the winter of 1991-1992] was geared for the Serbs in Bosnia, not for Serbia."[106]

---

[104] Malcolm, supra note 5 at 225.

[105] R Duric, "Banja Luka war diary", *Bosna Press*, (Frankfurt), 21 Oct. 1993.

[106] P Luković to author, 14 Oct. 1993.

At the end of September 1991, with war raging in nearby Croatia, General Uzelac of the JNA was given the hospitality of the local radio station, Radio Banja Luka, to issue a general mobilization to fight in Croatia. President Izetbegović immediately appeared on TVSA to declare the mobilization illegal. The collective Presidency of the republic, sitting in Sarajevo, demanded General Uzelac's resignation, but was powerless to enforce its demand. The Minister of Information in the coalition government, Velibor Ostojić, an SDS leader, announced that the mobilization was legal.[107] Uzelac stayed, the mobilization went ahead, and the government was powerless to prevent it.

On 1 March 1992, the SDS seized the RTVSA studio and equipment in Banja Luka. Employees found a message when they came to work next morning: "If you are willing to work with us, you are welcome. If not, find yourselves a new job!"[108] The timing of their seizure of local media reveals the SDS strategy very plainly; 1 March was the second day of the referendum on sovereignty and independence, which the party knew would produce an unwelcome result.

Meanwhile the regional daily newspaper *Glas* had come under intense pressure to serve the SDS. After the 1990 elections, the paper passed into the ownership of the municipality, controlled by the SDS. In August 1992, the Minister of Information, Velibor Ostojić, attacked the editor-in-chief for being too critical and not a 'good Serb'. The editor was forced to leave and the paper became a hard-line nationalist organ. In August 1993, it changed its name to *Glas zapadne Srbije*. According to Nenad Zafirović in *Balkan War Report*, the paper and TV Banja Luka "compete in glorifying Karadžić's achievements, especially in conducting the war". Zafirović found few other news media in Banja Luka:

> The fledgling Liberal Party of Banja Luka, the only opposition party in the self-proclaimed State, was granted a permit last December [1992] to publish its own newspaper, *The New Lay-Out*. It had an open

---

[107] *The Guardian*, 1 Oct. 1991. Ostojić was to play an odious role in the 'ethnic cleansing' of Foča a few months later.

[108] The Forum of Muslim Intellectuals in Banja Luka, report by the Committee to Protect Human Rights dated 20 March 1992. The quotation comes from the list "Examples of Obstruction of Work and Harrassment of TV Sarajevo Journalists", supra note 51.

spirit, and for a time allowed a voice of sanity to surface. But after seven issues the authorities shut the paper, allegedly because of unauthorized use of offices. Other papers that did not sufficiently follow the line of the SDS have suffered a similar fate.[109]

In September 1993, about 1,000 mutinous Serb troops descended on Banja Luka from the front lines. They blocked the access roads, and effectively captured the town without firing a shot. Their headquarters issued a statement denouncing corruption and war-profiteering. When the rebels started to broadcast from Banja Luka's television studio, the order swiftly came from Pale that "loyal" troops must seize and block the transmitters at Majevica and Kosaro, to prevent viewers in the rest of the 'Serb Republic' from seeing the rebellion for themselves. The transmitters were blocked. Meanwhile, Kanal S television studio in Pale gave the 'official' version of events: the rebellion was mentioned "somewhere near the end" of the evening news, and "in the familiar format: 10 seconds for the event itself, then five minutes for Karadžić, and lastly an editorial commentary".[110] In Serbia, the government-controlled media were likewise playing down the rebellion; during the week that it lasted, Tanjug and *Večernje novosti* announced no less than four times that it was already over.[111] The rebels initially refused to negotiate until the transmitters were unblocked. They failed in this demand, and yielded, but not before proving that everyone in the 'Serb Republic', down to the cannon-fodder, recognized the power of the media.

The SRNA News Agency and Kanal S Television

Srpska Republika Novinska Agencija (SRNA, Serb Republic News Agency) was established as the news agency of the 'Serb Republic of Bosnia-Hercegovina' on 8 April 1992, one day after the independence of the 'republic' was proclaimed by its leadership, under 'President' Karadžić.

---

[109] N Zafirović, "Recently in Banja Luka", 21 *Balkan War Report*, Aug-Sept. 1993.

[110] *Vreme*, 20 Sept. 1993.

[111] Id.

SRNA has lied more consistently and on a bigger scale than its Croat rival, the Herceg-Bosna News Agency (HBNA), or even than Tanjug. SRNA, based in Pale, the mountain resort near Sarajevo which has become the Bosnian Serb 'capital', shares a building with Kanal S television and Radio Republika Srpska, whose parent body is Srpska Radio-Televizija (SRT, Serb Radio-Television). The radio station began broadcasting several weeks before the attack on Sarajevo in April 1992, and the television channel started up about a month after, allegedly using equipment stolen from RTVBH and donated by the JNA and RTS.

The agency and the radio-television service are not distinguishable on any level. As the tools of the SDS they interlock with SRT's other media (TV Banja Luka, and captured local radio stations), as well as with Tanjug and RTS, to monopolize coverage of Bosnia for Serbs inside the republic and in Serbia. For the first year or so of the war, Kanal S evening news was rebroadcast every night on TV Belgrade.

Tanjug and RTS use SRNA, unadulterated, as a first-hand source. Following are two examples of their use:

* A typical example of SRNA and Tanjug acting hand-in-glove came in a routine Tanjug bulletin datelined Sarajevo, 11 May 1992: "Citing information received from the Interior Ministry of the Serb Republic of Bosnia-Hercegovina, SRNA said Muslim paramilitary formations relentlessly attacked positions of the Serbs' defence forces."

* On 7 May 1992, Tanjug ran a SRNA report that five leading members of the SDA in the northern Bosnian town of Bosanski Šamac had been sentenced to death by the SDA leadership for revealing secret plans, "prepared by the crisis headquarters of Muslims and Croats", for "genocide" against Serb citizens in that town. A report from Human Rights Watch/Helsinki gives a very different picture of what was happening in Bosanski Šamac during this period.

Serb forces, the JNA and paramilitary groups from Serbia attacked Bosanski Šamac on 17 April with light and heavy artillery.[112] The offensive did not meet with any armed resistance and its sole purpose was to displace the non-Serb population. During the brutal 'ethnic cleansing'

---

[112] The 1991 census figures for Bosanski Šamac were 41.5 per cent Serb, 44.7 per cent Croat and 6.8 per cent Muslim.

that followed, Serb forces were responsible for violations of human rights and humanitarian law including attacks against civilian targets, summary executions and abuses in detention. Among the first to be targeted were members of the HDZ and SDA. Summary executions were carried out in the municipality and some detainees were executed or beaten to death. In addition, "forced 'confessions', in which non-Serbs declared themselves guilty of anti-Serb activities, were recorded [including by television cameras] and later used as propaganda material and justification for the invasion".[113] Witnesses identified the television cameras as those of TV Novi Sad, a branch of RTS.[114]

Thus the SRNA report has all the hallmarks of disinformation, and Tanjug published it with no attempt to check its validity. The use of Serbian television cameras to record forced confessions is further proof of the close collaboration between Bosnian Serb and Serbian television in disseminating disinformation and propaganda about Serb activities in the war. In addition, much of SRNA's output during the early months of the war in Bosnia would appear to have been intended primarily for use by Tanjug and Serbian media.

Borba's monitors of TV Belgrade news programmes found no difference between TV Belgrade's and Kanal S's reporting about Sarajevo.[115] There was always the same frigid description of artillery fire, which always came from the enemy's direction; the screen always showed a picture of a carefully selected part of the city, with a destroyed house or an overturned car, or very occasionally something stronger.[116] As for SRNA's contributions to TV Belgrade's coverage, it was so pervasive on the news that the monitors noted an occasion when TV Belgrade omitted a SRNA report.[117]

Kanal S journalists such as Ilija Guzina and Risto Djogo double as RTS correspondents. When a Sarajevo marketplace was bombarded on 30

---

[113] Human Rights Watch/Helsinki, *War Crimes in Bosnia-Hercegovina: Bosanski Šamac* (New York: April 1994), 9.

[114] Id.

[115] See Ch. 3, section on 'Coverage of the War in Bosnia'.

[116] See M Pešić & B Mihajlović, *Republika*, 1-15 Dec. 1992.

[117] The report in question discussed the US army's technical capacity to shut down communications and electricity grids throughout Serbia. (*Borba*, 21 Aug. 1992.)

August 1992, Ilija Guzina merely mentioned in the middle of his report from Pale that 15 people had been killed, and the Muslims had carried out the attack themselves. On 16 October, Risto Djogo reported from Pale that 274 Serbs in Sarajevo were soon to be liquidated. This report was unsubstantiated, and later neither withdrawn nor confirmed.[118]

Kanal S uses the standard repertory of manipulation techniques. When a visiting Russian diplomat's remarks were translated on Kanal S, 'former' was inserted before every mention of 'Bosnia-Hercegovina', as if the Russian had chosen the standard Serb formula. When Serbs from Sarajevo, whose exit by convoy on 8 November had been negotiated by both sides, were interviewed about life in the city, they were not asked *why* conditions were so terrible; so their replies strongly implied that the government or the city authorities were to blame.

The same day, 8 November, shells killed several children as they sat in their improvized classroom near the edge of Sarajevo. The shells had clearly been fired from the Serb-held territory of Nedžarići. That night, Kanal S 'proved' by a fairly elaborate montage that the HVO had fired the shells from their artillery in Kiseljak, to avenge the recent dissolution of the HVO unit in Sarajevo (a dissolution which had been peacefully achieved by the Bosnian authorities).

SRNA and Kanal S are more aggressive and cynical than Tanjug; they make even less effort to produce plausible, coherent stories. Indeed, sometimes their reports seem deliberately excessive and contradictory. A SRNA bulletin can announce that "Serbian defenders take all vantage points around Goražde".[119] In a typical spirit of provocation, on 2 December 1992, Kanal S "broadcast a movie about Sarajevo in its heyday, underscored by a love song to the city and its beauties, which we, who are here [in Sarajevo] now, 'have destroyed'".[120]

Most journalists in Pale arrived from Sarajevo shortly before or after the onslaught against Bosnia began. Editor Risto Djogo (formerly an editor at Radio Sarajevo) is responsible for the most outrageous items on Kanal S news. He is renowned for the satirical sketches with which he closes his news broadcasts. He once played a film of chattering

---

[118] *Borba*, 1 Sept. 1992 and 19 Oct. 1992.

[119] R Bugarski, *Intelektualci i rat* (Belgrade: Beogradski krug-Centar za antiratnu akciju, 1993).

[120] Dizdarević, supra note 22, diary entry for 2 Dec. 1992.

chimpanzees 'miming' to the voice of TVBH newscaster Mile Djurdjević, a Serb by nationality. 'Traitorous' Serb journalists are a favourite theme with Kanal S and SRNA.[121] (See section on 'TV Journalists and the Question of Impartiality' above for the case of SRNA attacks against Rade Trbojević.)

On another occasion, Djogo had his face darkened with cosmetics before solemnly reading an item about the allegations that Serb forces had used rape as a means of terror against Bosnian Muslim women. But what, asked Djogo, about the refugee woman in Switzerland who delivered a black baby? Well, it's true she was raped because it is well known, he said, looking at the camera, that Serbs are Blacks!

More provocative still was the time when Djogo, quoting the Italian newspaper *Il Giornale*, stated that nothing remained to be done for Bosnia except to bury it. He then put aside his script, extended his hands with palms upturned, bowed his head, and began to mutter phrases from Muslim burial rites. Then he looked up blandly and signed off, grinning as he made the Serbian salute with his right hand (thumb and two fingers splayed like a trident). It was an astonishingly offensive sketch. Kanal S can be seen in Sarajevo and other government-controlled areas, just as TVBH can be seen in Pale. Sarajevans do watch Kanal S, for a change, but also from appalled fascination. Many viewers of Djogo's mock burial would have spoken the burial rites over family and friends killed by Serb forces.

Risto Djogo's sketches against Bosnian Muslims serve two propagandistic purposes. While outraging Muslims *en masse* and others loyal to the Sarajevo government, he is appealing to his audience to remember that those Muslims are absurd, ridiculous, the natural butts of jokes. 'Their' suffering is not human suffering, not like 'ours'. In this sense, Djogo appeals to a lurking Yugoslav and Serb prejudice, absorbed through folklore and popular culture, of Muslims as stupid, good-natured (because too dim not to be good-natured), and fundamentally inferior.

The British war correspondent Ed Vulliamy writes: "In two years I never heard a single derogatory remark from a Serb about the Croats as people. Hatred, yes; contempt, never. But the Muslims are another matter, they are 'gypsies', 'filth', 'bitches', 'animals'. The Bosnian project did not

---

[121] See *Dani* magazine, 30 July 1993.

entail seeing the Muslims as an enemy — the threat of the Jihad was all hot air — so much as subhuman."[122]

A further point about SRNA and Kanal S is that their cynicism indicates a deeper truth about Serb expansionism in Bosnia. From the outset, this project used propaganda about the Bosnian Muslim people and leaders which was extreme and token at the same time. The anti-Muslim propaganda was transparently incredible.[123] The Bosnian state was so weak, the Bosnian Serb leaders were so confident of unquestioning support from masses of their people, and their military resources were (thanks to Serbia and the JNA) so overwhelmingly superior, that the propaganda did not need to be clever. What SRNA and Kanal S gives its audience is news as sedative entertainment, or entertainment as information, which always implies that one thing matters: we're winning and they're at their last gasp. Anything else is trivia, and can be treated as such.

These media reproduce the Bosnian Serb leadership's own stance toward truth. Radovan Karadžić told the press that Serbs aren't besieging Sarajevo, they were simply protecting Serbian suburbs from Muslim attack; that "the Bosnian Serbs have no armed forces"; that Serbs could not be attacking Sarajevo because you can't attack what belongs to you already.[124] He wasn't attempting to be plausible; he was causing a diversion, drawing gasps of surprise, generally serving as a focus of attention while the troops in the field got on with the 'ethnic cleansing'.

---

[122] Vulliamy, supra note 63 at 46-47.

[123] For example: the police chief in Prijedor, a 'cleansed' town in northern Bosnia, claimed that Serbs had found 'proof' that Muslims planned "to circumcise all Serb boys and kill all males over the age of 3, and send the women between the ages of 15-25 into a harem to produce janissaries", a reference to a Turkish medieval practice of forcing Serb women to bear children for use in the military. Asked for evidence, the chief said "it was elsewhere in Bosnia". R Gutman, *A Witness to Genocide. The first inside account of the horrors of 'ethnic cleansing' in Bosnia* (Dorset, UK: Element Books, 1993), 113.

[124] The first claim was cited by Bugarski, supra note 118. The second claim was quoted by Vulliamy, supra note 63 at 48. The third was recorded in the BBC Bookmarks film, *Serbian Epics* broadcast on 16 December 1992.

Radio

In the hands of Serb forces, local radio stations from the RTVBH network have been used as paramilitary loud hailers.

* Radio Trebinje, serving a community whose 70 per cent Serb electorate had turned the town into the SDS stronghold in Hercegovina, joined a local propaganda campaign against TVSA in November 1991, because of its coverage about the nearby majority-Croat village of Ravno. Ravno had been destroyed by the JNA on the pretext that the Croatian Army was using it. The TVSA report, which accurately reported what happened, had not met with SDS approval.[125]

* The capture of the town of Foča in eastern Bosnia began on 7 April 1992 and was soon completed. "When Radio Foča fell into Serbian hands, Velibor Ostojić [Minister of Information in the 'Serb Republic of Bosnia-Hercegovina'] declared over the radio that the township of Foča was Serbian. He said that Muslims would no longer be permitted to live in Foča. And he added that every Serbian woman would have to bear seven children."[126]

* Serb forces took power in Prijedor, north of Banja Luka, on 29 April 1992. Next day, the new authorities ordered Muhamed Čehajić, a Muslim and Mayor of the town, to broadcast on radio an instruction to the townspeople to surrender all arms to the Serbs. Instead, "he called on the citizens to preserve the peace, to act with dignity and to conduct a Ghandian resistance to the illegal government".[127] He was arrested the following month and charged with organizing an attack on Serb soldiers. According to Roy Gutman, other charges began to be added to the list, while "Radio Prijedor, under Serb control, alleged that Čehajić was the son of a war criminal".[128]

---

[125] From "Examples of obstruction of work and harrassment of TV Sarajevo journalists" supra note 51.

[126] I Kajan, in Ali & Lifschutz, supra note 14 at 89.

[127] Gutman, supra note 123 at 113-114.

[128] Id.

With Prijedor taken, attention shifted to the smaller town of Kozarac, 10 kilometres down the road. The 24 days after 29 April "were punctuated by frantic negotiations, ultimatums, and threats made against the background of aggressive Serbian music blaring out of Radio Prijedor. Songs like 'Who says Serbia is small'. Later, in the camps, Muslims were forced to sing these songs."[129]

* Radio Brčko was used by its Serb captors on 5 May 1992 to announce that 5,000 Muslims had been killed during the battle for the town.[130]

* Vid Blagojević, a front-line correspondent for both TV Belgrade and for SRNA, used 'Free Serb Radio Modriča' to intimidate his Croat and Muslim neighbours every day, during the final struggle for the region. "Dear neighbours," he would say, "hurry up and flee across the Sava to 'your beautiful homeland', because soon, I'm afraid, it will be too small to take you all."[131]

Croat Media

The Croat equivalents of SRNA and Kanal S are HABENA and TV Široki Brijeg. HABENA (Hercegbosanska Novinska Agencija, the Herceg-Bosna News Agency) was founded after the proclamation of the 'Croat Republic of Herceg-Bosna' on 28 August 1993. Its headquarters are in Medjugorje, the dusty village-cum-Marian shrine on the high plateau behind Mostar.

HABENA is owned by the self-constituted 'government' of the self-proclaimed republic. Its director, Božo Rajić, is a prominent HDZ

---

[129] I Traynor, *The Guardian*, 17 Oct. 1992.

[130] Information from a resident of Brčko who lived through the capture of the town. Quoted by W Tribe, supra note 21. There are no official casualty figures for Brčko or other 'cleansed' towns. However, evidence of a mass grave in Brčko came to the notice of *New York Times* reporters later in 1992; they estimated that it contained 3,000 corpses. (Vulliamy, supra note 63 at 90.)

[131] Čolić, supra note 88 at 55. The Croatian national anthem begins with the words "Our Beautiful Homeland".

member who had served the coalition government of Bosnia as Minister of Defence in the same undermining spirit that Velibor Ostojić had served as Minister of Information.[132] Rajić rarely left his base in Mostar whence, on 16 January 1993 (whilst still the Minister of Defence) he issued the fateful order for ABH forces in central Bosnia and western Hercegovina to submit to HVO command. The ABH's refusal triggered large-scale fighting between the two allies in Gornji Vakuf, central Bosnia, which later spread and intensified until the March 1994 ceasefire.

By 24 September 1993 HABENA claimed that, already "hundreds of news items have been sent into the world about the just struggle of the Croat people in their centuries-old areas".[133] That sentence epitomizes the agency's aspirations. Its bulletins are carried extensively by Croatian media, both under its own name and under the rubric of Hrvatska Izvjestajna Novinska Agencija (HINA, the Croatian News Reporting Agency).

HABENA boasted that, with an agency, a television studio, and a weekly paper, *Hrvatski list*: "The media system of the republic of the Croat people of Bosnia-Hercegovina is complete."[134] HABENA might also have mentioned a fourth element in the system: the HVO press centre in Mostar managed by Veso Vegar.[135] Within a few months, a radio station, Radio Herceg-Bosna, began broadcasting from Mostar. Radio Herceg-Bosna was set up at the initiative of a former Hrvatski Radio news journalist who had been born in Hercegovina. Reputedly much of the studio's equipment was donated from Zagreb.

The newspaper *Hrvatski list* was launched in Mostar in May 1993 by the 'government' of 'Herceg-Bosna', which never concealed its determination to have Mostar as its eventual capital. It was on 9 May 1993 that the HVO moved to take complete control of western Mostar. On that date, the Croats took prisoner eight radio journalists who had been working for RTVBH in and around the city. The journalists, all Muslim

---

[132] On Velibor Ostojić, see section on 'Serb Radio' supra .

[133] *Slobodna Dalmacija*, 24 Sept. 1993.

[134] *Vjesnik*, 11 Sept. 1993.

[135] In 1993, the HVO also launched a weekly paper in the tiny Croat-controlled enclave of Posavina, northern Bosnia. Called *Posavski glasnik*, this paper is edited in Posavina and printed in Zagreb. Its political line is milder than that of the 'Herceg-Bosna' media, due to the fact that the HVO in Posavina had opted to preserve its alliance with the ABH.

by nationality, were kept in extremely harsh conditions for several months; they were regularly beaten and interrogated, and the males were sent to dig trenches at the front, and used as human shields during offensives against the ABH.[136] Thus the newspaper was founded at the earliest possible moment after taking western Mostar. It is printed at the *Slobodna Dalmacija* plant in Split, Croatia, and distributed by the same company, so its access to the Croatian market is good. *Hrvatski list*'s political stance is unremittingly hard line, even after the March 1994 truce between the ABH and the HVO. Its editorial office is not in Mostar, however, but, significantly, in the nearby little town of Široki Brijeg.

The first Croatian newspaper to open a bureau in 'Herceg-Bosna' was *Slobodna Dalmacija*, owned by Miroslav Kutle, the entrepreneur and HDZ member who acquired a controlling share of the paper (including its printing and distribution businesses) in such dubious circumstances in March 1993.[137] The bureau is situated in Široki Brijeg, the birthplace of its owner, Kutle, and also that of Gojko Šušak (Croatia's Minister of Defence, the man who, in President Tudjman's own words "really implemented HDZ's policy in Bosnia-Hercegovina").[138] The web of Croatia's strategy in this war, including certainly the "media system of the republic of the Croat people of Bosnia-Hercegovina", is woven of such official and informal (ministerial and tribal) connections.

Široki Brijeg is also the site of the newly-built 'Herceg-Bosna' television station, HTV Široki Brijeg (unlike the Serb side, Croat-held territory did not contain a TVBH studio which could have been taken over). Remarkably, although it is situated in a different state (which has been recognized by the Republic of Croatia), it belongs to the Croatian government-controlled radio and television network, HRT: its staff are employed by HRT and directly responsible to Tomislav Marčinko, the news editor-in-chief of HRT television in Zagreb. There was no attempt to disguise it as a separate enterprise.

---

[136] Information from the Co-ordinating Centre for Independent Media of the Balkan Region, in Ljubljana and from *La Lettre de Reporters Sans Frontières*, March 1994. The journalists' own testimony has been corroborated by the Medjugorje office of the International Committee of the Red Cross.

[137] On the dubious nature of the paper's sale, see Ch. 4, section on '*Slobodna Dalmacija*'.

[138] Quoted in *Vjesnik*, 10 April 1994.

The studio produces a brief daily bulletin of news from 'Herceg-Bosna', which is sent via a microwave link to Split and thence to the HTV centre in Zagreb, for possible inclusion in its evening news or in *Slikom na sliku*, its current affairs programme. It started production in December 1992. This date too is remarkable, for less than a month later the leadership of 'Herceg-Bosna' went on the offensive against the ABH and the Muslim civilian population.

The station channelled a torrent of vicious propaganda and disinformation into HRT's news programmes. The key bridging figure in this effort was Smiljko Šagolj. Formerly a high-ranking journalist at TVSA, Šagolj gained renown in 1989 for reporting from the Berlin Wall without ever leaving Sarajevo. (A new slang expression was coined in media circles: '*šagoljica*', a blatant lie.) He bounced back with the 1990 election campaign, becoming HTV's correspondent in Bosnia. By the spring of 1992, Šagolj was committed to 'Herceg-Bosna' and the HVO. *Oslobodjenje* of 27 April reports his appearance at a press conference in Mostar, reading out the HDZ's denial of accusations that an autonomous Croat army (the HVO) was afoot in Bosnia.

Šagolj heads a small team of propagandists, young and inexperienced journalists, such as Marija Topić, whose reports are often barely audible and always wholly one-sided. Šagolj came into his own when the HVO broke its alliance with the ABH. Independent Croatian journalist Vesna Roller described in *Vreme* how Šagolj and "the followers in his 'school' manipulate the tragedy of Bosnian Croats for Croatian television: all their interviewees — expelled Bosnian Croats — repeated to TV viewers day after day, full of grief and anger, how they want to stay in Croatia and asked for the eviction [from Croatia] of Muslim refugees, 'whose fathers and sons are guilty of expelling us'."[139] During 1993 Šagolj sent dozens of inflammatory reports from 'Herceg-Bosna' and central Bosnia, ranting against the *mujahedin* and 'Islamic fanatics'. Staff at HTV say, off the record, that Šagolj has even portrayed destroyed Muslim houses as Croat dwellings ravaged by "the Muslims".

HRT's news and current affairs programmes seem wholly open to Šagolj's reports and he benefits from excellent connections. He is believed to be close to Mate Boban, the former 'president' of 'Herceg-Bosna', who in turn was close to President Tudjman of Croatia. The Croatian Ministry

---

[139] *Vreme*, 20 Sept. 1993.

of Defence gave Šagolj a flat in Split, publicly justifying the act on the ground of his obligations to the HV (note, not to the HVO).[140] Other recipients of HV flats in Split at the same time were the HVO general Milivoj Petković and Boris Boban, son of the Herceg-Bosna 'president'. One leak elicited another; it emerged that the HVO had given Šagolj the tidy sum of 25,000 Deutschmarks to furnish his new property.

Conclusions

* The media space in Bosnia was shattered by force, before the territorial space was shattered by much greater force, in order to create exclusive national zones. While no-one can be sure that the former conquest was a precondition of the latter, it is true that in Sarajevo, where the key media successfully resisted fragmentation, there was powerful civic resistance — also successful — to territorial and national division.

* During the transition to multiparty government and the run-down to war (1990 to 1992), the media in Bosnia — in so far as they identified with Bosnia as a country, a republic — did not try to win public support for sectarian nationalism. This was not because journalists were more independent-minded than in Serbia and Croatia. Rather, it reflected two facts of political life in the republic:

1) The new multiparty government could not agree on anything, including how to subjugate the media to its control.

2) The largest party (the Muslim SDA) became increasingly opposed to sectarianism, because it contradicted the party's overriding goal: to preserve the republic.

Institutions whose identity and purpose were inseparable from the legitimacy, continuity and survival of the republic, therefore, were anti-nationalist by definition. Hence the key media, RTVSA and *Oslobodjenje*, psychologically disarmed the public, rather than arming it.

---

[140] *Feral Tribune*, 7 Sept. 1993.

*　　Serb media inside Bosnia and in Serbia converged to produce a seamless unity of coverage. The aim of this coverage was to justify war against Muslims and Croats by outrageous propaganda and disinformation which would mobilize Serbs in Bosnia while reassuring and distracting public opinion in Serbia.

It succeeded on both counts. Survivors of Serb-run concentration camps have described how their interrogators accused them of the same offences which Serb media were baselessly alleging; that Muslim leaders wanted to turn Bosnia into an Islamic fundamentalist state.[141] The seamless whole was, in another image, a closed circuit of lies, in which the media linked the military with the wider public. This is why the following scene, described by Roy Gutman, the Pulitzer Prize-winning reporter for the New York *Newsday* newspaper, is so memorably emblematic:

> At the [Serb army] headquarters in Banja Luka, Major Milovan Milutinović sat behind a portable typewriter churning out lurid diatribes. 'Under such a hot, Balkanic sky,' began one tract, 'necklaces have been strung of human eyes and ears, skulls have been halved, brains have been split, bowels have been torn out, human spits and children's bodies have been pierced by bayonets, once again have become a part of the Serbian people's enemies' folklore.' The

---

[141] The captured Bosnian Serb soldier and self-confessed war criminal, Borislav Herak, has recounted how Serb commanders inflamed their men by telling them about Muslim-run prisons and concentration camps for Serbs, about pregnant Serb women thrown to the lions and tigers in the zoo. Z Filipovic, *Izlet u pakao* (Zagreb: Durieux, 1993).

According to *New York Times* reporter John Burns (who shared the Pulitzer Prize with Gutman) the young soldier had "absorbed and accepted a view of Muslims which wholly contradicted his own experience of growing up in a nationally-mixed part of Sarajevo. From Serbian radio and television and in gatherings with other Serbian fighters, particularly the older generation steeped in Serbian folklore going back to Serbian defeats by the Ottoman Turks in the Middle Ages, [Herak] said he learned that Muslims posed a threat to Serbs. Serbian political leaders and commanders told fighters that Muslims ... were planning to declare 'an Islamic republic' in Bosnia. ... Muslims would also require Serbian children to wear Muslim clothing." (J Burns, *The Guardian*, 3 Dec. 1992)

document was titled 'Lying [sic] Violent Hands on
the Serbian Woman'.[142]

The military status of the 'journalist', the incredibly crude and evil
nonsense of the bulletin (expressing the agenda of victorious power): right
down to that reflex-seeking mention of folklore, Gutman's tableau of Serb
media life in the republic is complete in the essentials.

*   Croatia's policy towards Bosnia has been ambiguous, reflecting
political differences within the Croat population inside Bosnia. Coverage
of the war by media in the Croat-controlled territory in Bosnia, and by
government-controlled media in Croatia, has, however, not really portrayed
these differences; and they portrayed them least when they were greatest,
during 1993. Throughout that year, and into 1994, these media consistently
justified and obscured the most radical policy of territorial control
(entailing 'ethnic cleansing') as practised by the HDZ-HVO leaders of
'Herceg-Bosna'.

This unanimity proves as well as anything that 'Herceg-Bosna' has
executed the will of the parent HDZ party in Croatia, led by Franjo
Tudjman. Like the policy it shadows, the media coverage has abandoned
those Croats (over two-thirds of the prewar total of 750,000) who lived
outside 'Herceg-Bosna'. Above all, it abandoned the Croats of central
Bosnia, who were sacrificed to the fanaticism of the HDZ-HVO clique.
When the HVO tried to take total control of those areas in central Bosnia
which it held jointly with the ABH, the inevitable reaction was that the
ABH took total control wherever it could, expelling and sometimes
massacring Croat civilians. The Croat media presented the plight of these
civilians as the result of Muslim perfidy and 'fundamentalism', without
even implicating heedless Croat ambition.

*   In the wake of the March 1994 ceasefire between the HVO and the
ABH, journalists from the two sides in Mostar held a first 'post-war'
meeting. According to *Hrvatski list*, the official 'Herceg-Bosna' newspaper,
the atmosphere of the meeting was "rather cordial", as if the "venom and

---

[142] Gutman, supra note 123 at ix. By March 1994, Milutinović had been
promoted to colonel and, as "the linchpin of the Serb propaganda drive", was working
out of Radio Doboj's sand-bagged studios. (*Guardian*, 19 March 1994).

accusations of the media war had never existed".[143] Journalists who have followed one set of orders may well switch with such facility to another set. The negative effect on the Bosnian media of the HDZ-HVO switchback, from support for the Bosnian government, to aggression against it, then to alliance in the proposed new federation, will, however, probably be longer lasting. The onset of SDA control in RTVBH coincided with the onset of HDZ-HVO aggression, early in 1993. This control hardened through the following year, and is not likely to be reversed by the ceasefire and federal declaration. According to Nijaz Duraković, leader of the opposition SDP party and a member of the collective presidency, the SDA carried out a "new media purge" in March 1994, "eliminating people from TVBH [and] tomorrow it will be the same with *Oslobodjenje*".[144]

*	Unless an overall political solution for Bosnia is soon found, Duraković's worst predictions will come true. Until the fate of the republic has been settled, its media will not be independent. On the contrary, they will continue to be, or will finally become, subjugated to politico-military projects on all sides.

---

[143] *Hrvatski list*, 13 April 1994.

[144] *Arkzin*, April 1994.

GLOSSARY

Note on pronunciation in the Serbo-Croatian language

c	"ts" as in flats
č	"ch" as in church
ć	"tj", or "tu" as in tune
dj	approximately a crisp "j" as in jeans
dž	approximately a soft "g" as in gentle
j	"y" as in yes
lj	"liyuh", like the middle sound of "million"
nj	"ny" as in canyon
š	"sh" as in shot
ž	"zh" as in plea*su*re

Other letters are pronounced much as in English.

ARD   Agencija za Restrukturiranje i Razvoj, Agency for Restructuring and Development in Croatia.

ABH   Armija Bosne i Hercegovine, Army of Bosnia-Hercegovina (Bosnian Army).

BBC   British Broadcasting Corporation.

Bosnia   The Republic of Bosnia-Hercegovina.

četnik   Before the formation of the Yugoslav state in 1918, *četniks* (*četnici*) were irregular units within the Serbian army. In royal Yugoslavia (1918-1941) the name was linked with Serb nationalist paramilitarism. In the Second World War, the term came to mean the guerrilla forces of Serbs and Montenegrins, including officers and men of the former royal Yugoslav army, which wanted to restore the kingdom of Yugoslavia with its Serbian dynasty. These forces committed many atrocities against Bosnian Muslims; some of them collaborated with German and Italian commanders against the Partisan forces led by Josip Broz-Tito. Taboo in Tito's Yugoslavia, in 1990 the name was rehabilitated by extreme nationalist groups in Serbia, paving the way for armed irregular bands of volunteers to be raised and armed to fight in Croatia (and later in Bosnia). Vosilav Šešelj of the SRS is the best-known leader (*vojvoda*) of the latter-day *četniki*. In Croatia, by 1991 the name had become an all-purpose description of any Serb irregular, with or without *četnik* insignia. Croat nationalists are liable to apply the term to any Serb who does not denounce Serb nationalism.

CIFE — Civic Initiative for Freedom of Expression.

CNN — Cable News Network.

CSCE — The Conference on Security and Cooperation in Europe.

EC — The European Community (now the EU, European Union).

HABENA — Hercegbosanska Novinska Agencija, Herceg-Bosna News Agency. HABENA is the news agency of the self-proclaimed 'Croat Republic of Herceg-Bosna'.

Herceg-Bosna — The name given by Croat leaders to the Croat-controlled region in western Hercegovina (i.e. south-western Bosnia).

HDZ — Hrvatska Demokratska Zajednica, the Croatian Democratic Community. Under Franjo Tudjman, the HDZ won the first multiparty elections in Croatia. A branch of the party was founded in Bosnia early in 1990.

HINA — Hrvatska Izvještajna Novinska Agencija, the Croatian News Reporting Agency.

HOS — Hrvatske Oružane Snage, Croatian Armed Forces. A militia mustered and deployed by the extreme nationalist HSP (Hrvatska Stranka Prava, Croatian Party of Right) in Croatia in 1991 and in Bosnia in 1992.

HRT — Hrvatska Radio-Televizija, Croatian Radio-Television (formerly RTZ).

HTV — Hrvatska Televizija, Croatian Television.

HV — Hrvatska Vojska, Croatian Army (the army of the Republic of Croatia).

HVO — Hrvatsko Vijeće Obrane, the Croatian Defence Council. The HVO is the army established by the HDZ in Bosnia, under the tutelage of the HV.

Glossary

JNA — Jugoslovenska Narodna Armija, Yugoslav People's Army. As the successor to Tito's Partisan movement, the JNA was an institutional and ideological pillar of Yugoslavia. The JNA ceased to exist in May 1992, when the VJ was formed as the army of the 'new' Yugoslavia, the SRJ.

JRT — Jugoslovenska Radio-Televizija, Yugoslav Radio-Television.

KOS — Kontra Obavještajna Sluzba, the military counter-intelligence service in the SFRY.

mujahedin — Islamic paramilitary forces in Bosnia, comprising several hundred volunteers from Middle Eastern states, as well as some native Bosnian Muslim volunteers. In Serb and Croat media, the term has been used to describe any and all Muslim soldiers in Bosnia, including the multi-national ABH.

MUP — Ministarstvo Unutarnjih Poslova, Ministry of the Interior in Croatia.

NDH — Nezavisna Država Hrvatska, Independent State of Croatia (1941-5).

RSK — Republika Srpska Krajina, the Serb Republic of Krajina, the self-proclaimed Serb state in Croatia.

RTB — Radio-Televizija Beograd, Belgrade Radio-Television (now RTS).

RTS — Radio-Televizija Srbija, Serbian Radio-Television (formerly RTB).

RTVBH — Radio-Televizija Bosne i Hercegovine, Radio-Television of Bosnia-Hercegovina (formerly RTVSA).

RTVSA — Radio-Televizija Sarajevo, Sarajevo Radio-Television (now RTVBH).

RTZ — Radio-Televizija Zagreb, Zagreb Radio-Television (now HRT).

SAWP — Socialistički Savez Radnih Naroda, Socialist Alliance of Working People. The SAWP was a "socio-political" mass organization comprising trade union, youth, student, women's and war veterans' associations in each republic, under the political 'guidance' of the League of Communists; the SAWP was a typical device of Tito's

269

'self-management socialism', which extended one-party power under the guise of devolving it.

SDA   Stranka Demokratske Akcije (Party of Democratic Action), the party supported by the majority of Muslims in Bosnia's 1990 elections.

SDS   Srpska Demokratska Stranka, Serb Democratic Party. The extreme nationalist Serb parties, which contested the 1990 elections, in Croatia and Bosnia both bore this name. (There is no connection between these parties and the third party with this name, in Serbia proper. On the contrary, the SDS in Croatia and Bosnia enjoyed the backing of the ruling SPS in Serbia.)

SFRY   Socialisticka Federativna Republika Jugoslavija, Socialist Federative Republic of Yugoslavia. Established under the last, 1974 Federal Constitution, the SFRY comprised six republics (Bosnia-Hercegovina, Croatia, Macedonia, Montenegro, Serbia and Slovenia) and two 'autonomous provinces' within Serbia (Kosovo and Vojvodina).

Šiptars   A standard term for Kosovo Albanians in the former Yugoslavia, it is now commonly used with perjorative intent.

SPO   Srpski Pokret Obnove, Serb Movement of Renewal. Led by the charismatic Vuk Drašković, the SPO has evolved from a radical anti-nationalist movement, with *četnik* connections, into the most outspoken party in the Serbian opposition.

SPS   Socialistička Partija Srbije, Socialist Party of Serbia. As the renamed League of Communists of Serbia, the SPS won the 1990 multiparty elections in Serbia; it also won the 1992 and 1993 elections.

SRJ   Savezna Republika Jugoslavija, Federal Republic of Yugoslavia. Proclaimed on 27 April 1992 by Serbia and Montenegro, the new federation's claim to be a successor state of the SFRY has been rejected by the United Nations and the European Union.

SRNA   Srpska Republika Novinska Agencija, Serb Republic News Agency. SRNA is the news agency of the self-proclaimed 'Serb Republic of Bosnia-Hercegovina'.

Glossary

SRS   Srpska Radikalna Stranka, Serb Radical Party.

SRT   Srpska Radio-Televizija, Serb Radio-Television. The broadcasting network of the self-proclaimed 'Serb Republic' in Bosnia.

Tanjug   Telegrafska Agencija Nove Jugoslavije, Telegraph Agency of New Yugoslavia. Formerly the news agency of the SFRY, Tanjug is now the news agency of the SRJ.

TVB   TV Beograd, TV Belgrade.

TVBH   Televizija Bosne i Hercegovine, Bosnian TV (formerly TV Sarajevo).

TVSA   Televizija Sarajevo, TV Sarajevo (now TVBH).

UN   United Nations.

UNCHR   United Nations Commission on Human Rights.

UNHCR   United Nations High Commissioner for Refugees.

UNPROFOR   United Nations Protection Force, the UN peacekeeping operation in former Yugoslavia.

ustaša   The *ustaša* movement was a Croat extreme nationalist grouping which practised terrorism against royal Yugoslavia in the 1930s, with the aim of winning full independence for Croatia. In 1941, the invading Nazis installed the *ustaše* to govern the puppet NDH, including the territories of Croatia and Bosnia. The *ustaša* regime was responsible for the murders of several hundred thousand Serbs, Jews, Gypsies, and political enemies in 1941-1945. Among its concentration camps, the most infamous was at Jasenovac, where as many as 150,000 were killed.There have been attempts to rehabilitate the movement and the NDH by some members of the ruling HDZ, including Franjo Tudjman himself. Since 1990 or earlier, the term and its cognates (*ustašoid, ustašism*) have been widely used in Serbia to describe all Croat nationalists.

VJ   Vojska Jugoslavije, Army of Yugoslavia. Formed in May 1992 from the JNA, as the army of the SRJ.

ARTICLE 19

The International Centre Against Censorship

ARTICLE 19 takes its name and purpose from Article 19 of the Universal Declaration of Human Rights which states:

Everyone has the right to freedom of opinion and expression; this right includes freedom to hold opinions without interference and to seek, receive and impart information and ideas through any media and regardless of frontiers.

ARTICLE 19, the International Centre Against Censorship, works impartially and systematically to identify and oppose censorship world-wide. We believe that freedom of expression and information is a fundamental human right without which all other rights, including the right to life, cannot be protected. ARTICLE 19 defends this right when it is threatened, opposes government practices which violate it and exposes censorship.

ARTICLE 19 works on behalf of victims of censorship: individuals who are physically attacked, killed, unjustly imprisoned, banned, restricted in their movements or dismissed from their jobs; publications which are censored or banned; media outlets which are closed, suspended or threatened with closure; organizations, including political groups or trade unions, which are harassed, suppressed or silenced.

ARTICLE 19 monitors individual countries' compliance with international standards protecting freedom of expression; prepares reports for inter-governmental organizations such as the United Nations Human Rights Commission and Committee; and files legal interventions on behalf of individuals with the European Court of Human Rights, other international bodies and national courts.

ARTICLE 19 has established a growing international network of individuals and concerned organizations who promote awareness of censorship issues and take action on individual cases.

ARTICLE 19 is a registered charity in the UK (Charity No. 327421) and is entirely dependent on donations.

For more information and membership details please contact:

ARTICLE 19
33 Islington High Street, London N1 9LH
Tel. 071 278 9292   Fax. 071 713 1356
Executive Director: Frances D'Souza